Soviet and Post-Soviet Politics and Socie...
ISSN 1614-3515

General Editor: Andreas Umland,
Stockholm Centre for Eastern European Studies, andreas.umland@ui.se

Commi...
London,...

EDITORIAL COMMITTEE*

DOMESTIC & COMPARATIVE POLITICS
Prof. **Ellen Bos**, *Andrássy University of Budapest*
Dr. **Gergana Dimova**, *Florida State University*
Prof. **Heiko Pleines**, *University of Bremen*
Dr. **Sarah Whitmore**, *Oxford Brookes University*
Dr. **Harald Wydra**, *University of Cambridge*

SOCIETY, CLASS & ETHNICITY
Col. **David Glantz**, *"Journal of Slavic Military Studies"*
Dr. **Marlène Laruelle**, *George Washington University*
Dr. **Stephen Shulman**, *Southern Illinois University*
Prof. **Stefan Troebst**, *University of Leipzig*

POLITICAL ECONOMY & PUBLIC POLICY
Prof. **Andreas Goldthau**, *University of Erfurt*
Dr. **Robert Kravchuk**, *University of North Carolina*
Dr. **David Lane**, *University of Cambridge*
Dr. **Carol Leonard**, *University of Oxford*
Dr. **Maria Popova**, *McGill University, Montreal*

FOREIGN POLICY & INTERNATIONAL AFFAIRS
Dr. **Peter Duncan**, *University College London*
Prof. **Andreas Heinemann-Grüder**, *University of Bonn*
Prof. **Gerhard Mangott**, *University of Innsbruck*
Dr. **Diana Schmidt-Pfister**, *University of Konstanz*
Dr. **Lisbeth Tarlow**, *Harvard University, Cambridge*
Dr. **Christian Wipperfürth**, *N-Ost Network, Berlin*
Dr. **William Zimmerman**, *University of Michigan*

HISTORY, CULTURE & THOUGHT
Dr. **Catherine Andreyev**, *University of Oxford*
Prof. **Mark Bassin**, *Södertörn University*
Prof. **Karsten Brüggemann**, *Tallinn University*
Prof. **Alexander Etkind**, *Central European University*
Prof. **Gasan Gusejnov**, *Free University of Berlin*
Prof. **Leonid Luks**, *Catholic University of Eichstaett*
Dr. **Olga Malinova**, *Russian Academy of Sciences*
Dr. **Richard Mole**, *University College London*
Prof. **Andrei Rogatchevski**, *University of Tromsø*
Dr. **Mark Tauger**, *West Virginia University*

ADVISORY BOARD*

Prof. **Dominique Arel**, *University of Ottawa*
Prof. **Jörg Baberowski**, *Humboldt University of Berlin*
Prof. **Margarita Balmaceda**, *Seton Hall University*
Dr. **John Barber**, *University of Cambridge*
Prof. **Timm Beichelt**, *European University Viadrina*
Dr. **Katrin Boeckh**, *University of Munich*
Prof. em. **Archie Brown**, *University of Oxford*
Dr. **Vyacheslav Bryukhovetsky**, *Kyiv-Mohyla Academy*
Prof. **Timothy Colton**, *Harvard University, Cambridge*
Prof. **Paul D'Anieri**, *University of California*
Dr. **Heike Dörrenbächer**, *Friedrich Naumann Foundation*
Dr. **John Dunlop**, *Hoover Institution, Stanford, California*
Dr. **Sabine Fischer**, *SWP, Berlin*
Dr. **Geir Flikke**, *NUPI, Oslo*
Prof. **David Galbreath**, *University of Aberdeen*
Prof. **Frank Golczewski**, *University of Hamburg*
Dr. **Nikolas Gvosdev**, *Naval War College, Newport, RI*
Prof. **Mark von Hagen**, *Arizona State University*
Prof. **Guido Hausmann**, *University of Regensburg*
Prof. **Dale Herspring**, *Kansas State University*
Dr. **Stefani Hoffman**, *Hebrew University of Jerusalem*
Prof. em. **Andrzej Korbonski**, *University of California*
Dr. **Iris Kempe**, *"Caucasus Analytical Digest"*
Prof. **Herbert Küpper**, *Institut für Ostrecht Regensburg*
Prof. **Rainer Lindner**, *University of Konstanz*

Dr. **Luke March**, *University of Edinburgh*
Prof. **Michael McFaul**, *Stanford University, Palo Alto*
Prof. **Birgit Menzel**, *University of Mainz-Germersheim*
Dr. **Alex Pravda**, *University of Oxford*
Dr. **Erik van Ree**, *University of Amsterdam*
Dr. **Joachim Rogall**, *Robert Bosch Foundation Stuttgart*
Prof. **Peter Rutland**, *Wesleyan University, Middletown*
Prof. **Gwendolyn Sasse**, *University of Oxford*
Prof. **Jutta Scherrer**, *EHESS, Paris*
Prof. **Robert Service**, *University of Oxford*
Mr. **James Sherr**, *RIIA Chatham House London*
Dr. **Oxana Shevel**, *Tufts University, Medford*
Prof. **Eberhard Schneider**, *University of Siegen*
Prof. **Olexander Shnyrkov**, *Shevchenko University, Kyiv*
Prof. **Hans-Henning Schröder**, *SWP, Berlin*
Prof. **Yuri Shapoval**, *Ukrainian Academy of Sciences*
Dr. **Lisa Sundstrom**, *University of British Columbia*
Dr. **Philip Walters**, *"Religion, State and Society", Oxford*
Prof. **Zenon Wasyliw**, *Ithaca College, New York State*
Dr. **Lucan Way**, *University of Toronto*
Dr. **Markus Wehner**, *"Frankfurter Allgemeine Zeitung"*
Dr. **Andrew Wilson**, *University College London*
Prof. **Jan Zielonka**, *University of Oxford*
Prof. **Andrei Zorin**, *University of Oxford*

---

* While the Editorial Committee and Advisory Board support the General Editor in the choice and improvement of manuscripts for publication, responsibility for remaining errors and misinterpretations in the series' volumes lies with the books' authors.

Soviet and Post-Soviet Politics and Society (SPPS)
ISSN 1614-3515

Founded in 2004 and refereed since 2007, SPPS makes available affordable English-, German-, and Russian-language studies on the history of the countries of the former Soviet bloc from the late Tsarist period to today. It publishes between 5 and 20 volumes per year and focuses on issues in transitions to and from democracy such as economic crisis, identity formation, civil society development, and constitutional reform in CEE and the NIS. SPPS also aims to highlight so far understudied themes in East European studies such as right-wing radicalism, religious life, higher education, or human rights protection. The authors and titles of all previously published volumes are listed at the end of this book. For a full description of the series and reviews of its books, see www.ibidem-verlag.de/red/spps.

Editorial correspondence & manuscripts should be sent to: Dr. Andreas Umland, Department of Political Science, Kyiv-Mohyla Academy, vul. Voloska 8/5, UA-04070 Kyiv, UKRAINE; andreas.umland@cantab.net

Business correspondence & review copy requests should be sent to: *ibidem* Press, Leuschnerstr. 40, 30457 Hannover, Germany; tel.: +49 511 2622200; fax: +49 511 2622201; spps@ibidem.eu.

Authors, reviewers, referees, and editors for (as well as all other persons sympathetic to) SPPS are invited to join its networks at www.facebook.com/group.php?gid=52638198614
www.linkedin.com/groups?about=&gid=103012
www.xing.com/net/spps-ibidem-verlag/

Recent Volumes

270   *Jakob Hauter*
Russia's Overlooked Invasion
The Causes of the 2014 Outbreak of War in Ukraine's Donbas
With a foreword by Hiroaki Kuromiya
ISBN 978-3-8382-1803-8

271   *Anton Shekhovtsov*
Russian Political Warfare
Essays on Kremlin Propaganda in Europe and the Neighbourhood, 2020-2023
With a foreword by Nathalie Loiseau
ISBN 978-3-8382-1821-2

272   *Андреа Пето*
Насилие и Молчание
Красная армия в Венгрии во Второй Мировой войне
ISBN 978-3-8382-1636-2

273   *Winfried Schneider-Deters*
Russia's War in Ukraine
Debates on Peace, Fascism, and War Crimes, 2022–2023
With a foreword by Klaus Gestwa
ISBN 978-3-8382-1876-2

274   *Rasmus Nilsson*
Uncanny Allies
Russia and Belarus on the Edge, 2012-2024
ISBN 978-3-8382-1288-3

275   *Anton Grushetskyi, Volodymyr Paniotto*
War and the Transformation of Ukrainian Society (2022–23)
Empirical Evidence
ISBN 978-3-8382-1944-8

276   *Christian Kaunert, Alex MacKenzie, Adrien Nonjon (Eds.)*
In the Eye of the Storm
Origins, Ideology, and Controversies of the Azov Brigade, 2014–23
ISBN 978-3-8382-1750-5

277   *Gian Marco Moisé*
The House Always Wins
The Corrupt Strategies that Shaped Kazakh Oil Politics and Business in the Nazarbayev Era
With a foreword by Alena Ledeneva
ISBN 978-3-8382-1917-2

278   *Mikhail Minakov*
The Post-Soviet Human
Philosophical Reflections on Social History after the End of Communism
ISBN 978-3-8382-1943-1

Natalia Kudriavtseva, Debra A. Friedman (eds.)

LANGUAGE AND POWER IN UKRAINE AND KAZAKHSTAN

Essays on Education, Ideology, Literature, Practice, and the Media

With a foreword by Laada Bilaniuk

Bibliographic information published by the Deutsche Nationalbibliothek

Die Deutsche Nationalbibliothek lists this publication in the Deutsche Nationalbibliografie; detailed bibliographic data are available on the Internet at http://dnb.d-nb.de.

Bibliografische Information der Deutschen Nationalbibliothek

Die Deutsche Nationalbibliothek verzeichnet diese Publikation in der Deutschen Nationalbibliografie; detaillierte bibliografische Daten sind im Internet über http://dnb.d-nb.de abrufbar.

Cover picture: "Russians, give up", © by Natalia Kudriavtseva, 2022

ISBN (Print): 978-3-8382-1949-3
ISBN (E-Book [PDF]): 978-3-8382-7949-7
© *ibidem*-Verlag, Hannover • Stuttgart 2024
All rights reserved.

No part of this publication may be reproduced, stored in or introduced into a retrieval system, or transmitted, in any form, or by any means (electronic, mechanical, photocopying, recording or otherwise) without the prior written permission of the publisher. Any person who commits any unauthorized act in relation to this publication may be liable to criminal prosecution and civil claims for damages.

Alle Rechte vorbehalten. Das Werk einschließlich aller seiner Teile ist urheberrechtlich geschützt. Jede Verwertung außerhalb der engen Grenzen des Urheberrechtsgesetzes ist ohne Zustimmung des Verlages unzulässig und strafbar. Dies gilt insbesondere für Vervielfältigungen, Übersetzungen, Mikroverfilmungen und elektronische Speicherformen sowie die Einspeicherung und Verarbeitung in elektronischen Systemen.

Printed in the United States of America

Acknowledgement

This collected volume was prepared for publication during Natalia Kudriavtseva's research leave as part of the Centre for Advanced Study Sofia Fellowship for the project "Switching to Ukrainian from Russian in Wartime: Linguistic Conversion in Eastern Ukraine." The preparation of the volume primarily benefited from collaborative involvement in the production of the special issue of the *Ideology and Politics Journal* "Critical Perspectives on Language and Power in Ukraine and Kazakhstan" (2023). The editors of the volume extend their thanks to Mikhail (Mykhailo) Minakov, the editor-in-chief of the *Ideology and Politics Journal*, for his assistance and help with the special issue and to the reviewers for the special issue for their insightful feedback on earlier drafts of these chapters.

The editors would also like to acknowledge the financial support of VolkswagenStiftung, granted under the "Sustaining Ukrainian Scholarship — A fellowship programme for 3 years, 2023-2026", which has been jointly established by the Centre for Advanced Study Sofia and New Europe College Bucharest. The editors of the volume would like to thank these institutions as well as the Ibidem-Verlag editorial team who made this publication possible.

Contents

Acknowledgement 5

Foreword by *Laada Bilaniuk* 9

Natalia Kudriavtseva, Debra A. Friedman
Introduction: Critical Perspectives on Language and Power in
Ukraine and Kazakhstan 15

Svitlana Melnyk
Pen and Sword: Tracing the Ideological Dimension of Ukraine's
Language-in-Education Policy in Wartime 29

Maryna Vardanian
Translation as Ideology: Nation-Building vs Colonization
in Diasporic-Ukrainian and Soviet Literature for Young Adults . 61

Yuliia Soroka, Natalia Kudriavtseva, Igor Danylenko
Language and Social Inequalities in Ukraine: Monolingual and
Bilingual Practices 97

Elise S. Ahn, Juldyz Smagulova
School Language Choice in Almaty, Kazakhstan, and Emerging
Educational Inequality 137

Alla Nedashkivska
Pro-change or Safeguarding the Status-Quo:
Language Ideological Debates Surrounding the 2019 Ukrainian
Orthography 169

Lada Kolomiyets
Deconstruction of Russia's *Newspeak* in Ukrainian
Humorous Translation and Digital Folklore 201

Bridget Goodman
Conclusion: Future Perspectives on Language and Power in
Ukraine and Kazakhstan 257

Our Authors 261
Index 267

Foreword

Laada Bilaniuk

Language is at the core of who we are. Through language we come to understand and define ourselves, our place in the world, and our goals. As language flows between people, as it rolls off tongues and pages and screens and pours into minds, in and out again, it ties us together and binds us into communities. Language is the glue that holds society together. But it also builds walls between us. Differences of language — and just as importantly, differences of opinion about language — divide people.

As long as there are social differences, there will be linguistic differences. But language is not just a mirror of social realities — it is part of what makes up social realities. Linguistic differences allow us to perform, and to bring into being, social differences. Through the accumulation of the effects of myriad fleeting social interactions, larger social phenomena (such as gender, ethnicity, class, regional identities, and political groupings) come to exist, and continue to be recreated and transformed. How we choose to speak and write, which languages we learn, whose words we respect or disdain — all of these choices shape society. Those with institutional power or fame may sway usages and opinions more than those with less clout. But like drops eroding rock, the linguistic choices of the masses will also make their mark. The centripetal forces of language regulation and education are constantly up against the centrifugal forces of idiosyncrasy, innovation, rebelliousness, and irreverent play with words.

As language circulates through society, uniting and dividing, what we think about language is just as important as how we actually use language. Our language ideology is the prism through which we judge the words of others, both implicitly and explicitly. Are these words like ours, or are they "Other"? Are they worth listening to? Do they make our heart sing, or do they make us cringe, or laugh? Do they command respect, or can they be discounted? These judgements are just as central in the communicational work that language does as are the structural concerns of grammaticality.

Language ideology is not just about language. It is about social values and worldview. Our views on purism or hybridity in language are intertwined with beliefs about how categories of people, and societies, are defined. A language ideology is a personal belief system, based on a lifetime of accrued experiences, and individual views add up to the broader framework that underpins national laws regulating language use in government, education, media, and other public spheres. Regulation of language is regulation of society: which language is correct, which is taught, which language is to be used where—these designations shape access to social power.

This volume brings together studies that examine the political and ideological dimensions of language in societies that have been undergoing intense changes and that face existential threats to their languages and cultures. These societies are "post-Soviet," although now, more than thirty years after the dissolution of the Union of Soviet Socialist Republics, this label is problematic, in that it chains countries to a past that many consider a form of cultural imprisonment. The Soviet social experiment, officially intended to liberate and create equality for all people, in practice continued the imperialist and colonizing practices in which Russian was the language of power and prestige, the oxymoronic "first among equals." Languages other than Russian were ghettoized into rural and private spheres and state-approved folklore. Those who pushed those boundaries, let alone advocated for their own languages to play a more important role, faced serious and often brutal punishment. But linguistic diversity persisted, albeit in private, informal, less prestigious, and rural spaces.

All fifteen successor states enacted laws regulating language as part of their independence and nation-building, uplifting and formalizing the status of their titular languages as they confronted the historical dominance of Russian language when the USSR disintegrated. This legacy has been problematic even within the Russian Federation, which includes twenty-one republics identifying with non-Russian languages and cultures. In recent years, the central Russian government has eroded the autonomy of these republics and drastically limited support for their languages, threatening their survival. Outside of the Russian Federation, many in the independent successor countries view Russian as a colonizing language, and have put in force language policies that aim to decolonize. Such has been the case in Ukraine and Kazakhstan, the focus of the studies in this volume.

Ukraine and Kazakhstan have much in common. After the Russian Federation, which is the largest post-Soviet successor state in terms of both population and physical size, Ukraine and Kazakhstan are both the second largest: Ukraine in terms of population, and Kazakhstan in terms of geography. Both countries have very long borders with Russia — over half of Kazakhstan's border and over one third of Ukraine's. Both countries lost millions of people due to man-made famines during Stalin's rule in the early 1930s, known as the Holodomor in Ukraine and the Asharshylyk in Kazakhstan. These famines decimated the local populations, and set the stage for large influxes of ethnic Russians into their territories, drastically changing the demographic and linguistic makeup of the countries. During the Soviet era, as was the case in the other non-Russian Soviet republics, the indigenous languages and cultures were treated as second-rate, while Russian was promoted as a vehicle for social advancement. Both Kazakh and Ukrainian experienced manipulation of their alphabets, their vocabularies, and their grammars in order to bring them structurally closer to Russian. These changes were imposed most drastically in the 1930s, when certain letters and words were banned, but the pressures of structural linguistic Russification continued throughout the Soviet era, through the editing of publications, popular culture, and education. Russian language acted as a gateway to foreign languages and literatures as well, acting as a filter for the way foreign languages were taught and how literary works were translated.

Reversing Russification is a challenge, as any institutional change of standards runs up against the power of habit, even if it is a reversal of a top-down change that was imposed earlier. Much of our sense of what is linguistically correct operates below the threshold of awareness, and changes in rules make us consciously confront these rules. This can be an uncomfortable process, as most of us are habituated to react automatically when judging if something "feels" wrong or right. New rules disrupt the transparency and feeling of "naturalness" of language, and make us question how it works and the authority of those who would change the rules.

Both Kazakhstan and Ukraine have been dealing with the historical legacy of Russification, as well as ongoing pressures from Russia, which seeks to maintain its cultural and political influence, as they strive to reestablish their "own" languages and cultures. But what is one's "own" is a complicated question for many people. After decades of Russian as the language of power, prestige, and social advancement, many Kazakh and Ukrainian families were bilingual, or had even given up speaking the language of their parents and grandparents in favor of Russian. Both countries had sizeable ethnic Russian and other minorities, although the very concept of 'minority' has been shifting. In many contexts, identity (usually discussed in Soviet discourse as "nationality") is being reconceptualized as civic belonging rather than as a hereditary ethnic trait. The role of particular languages in defining ethnic and national identities is up for debate. Both countries are confronting the socioeconomic inequality that has paralleled language differences due to the historical low status of their titular languages. Other languages, in particular English, are rapidly taking on a more prominent role in education, international relations, and business. Bilingualism (which some under Soviet rule saw as a cover for Russification) and multilingualism are taking on new meanings in globalizing, market-oriented economies. The symbolic capital associated with language knowledge and use is shifting.

Language ideology is a complex and nuanced thing. The subtlest nuances of pronunciation can speak volumes (Ukraine's current wartime shibboleth 'palianytsia' comes to mind, where saying /pal'anyts'a/ or /paljanitsa/ determines friend or foe). Yet people can wield many varieties of language, and learn to communicate and connect across different language systems. Language rules and regimes can be rigid and oppressive, but language is also a means of resistance and liberation, a tool for empowerment. Its fluidity allows for interlingual play that defies authoritarian efforts to control meaning. This multifaceted nature of language, and the fact that language permeates individual selves and all of society, makes it such a powerful analytic lens. The works in this volume address many dimensions of language ideology and language politics, historical and contemporary, institutional and informal. Through the lens of language, they provide insight onto the social transformations that Kazakhstan and Ukraine experience as they chart their paths as sovereign countries. Since language is performative, these analyses become part of those paths, and we, their readers, are joining the journey.

Seattle, March 2024

Introduction
Critical Perspectives on Language and Power in Ukraine and Kazakhstan

Natalia Kudriavtseva, Debra A. Friedman

Contemporary notions of power go far beyond traditional views of authority legitimized by institutional social structures. In social sciences and humanities, power is understood as ingrained in all spheres of life, and even individuals are recognized as capable of exercising power by influencing beliefs and behavior of others. Significant in this respect is that social power can effectively be exercised via symbolic means, of which language constitutes an instrument of especial importance. These means may be realized by the state and embodied in legislation, dictionaries and grammars, or they may involve ideologically-mediated perceptions of language(s) promulgated through public discourses, language pedagogy, fiction, and popular culture, all of which employ language to (re-)structure the real world. As a crucial factor in making and unmaking groups, language is also a powerful means in creating identity and an instrument of mobilization, inclusion and exclusion.

Going beyond the limited definition of language as vocabulary and grammar, a focus on language as used by people in real life brings the perspectives of status and power relationships into the consideration of ways in which words and rules are employed. This focus involves conscious or subconscious decisions on how a language should be spoken, which linguistic variety should be used and whether the chosen form of expression is perceived as authoritative in a particular real-life situation. This inclusive perspective fosters the understanding of language as a kind of symbolic capital which grounds claims to position and power in social, cultural and political contexts. This means that a critical study of language as used in real life is always inevitably a study of underlying power relations.

The approaches that are pursued in this volume are "critical" because they focus on the social and ideological functions of language in the production, reproduction and contestation of social structures, identities and political institutions. In this respect, this special issue continues the tradition of research known as *critical linguistics* or *critical discourse analysis* (Fairclough & Wodak 1997) — a field of academic enquiry which produced a theory of language as a social practice where "the rules and norms that govern linguistic behavior have a social function, origin and meaning" (Hodge and Kress 1993: 204 cited in Simpson, Mayr & Statham 2019). This tradition was launched by the seminal volumes *Language and Control* (Fowler et al. 1979) and *Language as Ideology* (Hodge & Kress 1979) that challenged the Chomskian view of language as an abstract set of grammar rules. The critical analysis of language and power was taken up by books such as *Language and Power* (Fairclough 1989) and the series *Language, Power and Social Process* (Watts & Heller 1999–2011), which later transformed into *Language and Social Life* (Britain & Thurlow 2015). These volumes made a crucial contribution to the development of critical approaches in the sociolinguistic study of social problems by examining the ways in which language constructs identities, builds communities and mediates inequalities in social life. The field has since produced several introductory and comprehensive textbooks and coursebooks either presenting a broad consideration of language functioning in various social contexts, such as politics and the media (e. g. Thomas et al. 1999; Talbot, Atkinson & Atkinson 2003) or focusing on peculiarities of the application of critical discourse analysis to the contexts of institutions and organizations, gender, humor, race, the law and social media (e.g. Simpson, Mayr & Statham 2019; Kramsch 2020). However, there have been few case-specific volumes devoted to the study of language as situated in particular geographic contexts, such as *Language, Identity and Power in Modern India* (Isaka 2022) or *Language and Power* (Watzke, Miller & Mantero 2022), which included chapters focusing on a range of geographic contexts.

The authors in this special issue examine the exercise of power along the lines of leading traditions in critical research. The classic approach formulated by Weber in 1914 (Weber 1978) is concerned with the *corrective power* of the state and its institutions and investigates the ways in which powerful groups influence how language is used while also exercising control over access to language. Along with the tradition researching the exercise of power through the dominance of the state, there is a more recent approach exploring the exercise of power via *hegemony*. The concept of hegemony as advanced by Gramsci (1971) underscores the routine, "common sense" realizations of power whereby hegemonic opinions on language structure, nature and use are transmitted as "appropriate" and "natural." The concept of hegemony echoes what Bourdieu (1991) understood as *symbolic power*, which is always disguised as something else and requires the compliance of those subject to it to be exerted. Close to this stream of research scrutinizing power as exercised by consent is Foucault's (1972) methodological concept of *discourse* in which power is continuously produced, reinforced and contested in social communication. Being an instrument of power, discourse mediates ideological control as all spoken, written and visual texts are shaped and determined by political ideologies as well as by explicit and implicit attitudes and beliefs, i.e. ideologies, about language.

The six contributions to this volume represent the first collection of essays presenting a critical examination of language and power relations in Ukraine and Kazakhstan. The post-Soviet period in Ukraine and Kazakhstan has been characterized not only by changes in the economic marketplace in the transition from communism to capitalism, but also in the linguistic marketplace. During the Soviet period, Russian was the primary language of schooling, media, and government administration in both countries, leading to widespread language shift away from their titular languages, especially among the educated urban elites. In addition, following independence in 1991, both countries found themselves with a large ethnic Russian (and Russian speaking) diaspora. Since independence, Ukrainian and Kazakh, which occupied relatively peripheral positions in the Soviet-era marketplace, have been elevated to the status of national languages and institutionalized in government and schools, thus increasing their symbolic power. Nevertheless, the years since independence have also seen contentious debates around language. Employing various methodological tools ranging from surveys to critical discourse analysis of legislation, literary texts and social media products, the authors in this volume seek to demonstrate and explain how political relations and hegemonic ideologies have been reproduced and negotiated at both the macro-level in legislation on language and state-sponsored media channels and embodiments of political and linguistic ideologies in translations, as well as at the micro-level of everyday language practices, school choice, and discourses on social media platforms.

Much of the research presented in this volume was collected during the tumultuous decade beginning with the so-called "language Maidan" in Ukraine — a mass public protest against adopting the 2012 law "On the Principles of the State Language Policy," also known as the Kolesnichenko-Kivalov law, that was largely seen as a means of allowing Russian to function on a par with Ukrainian, or even to substitute for it, in official domains — and culminating in the full-scale Russian invasion of Ukraine in February 2022. This period also saw the 2013–2014 Euromaidan protests, a three-month mass protest triggered by the government's refusal to sign an association agreement with the European Union, followed by Russian aggression in the Donbas and Crimea, as well as the "Bloody January" protests in Kazakhstan in 2022, which were triggered by anger over economic conditions and government corruption and violently suppressed with the assistance of a military force from Russia. Although these events took place in the political sphere, they have also had profound effects on the linguistic marketplace. While largely focusing on Ukraine in the years leading up to the full-scale invasion, these contributions also relate to the current realities of the ongoing Russo-Ukrainian war as they critically analyze and dismantle Russian propagandistic narratives, expose the repercussions of the Russian invasion on Ukraine's occupied territories, and raise potential implications regarding the impact of the ongoing hostilities on language policies, attitudes, and practices in the region.

The volume opens with Svitlana Melnyk's comprehensive overview of the impact of these political events on the evolution of Ukrainian language-in-education policy and the shifting attitudes towards the status of Ukrainian, Russian, and minority languages (i.e., Hungarian, Polish, etc.) in the Ukrainian educational system and in Ukrainian society in general. Drawing from a wide range of policy documents and media commentary, the paper uses Churchill's (1986) model of education for linguistic and cultural minorities to trace recent changes in Ukraine's language-in-education policy away from "minority language immersion" (i.e., education in the mother tongue, including Russian) to "bilingual education" (instruction in the minority language along with Ukrainian) and to situate them within their historical, political, and ideological contexts. The analysis carefully documents the interconnections between events at the legislative level (e. g., the "Law on Education" of 2017) and the evolving sociolinguistic situation in the aftermath of Euromaidan and the occupation of Crimea and the Donbas, which intensified perceptions regarding the importance of the Ukrainian language in strengthening national identity and unity in the face of Russian aggression and transformed language choice from "a decision about expressing personal identity" or a "politically neutral code choice," to "an activity with real political repercussions" (Bilaniuk 2016: 141, 147). The full-scale invasion that began on February 24, 2022, on the pretext of "protecting" the Russian-speaking minority in Ukraine has provided further impetus for this trend. The scope of the paper also expands beyond state educational institutions to consider the impact of grassroots efforts such as *Free Ukrainian Language Courses* (Безкоштовні курси української мови). This is the first nationwide network of volunteer language instructors, who have been teaching Ukrainian to Ukraine's speakers of Russian since 2013, which has since transformed into an online project—the platform *Ye-Mova* (Є-Мова)—designed to target primarily Russian-speaking Ukrainians, including those residing in the occupied territories of Crimea and the Donbas (see also Kudriavtseva 2023). The language-of-education situation in these occupied territories is another crucial focus of this paper, which notes the ongoing "Russification" of education in these areas, a process that includes requiring local citizens to send their children to schools that follow the Russian curriculum and ending instruction in subjects such as the Ukrainian language, literature, and history, in effect, recolonizing Ukrainian consciousness as well as Ukrainian territory.

The second paper, Maryna Vardanian's study on translations of literary texts performed in Soviet Ukraine and Ukrainian Diaspora, is situated in an historical context, yet has clear repercussions for understanding how the corrective power of the state, reinforced by the exercise of power via hegemony, continues to hold sway in contemporary Russia and reinforces its ongoing neocolonialist project. The primary goal of the sovietization of literature for children and young adults in Soviet Ukraine was achieved through the state mechanism of censorship which pursued the implementation of communist ideology into children's books and curated the selection of texts for translation. The political ideology was reproduced via the strategy of literal translation carried out from a preceding Russian translation into the other languages of the USSR "faithfully" recreating the form and content of the Russian "original." The political ideology was further bolstered through the hegemonic policy of Russification whose aim was the assimilation of "fraternal nations" under Moscow's imperial rule. The author also shows the contestations of ideologies in children's translations. In the diasporic translation of Boussenard's *Le Capitaine Casse-Cou*, the Soviet colonial ideology was opposed by attributing the language of the original text to the so-called "cultural languages" and performing the translation from the French original work. The language ideology for the source language (French) is extended onto the target language—Ukrainian—and realized in compliance with the 1928 Ukrainian spelling, which also manifests a protest against the Soviet policy of Russification. The language ideologies of the diasporic translation serve to transmit the hegemonic diasporic view of the self-sufficiency of Ukrainian culture and identity and socialize young Ukrainians into an imagined community of a self-sustaining Ukrainian nation. Significantly, Vardanian reveals how both the Soviet and the diasporic translations of Boussenard's *Le Capitaine Casse-Cou* negotiated the ideologies of the French original. In the Soviet translation, the purpose of colonization as the goal in the Anglo-Boer War is discursively diluted and the focus is displaced to the French international help in the struggle of the Boers to gain independence, while the diasporic version of *Le Capitaine Casse-Cou* emphasizes the opposition of the colony to the metropolis stressing the idea that only natives of the land can defend it. This study on ideologies in translation remarkably resonates with the current realities of the Russo-Ukrainian war. The Soviet-cultivated image of a fully militarized child coming to rescue the poor and oppressed is harnessed by the Russian propaganda machine which discursively reshapes it into the "liberator of the Donbas bombarded for eight years." As many previous generations born in the USSR, new generations born in modern Russia are still brought up within the same ideological frame for them to be ready to continue the traditions of Soviet colonization.

The remaining papers in this volume remind us of the importance of shifting our gaze from the macro-level of state power and policy to also consider the diverse ways in which supposedly hegemonic state-sponsored ideologies, discourses, and policies are received and renegotiated by individual social actors. Using survey data (Soroka, Kudriavtseva & Danylenko; Ahn & Smagulova) and critical analyses of digital discourses (Nedashkivska; Kolomiyets), these studies highlight the power and limits of state policy and official discourses in legitimating certain languages and instilling them with symbolic power.

Soroka, Kudriavtseva, and Danylenko examine language practices in pre-2022 Ukraine based on data from a nationwide survey conducted in 2017–2018. The aim of the survey, among other things, was to measure social inequalities in Ukraine as related to language. While drawing on Bourdieu's notions of symbolic power and the legitimate language, the authors align with reconceptualizations of Bourdieu's framework, whereby more than one language can be considered legitimate (e. g., Woolard 1985). Examining the symbolic power of Ukrainian and Russian, with the former being legitimized by the state while the latter is endorsed as a habitual means of communication, the authors also probe into the linguistic capital of Ukrainian-Russian bilingualism in Ukraine by introducing an additional variable for Ukrainian-Russian bilinguals. The analysis of the survey results for the three identified groups (Ukrainian speakers, Russian speakers, Ukrainian-Russian bilinguals) as regards questions on self-assessed social status, material welfare, sectors of the economy where they are employed and opportunities for overseas travel shows no significant inequalities between the respondents in question. This means that neither linguistic competence (in Ukrainian or Russian) was perceived as linked to more opportunities in pre-war Ukraine, while at the same time neither language was viewed by respondents as a factor contributing to social tension. This is an important finding to be considered against the backdrop of Putin's "pretexts" for the ongoing war whereby "liberation of Ukraine's Russian speakers" was put forward as a justification for the 2022 full-scale Russian invasion. Similarly important is the conclusion that the authors draw on the traditional perception of Ukraine's south-eastern regions as largely Russian-speaking which, as they suggest, is no longer valid. The revealed bilingualism of the southeast is in line with earlier research on respondents coming from the Donbas while it also accords with another finding that Soroka, Kudriavtseva and Danylenko make on the linguistic capital related to Ukrainian-Russian bilingualism. The author's assumption that there may be greater symbolic power linked to bilingual practice, with bilingualism being achieved by adding Ukrainian to the already possessed knowledge of Russian, offers two important questions to be considered in future research: about the relevance of the label "Russian speaker" in terms of Ukraine, namely, the implication of monolingualism conveyed by this label; as well as about the relevance of the same implication conveyed by the term "legitimate language." While more research is needed in view of the changing realities influenced by the war, the findings of the study are already sufficient to raise these important questions.

Ahn and Smagulova offer another corrective to assumptions regarding the hegemonic power of the state in legitimating languages in their study of school choice in Almaty, Kazakhstan. In Kazakhstan, longstanding economic disparities between rural and urban areas have also shaped an imbalance between the symbolic power of Russian (spoken by urban residents, many of whom historically were ethnic Russians) and Kazakh (spoken by ethnic Kazakhs who tended to reside in villages). Based on a large-scale survey conducted in 158 classes in 29 comprehensive schools in Almaty between April and May 2014, their analysis demonstrates that despite efforts by the state to raise the symbolic capital accorded to Kazakh by making it the state language and encouraging Kazakh-medium education, Russian-speaking Kazakhs continue to favor Russian-medium education. Kazakh-medium institutions, on the other hand, seem to function almost as ghettoes for Kazakh-speaking rural migrants who, for historical reasons, lack the economic, cultural, and linguistic capital that would enable them to succeed academically. In other words, state-sponsored efforts to increase the symbolic capital accorded to Kazakh since independence do not appear to be reversing the process of language shift among Russian-speaking ethnic Kazakhs, nor are they creating a generation of new Kazakh speakers. In addition, although the expansion of Kazakh-medium schooling in Almaty has provided students with opportunities for mother-tongue education, it has failed to address the socioeconomic inequities that have relegated many students in these schools to the margins of society. As Ahn and Smagulova note, this raises questions regarding social cohesion and may have contributed to the outbreak of protests in January 2022. The effect of the Russian invasion of Ukraine on this delicate situation remains to be seen; however, some commentators have noted increasingly negative attitudes towards Russia as well as an increased sense of national consciousness among Kazakhs since the outbreak of the war, especially among young people (Dumoulin 2023), both of which have the potential to alter the perceived legitimacy of Russian and Kazakh in the Kazakh linguistic marketplace. Ahn and Smagulova's survey has laid the groundwork for future research to investigate how these developments play out over the coming years.

Alla Nedashkivska's paper focuses on an analysis of social media discourses around the introduction of the 2019 Ukrainian orthography, which reintroduced some aspects of the 1928 orthography that were later abandoned in the 1933 "Russified" version. Adapting Sebba's (2009, 2012) sociocultural model that sees orthography as embodying historical, social, and political meaning, the article explores the diversity of responses to the 2019 orthography and the multiple language ideologies through which individuals sought to justify these responses as reflected on the popular social media platforms *Facebook*, *Instagram*, and *TikTok* between May 2019 and March 2021. On the one hand, some commentators on *Facebook* supported the new orthography on the grounds that the changes are necessary to rid Ukrainian of "Russified" forms introduced in the 1933 version, thus revoicing dominant national ideologies and framing the new orthography as emblematic of "Ukrainianness" through the semiotic process of *iconization* (Sebba 2009, 2012). However, these are not the only voices. A fairly radical reframing of the debate over orthography is found in the comments of those who oppose the new orthography by characterizing it as the project of a (possibly foreign) elite and implying that it represents an artificial version of the language that does not represent "real" Ukrainian as it is actually used by ordinary people. This can be read as not just opposition to the new orthography as such, but as opposition to top-down prescriptions of how language should be used and, perhaps more importantly, who decides. And while the young people on *TikTok* tend to endorse the new orthography, they take their own unique approach. Rather than representing it as a return to an older more "authentic" past practice, they "rebrand" it as something cool and contemporary. The generational divide evident in these divergent discourses, in particular, the impassioned defense of and advocacy for Ukrainian on the part of young people on *TikTok*, raises some interesting questions regarding future direction and vitality of the language and also points to a shift in attitudes away from young people's preference for Russian as more prestigious that was found in earlier studies (Kulyk 2015; see also Friedman 2016). This is also in line with recent surveys that have revealed that the decade since Euromaidan has seen a trend for "popular Ukrainianization," with growing percentages of respondents who choose Ukrainian as the language of everyday use (Kulyk 2023).

The final paper by Lada Kolomiyets brings us full circle back to wartime Ukraine in a critical examination of current Russian propaganda discourses and their deconstruction in Ukrainian parodistic translation and digital folklore. Employing critical discourse analysis, the author reveals the role of Russian state media in the ongoing war as the media outlets reproduce Russia's political attitudes through their function as the ideological state apparatus (Althusser). Close linguistic analysis of their Orwellian *Newspeak* shows how the Kremlin's manipulative discourse on the ongoing Russia's war against Ukraine constructs a "correct" reality for the population of Russia whose only worthwhile life goal, as proclaimed, is to fall on the field of battle. While the Russian populace largely seems to consent to the power of the state in their routine reproduction of hegemonic opinions, Ukrainians are actively debunking imperial myths via humorous deconstructive translation on social media. Drawing on Derrida's deconstruction, Kolomiyets suggests that Russian political slogans and statements are deprived of their propagandistic effect through the procedures of neologization, borrowing with meaning transfer, alternative word formation and wordplay in the parodistic translation of Russian messages into Ukrainian. The deconstruction of propagandistic narratives is reinforced in Ukrainian digital folklore by creating new narrative frames and rendering the concepts of Russian *Newspeak* into anecdotal and facetious contexts. An invaluable component of the study is the multimodal analysis of visual images reflecting various episodes in the Russo-Ukrainian war whereby deconstruction is performed by graphically explicating the contradictoriness of Kremlin's messages and the realities. It is remarkable that, in the process of deconstruction in the digital space, Ukrainians overcome not only Russian imperial myths, but also their own centuries-old national traumas. The study raises an important and timely question of the cultures of war and the significance of digital discourse accompanying real warfare. Since the mankind has entered the new age of cyberwars, it is language that is being used as the main weapon in virtual battles.

Taken together, this collection of papers vividly illustrates Kroskrity's (2004) observations regarding the fluidity, multiplicity, and contestation among language ideologies and discourses and how these are employed by states, interest groups, and individuals as resources to construct or deconstruct power and negotiate their place in the social world. That is, the struggles over control of language that have taken place and continue to take place in educational institutions, in literature, on social media, and in everyday language practices that are documented in these papers are never only about language, but are intimately interconnected with larger social issues and political projects. While these struggles are hardly unique to Ukraine and Kazakhstan, the social upheavals and military aggression that have marked the past decade in the region bring them into high relief and underscore the need to move beyond the simplistic notions of language, identity, and power that sometimes characterize popular media discourses to consider the complex mechanisms through which power is exercised in societies undergoing profound social and political change.

Bibliography:

Bilaniuk, Laada. (2016). Ideologies of language in wartime. In *Revolution and war in contemporary Ukraine: the challenge of change*, Bertelsen, Olga (ed). Stuttgart: Ibidem Verlag, 139–160.

Bourdieu, Pierre. (1991). *Language and symbolic power*. Trans. by Gino Raymond and Matthew Adamson. Cambridge: Polity Press.

Britain, David & Thurlow, Crispin. (eds) (2015). *Language and social life*. Berlin: De Gruyter Mouton.

Churchill, Stacy. (1986). *The education of linguistic and cultural minorities in OECD countries*. San Diego: College-Hill Press.

Dumoulin, Marie. (2023). Steppe change: how Russia's war on Ukraine is reshaping Kazakhstan. *European Council on Foreign Relations*, 13 April, https://ecfr.eu/wp-content/uploads/2023/04/Steppe-chan ge-How-Russias-war-on-Ukraine-is-reshaping-Kazakhstan_1.pdf (accessed 28 March 2024).

Fairclough, Norman. (1989). *Language and power*. New York: Longman.

Fairclough, Norman & Wodak, Ruth. (1997). Critical discourse analysis. In *Discourse as social interaction*, van Dijk, Teun (ed). London: Sage, 258–285.

Foucault, Michel. (1972). *The archaeology of knowledge and the discourse on language*. New York: Pantheon.

Fowler, Roger, Hodge, Robert, Kress, Gunther & Trew, Tony. (eds) (1979). *Language and control*. London: Routledge & Kegan Paul.

Friedman, Debra A. (2016). Our language: (re)imagining communities in Ukrainian language classrooms. *Journal of Language, Identity and Education* 15(3): 165–179.

Gramsci, Antonio. (1971). *Selections from the prison notebooks*. Trans. by Hoare, Quintin and Smith, Geoffrey Nowell. London: Lawrence & Wishart.

Hodge, Robert & Kress, Gunther. (1979). *Language as ideology*. London: Routledge & Kegan Paul.

Hodge, Robert & Kress, Gunther. (1993). *Language and ideology*. London: Routledge.

Isaka, Riho. (2022). *Language, identity and power in modern India: Gujarat, c. 1850–1960*. London & New York: Routledge.

Kramsch, Claire. (2020). *Language as symbolic power*. Cambridge: Cambridge University Press.

Kroskrity, Paul. (2004). Language ideologies. In *A companion to linguistic anthropology*, Duranti, Alessandro (ed). Malden, MA: Blackwell, 496–517.

Kudriavtseva, Natalia. (2023). Ukrainian language revitalization online: targeting Ukraine's Russian speakers. In *Teaching and learning resources for endangered languages*, Valijärvi, Riitta & Kahn, Lily (eds). Leiden: Brill, 203–223.

Kulyk, Volodymyr. (2015). The age factor in language practices and attitudes: continuity and change in Ukraine's bilingualism. *Nationalities Papers* 43(2): 283–301.

Kulyk, Volodymyr. (2023). Ukrainians now (say that they) speak predominantly Ukrainian. *Ukrainian Analytical Digest* 001: 6–11.

Sebba, Mark. (2009). *Spelling and society: the culture and politics of orthography around the world*. Cambridge: Cambridge University Press (online).

Sebba, Mark. (2012). Orthography as social action: scripts, spelling, identity and power. In *Orthography as social action*, Jaffe, Alexandra, Androutsopoulos, Jannis, Sebba, Mark & Johnson, Sally (eds). Boston & Berlin: De Gruyter Mouton, 1–21.

Simpson, Paul, Mayr, Andrea & Statham, Simon. (2019). *Language and power. A resource book for students*. London & New York: Routledge.

Talbot, Mary, Atkinson, Karen & Atkinson, David. (2003). *Language and power in the modern world*. Edinburgh: Edinburgh University Press.

Thomas, Linda, Wareing, Shân, Singh, Ishtla, Peccei, Jean Stilwell, Thornborrow, Joanna & Jones, Jason. (1999). *Language, society and power. An introduction*. London and New York: Routledge.

Watts, Richard & Heller, Monica. (eds) (1999–2011). *Language, power and social process*. Berlin: De Gruyter Mouton.

Watzke, John L., Miller, Paul Chamness & Mantero, Miguel. (eds) (2022). *Language and power*. Charlotte, NC: Information Age Publishing Inc.

Weber, Max. (1978). *Economy and society: an outline of interpretive sociology*. Roth, Guenther & Wittich, Claus (eds). CA: University of California Press.

Woolard, Kathryn A. (1985). Language variation and cultural hegemony: toward an integration of sociolinguistic and social theory. *American Ethnologist* 12(4): 738–748.

Pen and Sword
Tracing the Ideological Dimension of Ukraine's Language-in-Education Policy in Wartime[1]

Svitlana Melnyk

Abstract. *This chapter considers the current language-in-education policy in Ukraine within the broad context of language ideologies and sociolinguistic developments which have taken place since Maidan. In particular, I draw attention to the most recent changes in language education that have occurred due to the full-scale Russian invasion. Since the declaration of its independence in 1991, Ukraine has tried to balance the protection and promotion of Ukrainian as the sole state language, with the preservation of education in national minority languages through immersion education and bilingual schools and classes. Russia's war against Ukraine and its temporary occupation of Ukrainian territories have brought changes to the domain of language education, which will be discussed.*

Key words: *Ukraine, language-in-education policy, Russian-Ukrainian war, linguicide, language policy, minority languages*

1. Introduction

Since Ukraine's declaration of independence in 1991, its language-in-education policy has been aimed at simultaneously revitalizing and promoting Ukrainian as the only state language and a marker of Ukrainian identity, while protecting and preserving national minorities' rights to education in their own languages. State and communal educational institutions have facilitated the implementation of policies preserving the linguistic educational rights of national minorities. Ukrainian has been taught as a separate subject in these institutions, rather than serving as the primary language of education. The system of these educational institutions has been non-

---

1   I would like to express my deepest gratitude to the editors and anonymous reviewers for their insightful and valuable comments.

uniform, and to a large extent, has depended on regional characteristics and the educational demands of one or another linguistic group. Additionally, Ukrainian language-in-education policy has been influenced by variations in population density, the existence of a collective will to maintain national language and culture, societal prejudices, and in some cases, the support of foreign countries.

This ethnic and linguistic diversity has piqued scholarly interests in recent years. Over the last few decades, language education in Ukraine has been the focus of several publications, which present both theoretical research and empirical studies. Applying a rich array of methodological frameworks, the authors of these publications incorporate analyses of many themes, such as language education of certain communities (Kulyk 2013, Csernicskó & Orosz 2019), language attitudes in the educational sphere (Friedman 2016), and language ideologies and practices (Kudriavtseva 2021). Bilaniuk & Melnyk (2008) look at the educational practices in Ukraine within the broad context of shifting Ukrainian-Russian bilingualism and minority language education.

The authors point out that, in the educational sphere, legislative and institutional changes post-independence aimed to increase the status of Ukrainian as the sole state language. At the same time, the authors made the prediction that Russian-language schools will remain for some time due to regional peculiarities and the social practices of the Russian-speaking population. They argued as well that non-Russian minority language education will continue. However, since this publication, many important events have occurred that have changed specific ideological dimensions and sociolinguistic practices related to the educational sphere. Among them are: Euromaidan, the Russian-Ukrainian war—which began in 2014 with the occupation of Crimea and the Donbas region—as well as the full-scale Russian invasion of Ukraine beginning February 24, 2022. At the state legislative level, a few important laws have been adopted, namely the "Law on Education" (2017) and the Law of Ukraine, "On Ensuring the Functioning of the Ukrainian Language as the State Language" (2019), which also affected language-in-education policy in Ukraine. Therefore, there is a need for an update to Bilaniuk & Melnyk's findings in the context of recent sociolinguistic changes.

This chapter aims to analyze language education in Ukraine using Churchill's (1986) model of education for linguistic and cultural minorities within a broad context of the profound changes that have taken place in Ukraine after 2014. In particular, special attention is paid to the contemporary situation and the impact that the full-scale Russian invasion has had on language practices and language ideologies in both the sociolinguistic and educational domains. After providing a brief background for the study, I will explain my approach and the Churchill's methodological framework. Then, I will examine the most recent ideological issues and sociolinguistic practices which take place in Ukraine due to the above-discussed events. Finally, I will analyze language-in-education policy after 2014 as well as the public initiatives in language education which occurred due to the full-scale invasion of Ukraine.

2. Background

The current Ukrainian sociolinguistic situation is deeply-rooted in its past. While a full account of the historical background of language policy in Ukraine is beyond the scope of this article, I will provide a brief overview to situate the current sociolinguistic changes within their historical context.

At many times in its history, the Ukrainian language has been subject to suppression and bans, including in the educational system. The website "Chronology of Linguistic Events in Ukraine: The External History of the Ukrainian Language", based on books by Kubaichuk (2004) and Masenko et al. (2005), provides information about such suppressions. In the 19th century, there were two imperial documents that introduced the policy of prohibiting the use of Ukrainian, which at that time was called "Little Russian." The so-called Valuev Decree (1863) stated that, "teaching in all schools is without exception in the common Russian language, and nowhere is use of the Little Russian language permitted" as well as "a Little Russian language has not, does not, and cannot exist" (Magocsi 2010: 393). The *Ems Ukase* (or Ems Decree) (1876), among other restrictions, outlawed the publication of "all original works or translations" in Ukrainian, the staging of all performances in Ukrainian, and the importation of Ukrainian language texts written abroad into the Russian Empire. The only exception to this were historical sources on some topics, provided they appeared in the "common Russian orthography". Moreover, no subject would be permitted to be taught in Ukrainian in lower-level schools (Magocsi 2010: 396).

In the early years of the Soviet Union, the policy of *korenizatsiya* (indigenization, rooting) was introduced. In Soviet Ukraine it was known as Ukrainianization. The main goals of this policy were to impose Soviet ideology on Ukrainian society through the Ukrainian language, as well as the strengthen socialism in the Soviet Empire at large (Masenko 2017; Martin 2019; Pavlenko 2008). When the regime succeeded in these aims, in the 1930s the policy of Ukrainianization was replaced by the policy of Russification. At that time Soviet propaganda introduced the idea of the special status of the Russian language as a language of inter-ethnic communication and the language of the "leaders of world proletariat" Lenin and Stalin, which made speakers of this language privileged (Masenko 2017). Historically, Russian speakers in Ukraine had enjoyed a privileged position, and as Mykola Riabchuk (2000) points out, the Russian-speaking minority in Ukraine was privileged not only politically and culturally — as a representative of the imperial majority — but also socially. A significant factor in Russophone social privilege is their status as a predominantly urban population, purporting them to be superior to the predominantly rural Ukrainophones enslaved by the collective farm system. Riabchuk's opinion echoes the opinion of the well-known Ukrainian dissident Ivan Dziuba, who pointed out that the real anti-Ukrainian policy was not to prohibit the use of Ukrainian (because that would be impossible), but to make it so that people themselves no longer wanted to speak it (Dziuba 1998).

As an independent state, Ukraine proclaimed Ukrainian as the sole state language. In many publications, the term "state language" is used as a synonym for "official language," but in the post-Soviet context, this concept carries a symbolic meaning (Hogan-

Brun & Melnyk 2012). The idea of 'a state language' and not just an official language reflects the ideology which acknowledges the prominent role that the language plays in the Ukrainian national identity and state formation. For Ukraine, the Ukrainian language became a symbol of statehood together with the national anthem, flag, and the coat of arms. As a result of this policy, Ukrainian obtained a higher status in the society and its usage has expanded, especially in the official and educational spheres. At the same time, before the war, Russian language usage prevailed in many spheres, such as business, sports, and in popular culture—especially in the south and east of the country and in many Ukrainian cities. Russian remained a popular tool of communication.

A large-scale asymmetrical Ukrainian-Russian bilingualism was a visible feature of sociolinguistic developments of the state and a substantial part of the country's linguistic landscape (Masenko 2004; Melnyk & Csernicskó 2010). This asymmetrical bilingualism was not only societal, but also regional. Much of the population spoke Russian fluently, but a significant percentage of the population did not speak Ukrainian. This was mainly due to many ethnic Ukrainians in the east and south, as well as other national minorities (Belarusians, Jews, Greeks), enduring russification. The situation with Russian-Ukrainian bilingualism became even more complicated because of *surzhyk*, which is a mixed Ukrainian-Russian vernacular, as well as a "high degree of code switching by bilinguals" (Bilaniuk 2005: 105). For more information about *surzhyk* see Bilaniuk (2005), Masenko (2019). After the declaration of independence, when the state faced the task of protecting the Ukrainian language and restoring its prestigious status, *surzhyk* was perceived negatively by linguists, writers, and other intellectuals.

For example, Yuri Andrukhovych called it *"krovozmisne dytya bilinhvizmu"* (an inbred child of bilingualism.) The negative attitudes towards *surzhyk* and the emphasis on purism were "part of efforts to elevate and define a prestigious Ukrainian language, to separate it from its connotation as a backward peasant language" (Bilaniuk & Melnyk 2008: 71). Gradually, with the strengthening of the Ukrainian language as the state language, attitudes toward *surzhyk* have been changing. Writers began to use it in their works as an authentic language (such as Les' Poderevianskyi, Saigon), and after the war began, discussions about *surzhyk* and negative attitudes toward it have decreased, perhaps because many Ukrainian defenders themselves speak *surzhyk*.

However, this sociolinguistic situation of bilingualism did not change the official language policy of monolingualism, and as Aneta Pavlenko (2006: 86) points out, the choice of a single, rather than dual, language policy can be understood as a strategy of resistance to the high degree of Russification. In Ukraine, there has been a powerful legislative framework that has regulated the status and functioning of languages. Ukrainian legislation has been aimed at strengthening the status of the Ukrainian language as the state language and protecting the development and use of languages of national minorities. The legal basis of language policy was established by many legal documents, among them the Ukrainian Constitution, language laws, and special laws and treaties with neighboring countries.[2] However, in many cases, these legal documents were prescriptive by nature and did not provide the requisite legal tools and mechanisms for regulating language situations or protecting language rights. Although they significantly changed the situation with the official use of Ukrainian language as the state language, only to a lesser extent did they influence the sociolinguistic situation and the real language practices of the population.

The situation however markedly changed following 2014, after Euromaidan and the occupation of Crimea and the Donbas, and especially after the start of the full-scale invasion by Russia on February 24, 2022. Language policy became a part of the national ideology "Army-Language-Faith" (*Armiya, mova, vira*) for the formation of contemporary Ukrainian identity (Ukrainska Pravda 2018). The peculiarity of this period in the sociolinguistic development of Ukraine lies within the combination of top-down efforts for strengthening the official status of the Ukrainian language in its

---

2   For more information regarding independent Ukraine's legislative action prior to 2014 see: Csernicskó & Fedinec (2016), Besters-Dilger (2008), Moser (2014).

combination with bottom-up public initiatives and activities in promoting its usage and development. These will be discussed below.

3. Methodology

Since the chapter considers the most recent changes in language education and linguistic practices in Ukrainian society related to the war, it relies on the most recent publications in Ukrainian media and social media platforms as well as on the information from official websites of the Ministry of Education and Science, Language ombudsman, city councils, etc. When analyzing these different primary and secondary sources, I examined references to education policy and changes in the education sphere occurring during the war that began in 2014 and from the time of the full-scale invasion. I searched for information on how this invasion changed the ideological dimension of the language issue in Ukrainian society and how these changes have influenced educational practices, including in the occupied territories. Thus, in terms of theoretical approach, this is a qualitative and interpretive study.

In this chapter, Ukraine's language-in-education policy since 2014 is analyzed using Churchill's (1986) framework of state responses to the education of cultural and linguistic minorities. This model is a complex taxonomy of six stages of policy responses to the educational and language needs of minority groups, including definitions, educational issues, and language outlook. Stephen May (2012), in his publication, *Language and Minority rights: Ethnicity, Nationalism and the Politics of Language*, provides a thorough analysis and explanation of these stages; for the purpose of this research, I will be using his simplified model:

- Stage 1 represents assimilation and submersion in the majority language in education.
- Stage 2 is a modified form of assimilation. This stage associates a minority group's educational disadvantage with family status. Some supplementary programs are promoted to facilitate adjustment to the so-called majority society.

- Stage 3 is so-called multicultural education. As May (2012: 185) points out, "the essence of this multicultural model is the recognition of the rights to be different and to be respected for it, not necessarily to maintain a distinct language and culture."
- Stage 4 recognizes the need for support of the minority language, at least as a transitional measure. In education, this is usually implemented through transitional bilingual education programs, which use a minority language in the initial years of schooling.
- Stage 5 recognizes the rights of minorities to maintain and develop their language and cultures in private life and corresponds to the maintenance of bilingual programs that teach through a minority language in schools.
- Stage 6 sees the granting of full official status to a minority language.

Later in this chapter I will show how this model correlates with language-in-education policy in Ukraine and what stage corresponds to the current Ukrainian situation.

4. Language Ideologies and Sociolinguistic Developments after 2014

The current situation in education should be discussed in the broader context of language ideologies and sociolinguistic practices, as educational practices are deeply rooted in language policy and the language use of Ukrainian society. These changes and tendencies in sociocultural and linguistic developments have become the subject of several national polls and surveys. The polls show the favorable attitude of Ukrainians towards the Ukrainian language as a single state language.

In 2019, the Ilko Kucheriv Democratic Initiatives Foundation and the Razumkov Ukrainian Centre for Economic and Political Studies conducted a survey on language preferences. The majority of Ukrainians surveyed believed that Ukrainian should be the country's only state language. At the same time, they held that the Russian language should not be subject to restrictions in the private communications of citizens. These data are consistent with the data of another poll conducted by the Ilko Kucheriv Democratic Initiatives Foundation in August 2020. The study showed that most Ukrainians in all regions supported the idea that all citizens of Ukraine should be able to speak the state language, that Ukrainian should be the language of communication for civil servants and officials, and that most subjects in all public schools should be taught in the state language.

Regarding the prestige of speaking Ukrainian and Russian, as well as their social roles, studies reveal that Ukrainian has been more often valued for its symbolic importance while Russian has been predominantly seen as a communicative tool (Kulyk 2019; Kudriavtseva 2021). Some research highlights positive language attitudes and shifts toward Ukrainian among Russophone citizens after Euromaidan (Seals 2019; Kulyk 2016). For some citizens, their language usage is a conscious choice (*svidomy vybir*); for others, it is part of their heritage; and for still others, it is a political statement.

Each of these narratives shows a key theme — the increasing importance of the Ukrainian language in national identity after Euromaidan and continued Russian aggression against Ukraine. However, despite these positive attitudes, a large number of Ukrainian citizens remained Russophone (or primarily Russian speaking), especially in the south and east. The ideology of "it does not matter what language one speaks" is reflected in the linguistic practices of many Russian speakers who view themselves as part of the Ukrainian nation but hesitate to change their daily language preferences (Kulyk 2016). As suggested by an anonymous reviewer, language is not an automatic marker of identity or national orientation (as Russian-speaking Ukrainians speakers see themselves *as Ukrainians* and are fighting to defend Ukrainian sovereignty).

Besides sociolinguistic changes in language choice and language attitudes, there were very also important changes in language policy after Maidan:

- In April 2019 the Ukrainian Parliament adopted the law "On Ensuring the Functioning of the Ukrainian Language as the State Language," which greatly expanded protections for the state language (see Kudriavtseva 2019);

- The position of State Language Protection Commissioner was established in 2019;
- In accordance with the Law of Ukraine "On Ensuring the Functioning of the Ukrainian Language as the State Language," the National Commission on State Language Standards was established. This commission develops and approves standards for the Ukrainian language as the state language, as well as develops methods for testing language proficiency.

As noted earlier, Russia's full-scale invasion of Ukraine, significantly changed the ideological dimension and sociolinguistic practices of Ukrainian society, both at the official and everyday levels. At the official level, the use of the Russian language continues to decrease. This is evidenced both from the data of sociological surveys and policies of the government, as well as city or municipal councils. As Ukrainian political analyst Mykola Riabchuk points out, we continue to observe the delegitimization of Russian on the official level (Riabchuk 2022). The most recent examples of such delegitimization include the following:

- New norms of the language law "On Ensuring the Functioning of the Ukrainian Language as the State Language" came into force in July 2022. They regulate the use of the state language on the Internet and the language of computer software. A computer program with a user interface deployed in Ukraine must have a user interface in the national language and/or English or other official languages of the European Union (Ukrinform, July 16, 2022);
- The Kyiv City Council renamed more than forty city objects (streets, squares etc.) as a part of de-Russification (*Kyyivs'ka mis'ka rada* (Kyiv City Council) September 8, 2022);
- In April 2023, President Zelensky signed the law "On the Condemnation and Prohibition of Propaganda of Russian Imperial Policy in Ukraine and the Decolonization of Toponymy" (Zakon 2023);

- On July 20, 2022, the mayor of the city of Dnipro announced "gentle Ukrainianization." According to the state official, this campaign aims to protect the language and unite Ukrainians, considering the multinational nature of the city (Dniprorada). Gentle Ukrainianization refers to measures aimed at gradually transitioning to the Ukrainian language in all spheres of life of Ukrainian society, both in official structures and in the population, as well as creating conditions and opportunities for such a transition.

At all stages of the implementation of language legislation, the Ukrainian state has provided a certain period of time to implement the relevant language norms. For instance, in May 2021, the Cabinet of Ministers of Ukraine approved the "Concept of the State Targeted National and Cultural Program to Ensure the Comprehensive Development and Functioning of the Ukrainian Language as the State Language in All Spheres of Public Life" until 2030. Then Minister of Culture and Information Policy Oleksandr Tkachenko noted that his ministry "adheres to soft Ukrainianization, which will have a long-term effect" (Ukrinform). The program presupposes the mandatory use of the Ukrainian language by civil servants, opening a network of Ukrainian language courses, improving the quality of teaching the state language in educational institutions, supporting and popularizing the Ukrainian language abroad, promoting research in the field of Ukrainian linguistics, supporting innovations and improving the quality of Ukrainian cultural products, encouraging dubbing of films into Ukrainian, supporting book publishing in Ukraine, and so on.

Specific actions of the official bodies of Ukraine to reduce the influence and use of the Russian language are visible. However, a new state channel FreeDom broadcasting in Russian appeared on Ukrainian television after February 24. Here we can observe a reconceptualization of the most important language function — language as a tool of communication. In the current situation, this language function transforms into a new ideology: language is not only a means of communication but is also a way of combating Russian propaganda. Since this Russian-language channel is viewed by

Russian-speaking audiences of Ukraine as well as Russophone audiences of the post-Soviet sphere, language appears as a real-time tool for conveying important information in the most efficient way.

The same ideology is observed at non-official levels and in private communication. For example, a military expert, Oleh Zhdanov, provides daily, real-time information on the war's operational situation via his own YouTube channel. Zhdanov speaks Ukrainian and uses Ukrainian in many of his media interviews. However, he speaks Russian on his channel. He begins his analytical report with a Ukrainian greeting, and then switches to Russian, as he prepares his reports not only for his Ukrainian listeners, but also for Russian speakers from Russia and the temporarily occupied territories.

The importance of language as an effective communication tool is especially evident when Ukrainian defenders use Russian on the battlefield to convey critical information quickly and effectively. This is also evident in situations of non-reciprocal bilingualism, when one soldier speaks Ukrainian and the other responds in Russian.

The ideological use of language as a weapon is also experiencing an observable re-conceptualization, such that a famous Ukrainian actor, Volodymyr Rashchuk, who is now fighting in the Armed Forces of Ukraine, encourages and calls on Ukrainians to speak Ukrainian. He observes that speaking Ukrainian helps in the battlefield, while associating every Russophone Ukrainian with an incoming artillery shell and with the horrors of the battlefield. He asks citizens to return to their roots, and thus to finally become Ukrainians. He stresses that this is imperative for Ukrainian defenders and that it assists them tremendously.[3] For Ukrainian society, the Ukrainian language is the language of resistance.

As for private communication, language usage depends primarily on such factors as personal language preferences, the temporary Russian occupation of the southern and eastern regions of

---

3   The video is available at https://www.youtube.com/watch?v=K6Z_u7AqrW
     4. The issue of language choice in the military is a very important one and requires further research. As noted by an anonymous reviewer of this chapter there is a "need to balance strategic considerations with complex issues of morale."

Ukraine, and, as a result, the resettlement of the population from these regions mainly to the western regions or abroad. On March 19, 2022, the sociological group Rating, a non-governmental, independent research organization, conducted a national poll titled "The Language Issue in Ukraine." According to the survey, the number of people who consider Ukrainian to be their native language increased from 57% in 2012 to 76% in 2022. However, this does not mean that these people use Ukrainian in their everyday interactions. Often people determine as native (*ridna mova*) the language which corresponds to their ethnic heritage, the language of their people; even if they speak this language poorly, they believe that this is "how things should be" (Bilaniuk & Melnyk 2008: 346). At the same time the study confirms a decrease in the percentage of self-identified Russian speakers among respondents (about 40% in 2012, 26% at the end of 2021, and 18% at the beginning of the war).

Nevertheless, despite the full-scale invasion, people still use Russian or both the Ukrainian and Russian languages in everyday communication. According to Rating's research, this is explained by the fact that the process of switching to another language requires some adaptation. It is also confirmed by my communications with some internally displaced people from the eastern and southern regions who are not able immediately switch to Ukrainian due to insufficient knowledge of the state language. In sum, Rating concludes that, even though the war is a challenge to the entire society, it has accelerated the process of Ukrainians' linguistic self-identification and the societal shift toward the Ukrainian language (Rating group 2022).

The situation with Ukrainian and Russian in social media also deserves special attention. In "Ukrainian Language in Social Networks: What Changed after Russian Invasion?" (June 2022), the Center for Content Analysis shows that, despite the fact that the number of Ukrainian-language posts on social media has grown significantly after the beginning of the full-scale invasion, it is still smaller than the number of Russian-language posts. The Ukrainian language prevails on Instagram, Facebook, and Twitter, while Russian prevails on TikTok and YouTube. On YouTube, only 5% of the content is in the Ukrainian language. According to the researchers, the level of Ukrainian language on YouTube is low due to the monetization algorithm. They also explain the trend in TikTok by the generation gap: this social platform is primarily a place for young people to communicate, and it shows a higher level of Russification among the young audience.

5. Language-in-education Policy after 2014

Ukraine inherited its system of national schools from the former Soviet Union (in the context of this research, "national schools" refers to schools where national or ethnic minority languages are the languages of instruction). At the same time, after independence, some new tendencies have appeared in the national school system. First, the number of Ukrainian schools has increased while the number of Russian schools has decreased. In addition, after independence, Crimean Tatar schools were opened due to the mass repatriation of Crimean Tatars to Ukraine. The structure of the minority educational system and the number of their educational institutions both depend on different factors such as: individual needs; the importance of a minority within a given region; minority demographic concentration; political power; the assistance of a corresponding kinstate.

In the Methodology section, I reviewed Churchill's model of state responses to minority education, which begs the question: per this model, what stage best describes Ukraine and its educational policy at the current moment? Although it is difficult to determine the clear boundaries of each stage, after independence, the Ukrainian language-in-education policy in general corresponded to stage 5 in this typology. Ukraine has recognized the importance of maintaining minority languages and cultures, and minority education could be described as "minority language immersion" where instruction in minority schools was in the minority language. In addition to the full-immersion educational establishments, Ukraine has had bilingual and trilingual schools with separate but parallel language classes. Also, the minority language was sometimes taught as a subject in schools with Ukrainian as the language of instruction.

However, important changes have occurred in the language-in-education policy after Maidan and, subsequently, 2017 when the new Law on Education (2017) was adopted. This law changed the model of language-in-education from full immersion to bilingual education for some linguistic minorities, and this step can be understood as a strategy for further protection and promotion of the state language.

Such a policy provides implementation of the Ministry of Education's key reform: the "New Ukrainian school." The primary goal is to create a schooling system where students enjoy studying and where they acquire not only knowledge, but also the ability to apply it in everyday life. According to the Ministry website, instead of memorizing facts and concepts, students will acquire competencies. Two prioritized competencies are fluency in the state language and the ability to communicate in native (if different from the state) and foreign languages (Ministerstvo). To develop these competencies, Ukraine has changed its language-in-education in minority schools from full immersion to bilingual education, which corresponds to stage 4 in Churchill's taxonomy. The Law on Education (Article 7) provides the following models for language education of national minorities:

- The first model provides the possibility of obtaining pre-school and general secondary education in the native language, along with the Ukrainian language, in schools for indigenous peoples of Ukraine.[4]
- The second model focuses on other national minorities. For them, pre-school and primary education will be conducted

---

4 According to the Law of Ukraine "On the Indigenous Peoples of Ukraine," these are Crimean Tatars, Karaims, and Krymchaks. The Law on Education applies to Crimean Tatars only since the other groups are too small numerically. As such, Crimean Tatars require a separate model of language education due to their special status in Ukrainian society. The people were deported from Crimea in 1944 by the Soviet authorities, and their mass repatriation became possible only in 1991. Before the occupation of Crimea there were 15 national schools with Crimean Tatar as the language of instruction. In 2021, 7 schools remained but, in those schools, Russian has become the language of instruction, and Crimean Tatar is taught only as a subject. https://qirim.news/novosti-uk/u-krymu-zalyshylysya-tilky-shkoly-dlya-krymskyh-tatar-umerov/

in the language of the national minority, with compulsory study of the Ukrainian language. In addition, "One or more subjects may be taught in two or more languages — the state language, English, and other official languages of the European Union" (Law).

Another important document which specifies the language education in Ukraine is the law "On complete general secondary education" (2020). Article 5 determines three models for language-in-education policy. The first model relates to the indigenous peoples of Ukraine who have the right to receive complete education in their native language along with the state language. The second model concerns national minorities whose languages are official languages of the EU. The representatives of these minorities have the right to receive education in elementary school in their native language where Ukrainian is taught as a subject. In the 5—9 grades, the instruction in Ukrainian is gradually increased from 20% in the 5th grade to at least 40 % in the 9th grade. In high school, at least 60% of school time should be taught in Ukrainian.

The third model pertains to "other national minorities" (these are Russian speakers in Russian schools). For them, at least 80% of school time in junior high and high schools should be taught in the state language. The law also states that these measures are related to state-funded schools. Private educational establishments have a free choice of language of instruction. However, according to this law, Ukrainian should be taught in these schools and students should acquire language proficiency according to the state standards (Law; see also Kudriavtseva 2020).

The information agency UNIAN, with reference to the Ministry of Education, has informed that, in the 2020–2021 academic year, the educational process in secondary education institutions was conducted in the following languages of indigenous peoples and national minorities: Bulgarian, Crimean Tatar, Moldovan, German, Polish, Russian, Romanian, Slovak, Hungarian, and Ukrainian. According to the same source, in the 2020–2021 academic year, there were 874 secondary education institutions (public, communal, and private) with classes in which education was provided in minority languages along with the state language. Of them, 671 are bilingual schools and 203 schools had instruction in only one language (Tables 1 and 2) (Leshchenko 2021).

Table 1.   National minority schools in 2020-2021 academic year

Language	Number of schools	Regions
Hungarian	73 (6 private)	Zakarpattia region
Romanian	69	Zakarpattia, Chernivtsi regions
Russian	55 (35 private)	Dnipro, Donetsk, Zaporizhzhia, Odesa, Kharkiv, Kherson, Chernivtsi, Chernihiv, and Kyiv
Polish	4	Lviv region
German	1	Kyiv
Moldovan	1	Odesa region
Total:	**203**	

Table 2.   Bilingual schools in 2020-2021 academic year

Languages	Number of Schools	Regions
Ukrainian and Russian	603 (22 private)	19 regions and Kyiv (excluding regions: Ivano-Frankivsk, Rivne, Ternopil, Khmelnytskyi, Chernivtsi)
Ukrainian and Hungarian	27	Zakarpattia region
Ukrainian and Romanian	19	Zakarpattia, Chernivtsi regions
Ukrainian and Moldavian	16	Odesa region
Ukrainian and Polish	2	Khmelnytsky region
Ukrainian and Bulgarian	1	Odesa region
Ukrainian and Crimean Tatar	1	Kherson region
Ukrainian, Russian and Crimean Tatar	1	Kherson region
Ukrainian and Slovak	1	Zakarpattia region
Total:	**671**	

Even though national minority schools still exist, the new Law on Education presupposes the transition from the immersion model to the bilingual model. The bilingual model of education was criticized by representatives of national minorities, especially Hungarian, Romanian, and Russian as well as representatives of the kin states in violation of linguistic rights (Csernicskó 2021; Kostyuk 2017; Prykhid 2017). Also, the law has been examined by the Parliamentary Assembly of the Council of Europe and the Venice Commission. The Parliamentary Assembly in its resolution 2189 (2017), acknowledged that "knowledge of the official language(s) of a State is a factor of social cohesion and integration and it is legitimate for States to promote the learning of their official language." At the same time, it expressed its concern that "these national minorities, who were previously entitled to have monolingual schools and fully fledged curricula in their own language, now find themselves in a situation where education in their own languages can be provided (along with education in Ukrainian) only until the end of primary education" (Resolution 2189). The Venice Commission has also recognized that "it is a legitimate and commendable aim for states to promote the strengthening of the state language and its command by all citizens, and to take action for its learning by all, as a way to address existing inequalities and to facilitate more effective integration of persons belonging to national minorities into society." At the same time the Commission has provided some recommendations, among them are "to continue ensuring a sufficient proportion of education in minority languages at the primary and secondary levels," to improve the quality of instruction of the state language, to provide more time for the educational reform, as well as to exempt private language schools from the new language requirements (for all recommendations, see European Commission, Opinion 902). Why has Ukraine, which has expressed its desire to join the European Union, taken these steps of changing its educational model that raises such concerns?

Changes in language-in-education policy can be explained by both internal and external factors, including the growing importance of language issues in the field of national security after the Russian-Ukrainian war began, the status of the study of the Ukrainian language in certain national communities, and the limited social mobility and integration of representatives of certain national minorities in Ukrainian society.

In Ukraine, the language issue has become a matter of national security after 2014. According to the Revolution of Dignity Project (Harvard Ukrainian Research Institute, n.d.) Russia has weaponized "the language question as a pretext for occupying or annexing Ukrainian territories, and actively exploited the issue in its propaganda war and disinformation campaign." Since the occupation of the Crimean and the Donbas regions, Russian officials have repeatedly declared their intention to "protect" the Russian-speaking population of Ukraine. This narrative continued even after the beginning of the full-scale invasion on February 24, though the population of the mainly Russian-speaking cities and towns in the east and south was under constant attacks and shelling. The Ukrainian State Language Protection Commissioner Taras Kremin argues that the protection of the state language is the protection of national interests, it is a matter of the constitutional order, it is a matter for Ukraine's strategies and, moreover, it is a matter for all those things that determine the development and success of the Ukrainian state (Pidsymky).

Another issue which drew the attention of the State Commissioner was the large number of violations of language legislation in Ukraine after 2019 when the law "On Ensuring the Functioning of the Ukrainian Language as the State Language" was adopted. In April 2021, he pointed out that local authorities in the southern regions were slow to implement the language law and did not want to transfer schools into Ukrainian as a language of instruction.

Another important factor about promoting Ukrainian language acquisition in minority schools through bilingual programs is the situation regarding the state language skills among the students in minority schools. After proclaiming independence, Ukraine has been implementing its language policy through balancing support and promotion of Ukrainian language with the development of minority education and minority linguistic rights. Kulyk (2013) argues that such an approach does not necessarily consider student progress and social mobility.

In October 2017, then Minister of Education Liliya Hrynevych pointed out that more than half of children attending schools with Hungarian and Romanian languages of instruction cannot pass the external examination in Ukrainian. This external examination serves as an entrance exam to Ukrainian universities. Thus, without this exam, students from minority schools have no access to higher education in Ukraine. This is especially true for schools in rural areas where, according to the minister, in places where the population density of national minorities is very high, a child does not hear the Ukrainian language at all. Almost the same results are presented in the investigation on the platform texty.org.ua. According to their investigation project, Hungarians are the least integrated into Ukrainian society, judging by the results of the external evaluation. 42% of Hungarian children do not take this test in any significant number. Romanians take the exam but, like Hungarians, have poor results. Bulgarians take external examinations at the national level.

The limited educational opportunities for national minorities bring up another issue — the limited integration of national minorities into the national context. Representatives of national minorities who are not able to pass the external examination and continue their education will not be able to build a successful career in Ukraine and participate in public life. It is expected that this social immobility of Ukrainian minorities, due to lack of state language skills, can be reduced or even eliminated with the implementation of the provisions of the new Law on Education (Hrynevych 2017). Having compared school systems of the two national minorities — the Hungarians and the Crimean Tatars — Kulyk argues that the introduction of bilingual education is the best way to solve the problem of limited social mobility for the first group and the vulnerability of cultural identity of the other (Kulyk 2013).

The situation with the Hungarian community is different than other national minorities. Hungarians in Ukraine have a full cycle of education in the national language — from kindergarten to the Ferenc Rakoczi II Transcarpathian Hungarian Institute. Thus, they can realize their intellectual potential without Ukrainian as a state language. This also causes another problem, namely, that of brain drain. Many students go to study in educational establishments in Hungary. Although there is no exact data on the number of graduates who choose education outside of Ukraine, the assumption can be made from the observation of the university entrance campaign in Transcarpathia. For example, in 2017 the regional state administration of the region pointed out that the number of university applicants was very insignificant. In Uzhhorod State University, the region's leading university, the competition for some majors was very low. In some cases, the university was not even able to fill the state funding quota (*byudzhetni mistsya*) (Texsty 2017).

Another important topic is public initiatives in language education, which have been growing since the full-scale invasion. In Ukraine, language education is not provided by state institutions alone. There are also language courses, free websites, phone apps and other public initiatives with which one can learn the official language, as well as the languages of national minorities. These public bottom-up initiatives are aligned with official state language policy.

Some examples of these initiatives are:

- *Free Ukrainian Language Courses.* This project started in 2013 in different cities of Ukraine under the slogan "Teach your friends to speak Ukrainian." This initiative was one of the first in Ukraine to provide opportunities to learn the Ukrainian language, modify teaching approaches, and promote the language. The instructors voluntarily created and launched the country's first Ukrainian language courses for all interested. From 2020, the instructors have been actively promoting Ukrainian language courses online on the educational platform *E-Mova* (E-language) as a full immersion program (see Kudriavtseva 2023).
- A school in the village of Chaiky near Kyiv founded by the Crimean Tatar Association "Birlik Center" opened in September 2021. This village is a place of compact residence of Crimean Tatars, as well as Muslims from post-Soviet and other countries. They began with grades 5 through 8, and they plan to expand.
- The mobile application "Yoi" created for primary school students who are native speakers of Hungarian or Romanian to facilitate the study of the Ukrainian language. Although the program is primarily aimed at the national minorities of Transcarpathia and Bukovyna, it can also be used to teach students who speak other languages.

- *Free English Language Learning Project* from Innovative and Digital Education Association.

After the beginning of the full-scale invasion in February 2022, these public initiatives in language education can be viewed as a method of civil resistance to the Russian occupation. Such public initiatives are a manifestation of language ideology—"language matters" (Bilaniuk 2016).

Sometimes these initiatives are the results of the activity of local authorities and volunteers. One of the examples is a free Ukrainian language course organized in Kryvyi Rih, a city near the front line and the city where President Zelensky was born and raised. From July 1, 2022, in Kryvyi Rih, every district of the city opened "*Spilkuimosia ukrainskoiu*" language clubs. 23 such clubs were located in libraries throughout the city. Community members have an opportunity to learn Ukrainian and meet with writers, artists, and public figures. For those who want to learn the language remotely, the city held two-month online courses "Speaking Ukrainian correctly" for which more than 500 residents of Kryvyi Rih had signed up. According to Oleksandr Vilkul, the head of the Kryvyi Rih military administration, the city wants to make the process of transition to Ukrainian "gentle" and comfortable. He also posits that, historically, the people of Kryvyi Rih would speak mostly in Russian, but now language is their weapon of agency (Novynarnya 2022).

Volunteer initiatives for studying Ukrainian are also mentioned on the website of the Ukrainian Language Ombudsman. The official page of the Commissioner's office hosts a collection of more than 250 free online resources, courses, conversation clubs, and online educational platforms for mastering the Ukrainian language. The title of this page, "Volunteer Initiatives to Study the Ukrainian Language Are a Powerful Language Front for Local Communities," underscores the importance of civil society actions and resonates strongly with the ideology of "language as a weapon."

6. Impact of the Full-scale Invasion on Language Education in Ukraine: Situation in temporarily occupied territories

Another important issue is the education situation in temporarily occupied territories, which were highly impacted by the full-scale invasion. According to the Ministry of Education and Science of Ukraine, which has created a webpage with updated information on the number of Ukrainian educational institutions destroyed by Russia's attack on Ukraine, 3,416 institutions have been damaged with 363 destroyed (Zaklady). In addition to reporting on the physical destruction of educational establishments, government officials also report on violations of the language rights of the Ukrainian-speaking population in occupied territories. The State Language Protection Commissioner Taras Kremin has noted that in April 2022, the Russians announced the resumption of education in the temporary occupied territories of the Donetsk and Luhansk regions. However, that education did not include the teaching of such subjects as the Ukrainian language, Ukrainian literature, and the history of Ukraine.

In July 2022, the press service of the Main Intelligence office of the Ministry of Defense informed that in the Polohy district of the Zaporizhzhia region the occupation authorities forced Ukrainian citizens to send their children to schools and pre-schools that operated according to the Russian curriculum. According to the office, teachers and educators in these educational establishments came from the Russian Federation. In case of disagreement, parents received threats that their children would be taken away from them and sent to boarding schools. Also, the occupation authorities implemented a punishment for parents who refused to send their children to these educational establishments — military service for men, and community work for women.

Serhiy Haidai, the then head of Luhansk military-civilian administration, in his interview to Freedom TV channel on July 31, 2022, reported that, in the occupied territories of the Luhansk region, punitive measures were being taken against people with a clear pro-Ukrainian position. In addition, Ukrainian-language literature as well as books about Ukraine in general were being destroyed (Haidai 2022). The mayor of Melitopol, Ivan Fedorov, reported in March 2022 that the occupational regime forced school educators to teach in the Russian language.

The Commissioner Taras Kremin has characterized the language policy of the Russian Federation in the temporarily occupied territories as linguicide.[5] On the State Language Protection Commissioner website, there is a page entitled "Russian Policy of Linguicide in the Occupied Territories of Ukraine as a Way of Dismantling the Constitutional Order of Ukraine and an Element of Genocide against the Ukrainian People." On this page, linguicide is described as "the aggressor nation's actions in the temporarily occupied territories aimed at removal of the Ukrainian language from public space and public use, as well as discrimination, harassment or persecution of Ukrainian citizens because of language." Also, this page reports on over a hundred violations of the linguistic rights of Ukrainian speakers and discrimination against people who openly express their pro-Ukrainian position.

7. Concluding Remarks

Russia's war against Ukraine and the full-scale invasion have highlighted the importance of expounding and tracking the progress of linguistic trends and practices in Ukraine. In addition, these factors continue to attract attention to contrasting language ideologies "language does not matter" and "language matters" (Bilaniuk 2016). Along with the existence of these two main ideologies, we may observe a rethinking of some functions of language, which acquire special importance in connection with the war and which may be shaped into separate ideologies — language as an effective tool of communication, and language as a weapon.

In the case of Ukraine, it can be predicted that the position of the Russian language in the official and, especially, educational sphere will decrease. At the same time, the Russian language continues to be present on television and on YouTube because the language serves as a tool for fighting Russian propaganda and conveying information in the most effective way. It is important to note

---

5   For more information about linguicide see: Rudnytskyj (1967), Ukrayins'ka mova (2005).

that Russian-language programs are designed not only for Ukrainians, but also for Russian speakers from Russia and other states. The reduction of Russian in the official sphere does not imply its complete displacement in private communication. The Russian language will not disappear for some time, as there are citizens who are not ready to switch to Ukrainian immediately. However, due to the invasion, there has been a decided trend in the decline in use of Russian in the private sphere.

Language-in-education policy in Ukraine, then, correlates with the ideology "language matters," where language is viewed as a matter of national security and as a tool of nation building and social mobility. Institutional changes in educational domains have aimed at strengthening the status and position of Ukrainian as the state language. Despite the existence of private Russian-language schools, it can be expected that, due to the full-scale invasion, the status of Russian as a language of instruction and a school subject will decrease. Also, we can expect to see the availability of minority language education. In this context, a challenge for Ukraine in its language-in-education policy will be a balanced policy in promotion of the Ukrainian language and the protection of the linguistic and educational rights of national minorities.

Although language education in Ukraine has recently been analyzed in several publications, there is room for deeper research in the following areas: empirical studies on changes of language practices in educational establishments due to the implementation of the new Law on Education (2017); language education of temporarily displaced children in Ukraine and abroad; comparative research on language developments in the educational domain, etc. The situation in the temporarily occupied territories deserves special attention. In this case, Russia is not only pushing its narratives, but also is once again trying to use language as a tool to exert pressure there. The impact of the war on the language practices of Ukrainian society and the educational sphere requires further careful documentation and research through qualitative and quantitative methods — surveys, interviews, and observations. These methods will allow deeper investigation into important questions, such as whether attitudes toward languages have changed among representatives of national minorities, or what the situation with the

54 SVITLANA MELNYK

Russian language is, or what the attitudes toward the Russian language in the Ukrainian school system in different regions are. They will also help to research the language situation in the communities of Ukrainian immigrants.

Bibliography:

Besters-Dilger, Yuliane. (2008). (red.) *Movna polityka ta movna sytuatsiya v Ukraini* [from Ukr.: Language policy and language situation in Ukraine]. Kyiv: Vydavnychyy dim "Kyevo-Mohylyanska Akademiya."

Bilaniuk, Laada & Melnyk, Svitlana. (2008). A tense and shifting balance: Bilingualism and education in Ukraine. *International Journal of Bilingual Education and Bilingualism* 11: 340–372.

Bilaniuk, Laada. (2005). *Contested tongues: language politics and cultural corrections in Ukraine*. Ithaca: Cornell University Press.

Bilaniuk, Laada. (2016). Ideologies of language in wartime. In *Revolution and war in contemporary Ukraine: The challenge of change*, Bertelsen, Olga (ed). Stuttgart: Ibidem Verlag, 139–160.

Churchill, Stacy. (1986). *The education of linguistic and cultural minorities in OECD countries*. San Diego: College-Hill Press.

Csernicskó, István & Fedinec Csilla. (2016). Four language laws of Ukraine. *International Journal of Minority and Group Rights* 23: 560–582.

Csernicskó, István & Orosz, Ildiko. (2019). The Hungarian language in education in Ukraine. Mercator European Research Centre on Multilingualism and Language Learning.

Csernicskó, István. (2021). Languages in conflict situations in the context of the Law of Ukraine "On Education" (2017). In *Language politics, language situations, and conflicts in multilingual societies: Case studies from contemporary Russia, Ukraine and Belarus*, Muller, Daniel & Wingender, Monika (eds). Wiesbaden: Harrassowitz Verlag.

Dniprorada. (2022). Filatov oholosyv u Dnipri «lahidnu ukrainizatsiyu» [from Ukr.: Filatov has announced gentle Ukrainization in Dnipro]. 20 July, https://dniprorada.gov.ua/uk/articles/item/50847/filatov -ogolosiv-u-dnipri-lagidnu-ukrainizaciyu (accessed 3 January 2023).

Dziuba, Ivan. ([1965]1998) *Internatsionalizm chy rusyfikatsiya?* [from Ukr.: Internationalism or Russification?]. Kyiv: Vydavnychyy dim "KM Academia."

European Commission for democracy through law (Venice Commission). Opinion #902 (2017). https://www.venice.coe.int/webforms/docu ments/default.aspx?pdffile=CDL-AD(2017)030-e (accessed 17 June 2023).

Friedman, Debra A. (2016). Our language: (Re)imagining communities in Ukrainian language classrooms. *Journal of Language, Identity, and Education* 15: 165–179.

Harvard Ukrainian Research Institute (n.d.). *Revolution of Dignity Project* (n.d.). https://gis.huri.harvard.edu/language-module (accessed 6 January 2023)

Haidai, Serhiy. (2022), FreeДом, https://www.youtube.com/watch?v=Hz N2EC-5t3o (accessed 19 September 2023).

Hogan-Brun, Gabrielle & Melnyk, Svitlana. (2012). Language policy management in the former Soviet sphere. In *The Cambridge handbook of language policy,* Spolsky, Bernard (ed). Cambridge: Cambridge University Press, 592–616.

Hrynevych, Liliya. (2017). Movna stattia Zakonu «Pro osvitu» ne shkodyt natsionalnym menshynam [from Ukr.: The language article of the Law "On Education" does not harm national minorities], *Oficiinyi sait Ministerstva osvity i nauky Ukrainy* [from Ukr.: The official website of the Ministry of Education and Science of Ukraine], https://mon.gov.ua/u a/news/usi-novivni-novini-2017-10-23-movna-stattya-zakonu-pro-os vitu-ne-shkodit-naczmenshinam (accessed 20 September 2023).

Ilko Kucheriv Democratic Initiatives Foundation, https://dif.org.ua/en/a rticle/pidsumki-dvokh-rokiv-dii-zakonu-pro-movu-uspikhi-ta-nev dachi (accessed 8 September 2022).

Kostyuk, Bohdana. (2017). Venetsianska komisiya i osvita v Ukraini: ukrainska mova — osnova derzhavy [from Ukr.: The Venice Commission and education in Ukraine: The Ukrainian language is the foundation of the state]. *Radio Svoboda,* 14 December, https://www.radios voboda.org/a/28917710.html (accessed 17 June 2023)

Kubaichuk, Viktor. (2004). *Khronolohiia movnykh podii v Ukraini: zovnishnia istoriia ukrainskoi movy* [from Ukr.: Chronology of linguistic events in Ukraine: the external history of the Ukrainian language]. Kyiv: "K.I.C."

Kudriavtseva, Natalia. (2019). Ukraine's language law: whose rights are protected? *A blog of the Kennan Institute,* 8 July, https://www.wilsonc enter.org/blog-post/ukraines-language-law-whose-rights-are-prote cted (accessed 22 July 2023).

Kudriavtseva, Natalia. (2020). Ukraine's Russian language secondary schools switch to Ukrainian-language instruction: A challenge? *Forum for Ukrainian Studies*, 1 August, https://ukrainian-studies.ca/202 0/08/01/ukraines-russian-language-secondary-schools-switch-to-u krainian-language-instruction-a-challenge/ (accessed 22 July 2023).

Kudriavtseva, Natalia. (2021). Standard Ukrainian in the multilingual context: Language ideologies and current educational practices. *Journal of Multilingual and Multicultural Development* 2(42): 152–164.

Kudriavtseva, Natalia. (2023). Ukrainian language revitalization online: targeting Ukraine's Russian speakers. In *Teaching and learning resources for endangered languages*, Valijärvi, Riitta & Kahn, Lily (eds). Leiden: Brill, 203–223.

Kulyk, Volodymyr. (2013). Combining identity and integration: Comparative analysis of schools for two minority groups in Ukraine. *Compare: A Journal of Comparative and International Education* 5(43): 622–645.

Kulyk, Volodymyr. (2016). National identity in Ukraine: Impact of Euromaidan and the war. *Europe-Asia Studies* 4 (68): 588–608.

Kulyk, Volodymyr. (2019). Identity in transformation: Russian-speakers in post-Soviet Ukraine. *Europe-Asia Studies* 1 (71): 156–178.

Kyyivska miska rada [from Ukr.: Kyiv City Council]. (2022) U Kyevi pereymenuvaly shche ponad 40 miskykh obyektiv, nazvy yakykh povyazani z rosiyskoyu federatsiyeyu ta yiyi satelitamy [from Ukr.: In Kyiv, more than 40 city objects related to the Russian Federation and its satellites were renamed], 8 September, https://kmr.gov.ua/uk/content/u-kyy evi-pereymenuvaly-shche-ponad-40-miskyh-obyektiv-nazvy-yakyh-p ovyazani-z-rosiyskoyu (accessed 3 January 2023).

Law of Ukraine "On Education" (2017). https://zakon.rada.gov.ua/laws/ show/en/2145-19#Text (accessed 17 June 2023).

Leshchenko, Lesia. (2021). V MON porakhuvaly, skil'ky shkil navchayut' ditey rosiys'koyu [from Ukr.: The Ministry of Education and Science has calculated how many schools teach children in Russian], UNIAN, 23 September, https://www.unian.ua/society/v-mon-porahuvali-s kilki-shkil-navchayut-ditey-rosiyskoyu-novini-ukrajini-11554858.ht ml?_ga=2.190060651.1553351087.1647532547-1567973390.1644770844 (accessed 3 January 2023).

Magocsi, Paul R. (2010). *A history of Ukraine: the land and its people*. Toronto: University of Toronto Press.

Martin, Terry. (2001). *The affirmative action empire: nations and nationalism in the Soviet Union, 1923-1939*. Ithaca: Cornell University Press

Masenko, Larysa. (2004). *Mova i suspilstvo: postkolonialnyi vymir* [from Ukr.: Language and society: A post-colonial dimension]. Kyiv: KM Akademiya.

Masenko, Larysa. (2005). (red.) *Ukrainska mova u XX storichchi: Istoriya linhvotsydu. Dokumenty i materialy* [from Ukr.: The Ukrainian language in the 20th century: The history of linguicide. Documents and materials]. Kyiv: Vydavnychyy dim "Kyyevo-Mohylyans'ka Akademiya."

Masenko, Larysa. (2017). *Mova radianskoho totalitaryzmu* [from Ukr.: The language of Soviet totalitarianism]. Kyiv: Klio.

Masenko, Larysa. (2019). *Surzhyk: mizh movoyu i yazykom* [from Ukr.: Surzhyk: Between the language and the tongue]. Kyiv: KM Akademiya.

May, Stephen. (2012). *Language and minority rights: ethnicity, nationalism and the politics of language*. New York: Routledge.

Melnyk, Svitlana & Csernicskó, István. (2010). *Etnichne ta movne rozmayittya Ukrainy* [from Ukr.: Ethnic and linguistic diversity of Ukraine]. Uzhhorod: PoliPrint.

Moser, Michael. (2014). *Language policy and the discourse on languages in Ukraine under president Viktor Yanukovych (25 February 2010-28 October 2012)*. Stuttgart: Ibidem-Verlag.

Nova ukrayinska shkola [from Ukr.: New Ukrainian school]. *Oficiinyi sait Ministerstva osvity i nauky Ukrainy* [from Ukr.: The official website of the Ministry of Education and Science of Ukraine], https://mon.gov.ua/ua/tag/nova-ukrainska-shkola (accessed 4 January 2023).

Novynarnya. (2022). Okupanty na Zaporizhzhi perevely shkoly na prohramu RF, zmushuyut viddavaty do nykh ditey, — rozvidka [from Ukr.: The occupiers in the Zaporizhzhya region transferred the schools to the program of the RF, they force children to be sent to them, — intelligence]. *Novynarnya*, 5 June, https://novynarnia.com/2022/07/05/okupanty-na-zaporizhzhi-perevely-shkoly-na-program u-rf-zmushuyut-viddavaty-do-nyh-ditej-rozvidka/ (accessed 11 September 2022).

Novynarnya. (2022). Vilkul anonsuvav "lahidnyy" perekhid na ukrainsku movu v Kryvomu Rozi [from Ukr.: Vilkul announced a "gentle" transition to the Ukrainian language in Kryvyi Rih]. *Novynarnya*, 4 July, https://novynarnia.com/2022/07/04/vilkul-anonsuvav/ (accessed 11 September 2022).

Parliamentary Assembly. Resolution 2189 (2017). The new Ukrainian Law on Education: A major impediment to the teaching of national minorities mother tongue.https://pace.coe.int/pdf/a60a2c87d60bceaa184b972e6f aeb7465b5559856494dc46b13b6745e5210870/res.%202189.pdf (accessed 22 July 2023).

Pavlenko, Aneta. (2006). Russian as a lingua franca. *Annual Review of Applied Linguistics* 26: 78–99.

Pidsumky dvorichnoyi diyi zakonu pro movu: uspikhy ta nevdachi [from Ukr.: Two years after the language law came into force: successes and failures], Fond Demokratychni initsiatyvy imeni Il'ka Kucheriva [from Ukr.: Ilko Kucheriv Democratic Initiative Foundation], https://www.youtube.com/watch?v=Uz-tRy9LZ1Y (accessed 22 July 2023)

Prykhid, Viktoriya. (2017). Osvitni superechky: natsmenshyny proty ukrainskoi? [from Ukr.: Educational controversies: are national minorities against Ukrainian?]. DW, 11 September. https://www.dw.com/uk/освітні-суперечки-національні-меншини-проти-української/a-40448854 (accessed 22 July 2023)

QirimNews. (2021). Krymski tatary vidkryly shkolu v peredmisti Kyyeva [from Ukr.: Crimean Tatars opened a school in the suburbs of Kyiv]. *QirimNews,* 18 August, https://qirim.news/krymski-tatary/krymski-tatary-vidkryly-shkolu-u-peredmisti-kyyeva/ (accessed 11 September 2022).

Rating Group. (2022). The sixth national poll: The language issue in Ukraine, 19 March, https://ratinggroup.ua/en/research/ukraine/language_issue_in_ukraine_march_19th_2022.html (accessed 4 January 2023).

Riabchuk, Mykola. (2000). *Dylemy ukrainskoho Fausta* [from Ukr.: Dilemmas of Ukrainian Faust]. Kyiv: Krytyka.

Riabchuk, Mykola. (2022, 16 July) À la guerre comme à la guerre: 140 days and 300 years of the Russo-Ukrainian war, lecture, Summer Language Workshop, Indiana University.

Rudnytskyj, Jaroslav. (1967). *Language rights and linguicide.* Munich: Ukrainisches Technisch-Wirtschaftliches Institut.

Russian policy of linguicide in the occupied territories of Ukraine as a way of dismantling the constitutional order of Ukraine and an element of genocide against the Ukrainian people. *State Language Protection Commissioner Website.* https://mova-ombudsman.gov.ua/en/news/russian-policy-of-linguocide-in-the-occupied-territories-of-ukraine-as-a-way-of-dismantling-the-constitutional-order-of-ukraine-and-an-element-of-genocide-against-the-ukrainian-people (accessed 11 September 2022).

Seals, Corinne. (2019). *Choosing a mother tongue: The politics of language and identity in Ukraine.* Bristol: Multilingual Matters.

TEXSTY.ORG.UA. (2017). Ne rozumiyut. Ukrayinski uhortsi ta rumuny u shkolakh praktychno ne vyvchayut ukrainsku [from Ukr.: They don't understand. Ukrainian Hungarians and Romanians practically do not teach Ukrainian in schools]. *TEXSTY.ORG.UA.,* 23 November, https://texty.org.ua/articles/81080/Ne_rozumijut_Ukrajinski_ugorci_ta_rumuny_u-81080/ (accessed 24 July 2023).

Tsentr kontent analizu. Ukrainian language in social networks: what changed after Russian invasion? https://ukrcontent.com/en/report s/ukrainska-mova-u-socmerezhah-shho-zminilosya-pislya-pochatk u-povnomasshtabnoi-vijni.html (accessed 30 May 2023).

Ukrainska Pravda. (2018). Poslannya Prezydenta Ukrainy Poroshenka do Verkhovnoyi Rady Ukrainy [from Ukr.: The address of the President of Ukraine Poroshenko to the Verkhovna Rada of Ukraine], *Ukrainska Pravda*, 20 September, https://www.pravda.com.ua/articles/2018/ 09/20/7192645/ (accessed 19 September 2023)

Ukrainska Pravda. (2022a). Rosiyany khochut skasuvaty ukrainsku movu, literaturu ta istoriyu u shkolakh pid okupatsiyeyu [from Ukr.: The Russians want to abolish the Ukrainian language, literature and history in the schools under occupation], *Ukrainska Pravda*, 16 March, htt ps://life.pravda.com.ua/society/2022/03/16/247835/ (accessed 11 June 2023).

Ukrainska Pravda. (2022b). U Melitopoli okupanty zmushuyut vchyteliv navchaty rosiyskoyu [from Ukr.: In Melitopol, the occupiers force teachers to teach in Russian], *Ukrainska Pravda*, 24 March, https://life .pravda.com.ua/society/2022/03/24/247952/ (accessed 11 September 2022).

Ukrinform. (2022). Nabuly chynnosti novi normy zakonu pro derzhavnu movu [from Ukr.: New norms of the law on the state language came into force], *Ukrinform*, 16 July, https://www.ukrinform.ua/rubric-so ciety/3530377-nabuli-cinnosti-novi-normi-zakonu-pro-derzavnu-m ovu.html (accessed 3 January 2023).

Ukrinfrom. (2021). Kabmin skhvalyv kontseptsiyu rozvytku i funktsionuvannya ukrainskoyi movy do 2030 roku [from Ukr.: The Cabinet of Ministers approved the concept of the development and functioning of the Ukrainian language until 2030], *Ukrinform*, 19 May https://www.ukrinform.ua/rubric-polytics/3248729-kabmin-shval iv-koncepciu-rozvitku-i-funkcionuvanna-ukrainskoi-movi-do-2030-roku.html (accessed 17 June 2023).

UNIAN. (2017). Polovyna uchniv uhorskykh i rumunskykh shkil Ukrainy ne mozhut zdaty ZNO — Hrynevych [from Ukr.: Half of the students of Hungarian and Romanian schools in Ukraine cannot pass the ZNO — Hrynevych], *UNIAN*, 31 October, https://www.ukrin-form.ua/ru bric-society/2334549-polovina-ucniv-ugorskih-i-rumunskih-skil-ukr aini-ne-mozut-zdati-zno-grinevic.html (accessed 11 September 2022).

UNIAN. (2020). Almost 70% of Ukrainians oppose granting Russian language official status — poll. *UNIAN*, 21 January, https://www.unian.info/socie ty/10839353-almost-70-of-ukrainians-oppose-granting-russian-languag e-official-status-poll.html (accessed 11 September 2022).

Volonterski initsiatyvy z vyvchennya ukrainskoi movy—potuzhnyy movnyy front dlya mistsevykh hromad [from Ukr.: Volunteer initiatives for learning the Ukrainian language is a powerful language front for local communities]. *State Language Protection Commissioner Website.* https://mova-ombudsman.gov.ua/news/volonterski-initsiatyvy-z-vyvchennia-ukrainskoi-movy-potuzhnyi-movnyi-front-dlia-mistsevykh-hromad (accessed 11 September 2022).

Zaklady osvity, yaki postrazhdaly vid bombarduvan ta obstriliv [from Ukr.: Educational institutions affected by bombing and shelling], https://saveschools.in.ua/en/ (accessed 19 September 2023).

Zakon Ukrainy "Pro zabezpechennya funktsionuvannya ukrainskoi movy yak derzhavnoi" [from Ukr.: The Law of Ukraine "On Ensuring the Functioning of the Ukrainian Language as the State Language"]. (2019). https://zakon.rada.gov.ua/laws/show/2704-19#Text (accessed 19 September 2023).

Zakon Ukrainy "Pro povnu zahalnu serednyu osvitu" [from Ukr.: Law of Ukraine "On complete general secondary education"]. (2020). https://zakon.rada.gov.ua/laws/show/en/463-20?lang=en#Text (accessed 22 July 2023)

Zakon Ukrainy "Pro zasudzhennya ta zaboronu propahandy rosiyskoi imperskoi polityky v Ukraini i dekolonizatsiyu toponimiyi" [from Ukr.: Law of Ukraine ""On the Condemnation and Prohibition of Propaganda of Russian Imperial Policy in Ukraine and the Decolonization of Toponymy"]. (2023). https://zakon.rada.gov.ua/laws/show/3005-20#Text (accessed 19 September 2023)

Translation as Ideology
Nation-Building vs Colonization in Diasporic-Ukrainian and Soviet Literature for Young Adults

Maryna Vardanian

Abstract: *This chapter examines the influence of ideologies on the translation of literature for children and young adults (YA). I discuss the novel Le Capitaine Casse-Cou by French writer Louis Boussenard, which was translated into Ukrainian twice using different strategies. The analysis combines Andre Lefevere's concepts of rewriting in translation with Lawrence Venuti's discussion of foreignization and domestication translation strategies, Gideon Toury's concept of norms of translation framed within postcolonial theory. Ideologies in translation are realized through the system of patronage, rewriting according to the system of social norms and through strategies of domestication and foreignization, which can shape colonial and national cultures. The chapter focuses on representation of colonial and nation-building ideologies in two translations for Ukrainian young adults, which I call Soviet-Ukrainian, or Russian assimilation, and Diasporic-Ukrainian translation. I suggest that Boussenard's novel is open to two opposite interpretations: from a metropolis and from a colonial viewpoint. I begin by examining representations of colonial and nation-building strategies used in the Soviet Union and in Ukrainian institutions abroad. I then explore how Boussenard's novel was adapted to these ideologies. The analysis shows that translation can be used strategically to adapt the ideological norms of society – foreignization and domestication; they describe different social and cultural models for children and YA; and also reproduce a status of translators and of using opposite language ideologies.*

Key words: *ideology in translation, translation for children and young adults, power and translation, Ukraine, war, nation-building, cultural colonialism.*

1. Introduction

Since the Russian Federation began the war against Ukraine in 2014, the international community has been carefully analyzing their ideologies as world view values of each of these societies. According to *Radio Liberty*, the goal of Russia's current war against Ukraine is the restoration of the former empire and the subjugation of Ukraine, to achieve the actualization of several ideologies, including *Russian world*, *pobedobesie* (the Victory cult), and *rashism* (the Russian political ideology) (Khotyn 2022).[1] Instead, significant global actors have come to associate Ukraine with resistance to colonialism and the nation's right to its identity. According to *the United Nations News*, the questioning and denial of the Ukrainian identity and history as a justification for war is a violation of Ukrainians' right to self-determination and their cultural rights; "self-identification is the paramount expression of these rights and all discussions, by States and in social media, should respect this" (Neskorozhana 2022). Both ideologies are implemented through different channels such as language, literature, and translation, and are also the focus of Ukrainian researchers about cultural colonialism and nation-building through literature (Yurchuk 2013; Pavlyshyn 2014; Vardanian 2018), language (Zabuzhko 2009), and translation (Shmiher 2009; Strikha 2020). However, the themes of war, colonization, and national identity are also relevant to children's and juvenile literature, which can also represent opposing ideologies through translations. To date, this issue has not yet been highlighted in Ukraine, but ideologies, manipulations, colonial, imperial, and national identity in translation are widely represented in Western translation studies (Lefevere 1992; Tymoczko 2002; Venuti 2005; Aksoy 2010; Oittinen 2014; Leonardi 2020; Goodwin 2020). As Maria Calzada Pérez (2014: 3) states, translation is an operation carried out on language use because "translation itself is always a site of ideological encounters." The norms and values of the target culture are adapted into the target text. In addition, the

---

1   All translations from Ukrainian, Russian, Polish, and French into English are my own.

educational role of children's and juvenile literature involves ideological manipulations during translation. This research shows how translating children's and juvenile literature promotes certain ideologies, which we need to be able to recognize and interpret. These ideologies are adapted to the norms of society in translated texts. The use of the Ukrainian language becomes another example of language ideology. Translation can contribute both to the formation of colonial discourse and to the formation of national identity.

In this chapter, I will consider two translations of the novel about the South African War (1899–1902), also called the Anglo-Boer War, the Boer War, titled *Le Capitaine Casse-Cou* by the French writer Louis Boussenard, who was quite famous in Eastern Europe in the twentieth century. One translation was published in the Soviet Union (Boussenard 1957), and the other was republished outside Ukraine a decade later (Boussenard 1965). Boussenard's novel shows how the same text can embody opposing ideologies in translation to influence young adults. I connect these translations with current events in Ukraine and the ideologies of post-Soviet societies. For my analysis, I use the ideological approach to translation, particularly in translation for children and young adults. Primarily, Boussenard's book, which he defined as adventure literature for young adults, describes all the challenging themes usually imposed on children's and juvenile literature, depicting war, violence, murder, weapons, and alcohol and smoking. Moreover, the novel ambiguously depicts the political and historical events and famous figures depicted therein. In this respect, political and historical contexts about war, violence, genocide, and racism are a fruitful line for various *rewritings* (according to Lefevere) from the standpoint of metropolis and colony. They demonstrate how translation is a part of the formation and embodiment of certain ideologies: from colonial to nation-building. Analyzing these two translations, I aim to show that the ideological messages of Soviet and Diasporic translations of Boussenard's novel *Le Capitaine Casse-Cou* are in opposition to one another. I will also test my hypothesis that translations for children and young adults correspond to the ideological norms of a certain society or group of people who choose a text for translation. Translations then promote their ideologies through it or

64   Maryna Vardanian

rewrite the target text to fit their ideologies. To test the hypothesis, I discuss the following questions: how are ideologies related to literature for children and young adults and its translations? How do power and institutions influence the rewriting of translations for young adults and implement language ideology? What strategies provide the implementation of ideological norms in Soviet and Diasporic translations into Ukrainian?

2. Language, Ideologies, and Literature for Children and Young Adults

Although it may seem unusual, ideologies are widely present in children's and YA literature. This is the nature of children's and YA literature as cultural practices work as a way of socialization. According to John Stephens (1992: 3):

> Writing for children is usually purposeful, its intention being to foster in the child reader a positive perception of some socio-cultural values which, it is assumed, are shared by author and audience. These values include contemporary morality and ethics, a sense of what is valuable in the culture's past (what a particular contemporary social formation regards as the culture's centrally important traditions), and aspirations about the present and future.

In children's and YA literature, ideology refers to "all espousal, assumption, consideration, and discussion of social and cultural values, whether overt or covert" (Sarland 1996: 41). Based on this account of ideology in children's literature, Charles Sarland (1996: 41) suggests that "all writing is ideological since all writing either assumes values even when not overtly espousing them, or is produced and also read within a social and cultural framework which is itself inevitably suffused with values, that is to say, suffused with ideology." However, ideologies are different in the manner of their implementation. Following Peter Hollindale (1988), John Stephens (1992) emphasizes that ideologies are present in children's and YA literature on three levels: (1) *active ideology* (ideology appears as an overt or explicit element in the text, disclosing the writer's social, political or moral beliefs, e.g., books which openly advocate progressive or enlightened ideas), (2) *passive ideology* (or the implicit presence in the text of the writer's unexamined assumptions), and (3) *ideology as inherent within language*, i.e., "the words, the rule-systems, the codes which constitute the text" (1992: 10–11). Here, it means that "language is not just a site of social struggle but also an object of struggle, since an important aspect of social power lies in the power to determine word meanings and legitimate communicative norms" (Stephens 1992: 11). Children's and YA literature is ideological because it plays socialization and education roles in addition to performing an aesthetic function. Ideology is a broad concept that may characterize not only beliefs related to the political dominance of a certain group, manipulations, and power. It also includes the social and cultural values of a certain society, which may be presented in children's and YA literature in an explicit and implicit way as well as in the structure of language as a language ideology.

For Kathryn Woolard (2021: 1), language ideology or ideological representations of language(s) is "enacted by ordinary community members as well as official institutions and elites, including academic scholars." It will be noted, according to both Hollindale (1988) and Stephens (1992: 11), "if children can be made aware of how such ideologies operate in fictional representations, they may be more empowered to identify equivalent ideological apparatuses in their experiences in the actual world." Thus, the language in children's and YA literature can not only embody a certain ideology of a group or a writer, but also reflect certain societal processes related to the consequences of language usage. In this instance, Judith Irvine and Susan Gal emphasize that colonialism can be studied through language ideologies "because of colonialism's obvious consequentiality, the clash of interests at stake, and the evident differences in points of view" (Irvine & Gal 2000: 72). The colonial status of Ukraine in the twentieth century have thus affected the translation strategies and language practices of children's and YA literature. However, before we compare Soviet-Ukrainian, or Russian assimilation, and Diasporic-Ukrainian translations, it is significant to consider the theoretical frameworks on translation issues in children's and YA literature.

3. Ideologies in Translation for Children and YA

Despite the existing opinion that translating children's and YA literature is not essentially different from translating other forms of literature, there are some distinct nuances that greatly impact the translation of children's and YA literature (O'Sullivan 2013). In Western translation studies, the study of translated literature for children and YA is based on an understanding of this literature's specific characteristics (Sarland 1996; O'Sullivan 2013; Oittinen 2014; Leonardi 2020; Goodwin 2020). Among the major features of children's and YA literature that should be considered as a part of translation: (1) the concept of childhood, (2) the inclusion of this literature to the literary and the socio-educational systems, and (3) a selection of texts and themes considered appropriate for children and YA. Contemporary studies of children's literature are based on the following developments in the field of translation studies: (1) Gideon Toury's (2000) concept of norms of translation with its emphasis on the place of the text in the relevant cultural system, with an attendant focus on translation shifts; (2) Lawrence Venuti's (2000, 2005) concept of the translator's (in)visibility and his discussion of foreignization and domestication translation strategies; (3) the concept of a polysystem introduced by Itamar Even-Zohar (2000) and Zohar Shavit (1981) who attempt to give children's literature, along with other minor literatures, a proper place in the literary system; and (4) Andre Lefevere's (1992) account of rewriting in translation, as well as Maria Tymoczko's (2002) concept of cooperation between translation and power. I will briefly describe these theoretical and methodological frameworks below.

Audience specificity and the concept of the child(hood) image influences the rationale behind many of the translation shifts that occur in the process of producing books for children (Oittinen 2014). In other words, when translating, we should consider the following questions: "how should we adapt or rewrite the original?", "to which norms of the target culture should we adhere?", "what strategies should be used to make the text understandable to the target audience?". The answers directly depend on what image of childhood exists in the target culture. Primarily, the concept of childhood is determined by the norms or social ideas of a particular community which are correct or acceptable for it in a certain period of a certain time. According to Toury (2000), translators make decisions within these norms. Toury (2000: 202–203) describes the following norms as the converting of the general values of a certain community: (1) *preliminary norms* which have to do with the choice of text types; (2) *initial norms* where a translator may subject themself either to the original text, with its norms, or to the norms active in the target culture; (3) *operational norms* consist of *matrical norms* relating to changes in the structure of the text, and *textual-linguistic norms* relating to changes in the text at the level of vocabulary and syntax. According to O'Sullivan (2013), the choice of translation strategy depends on the extent to which the translator seeks to adapt the original to the social, cultural, and educational norms, values, and ideas dominant in a given culture at that specific time. Venuti (2000) defines two strategies: *domestication* (or adaptation of the context of the original to the target culture) and *foreignization* (preserving the context of the culture of the original) which reflect the translator's ideology. So, the translator's ideology determines his strategy for adapting the original to the culture of the translation. In other words, the translator rewrites the original for the target culture.

As Lefevere (1992: vii) emphasizes, translations are rewritings which, "whatever their intention, reflect a certain ideology and poetics, and as such, manipulate literature to function in a given society in a given way". Moreover, Lefevere (1992: vii) considers *rewritings* as a *manipulation,* and defines their positive and negative aspects:

> Rewriting is manipulation, undertaken in the service of power, and in its positive aspect can help in the evolution of literature and a society. Rewritings can introduce new concepts, new genres, new devices, and the history of translation is the history also of literary innovation, of the shaping power of one culture upon another. But rewriting can also repress innovation, distort and contain, and in an age of ever-increasing manipulation of all kinds, the study of the manipulation processes of literature as exemplified by translation can help us towards a greater awareness of the world in which we live.

68   MARYNA VARDANIAN

Thus, depending on the role of translation in society and the influence of the power on it, translation can be considered either as a tool for acculturation and enrichment of native culture and language, or as a colonial enterprise, meaning a suppression of national identities and culture, when language is intimately bound up with the ideologies that legitimize colonization (Aksoy 2010: 441). The development of these processes, according to Lefevere (1992), is related to *control factors*. One control factor belongs squarely within the literary (it is represented by the professionals such as critics, reviewers, teachers, and translators); the other is to be found outside that system (*patronage* in the form of such as persons and institutions — academies, censorship bureaus, critical journals, and educational establishment) (Lefevere 1992: 14–15). In addition, Lefevere (1992: 15–16) emphasizes that "patron(s) count on these professionals to bring the literary system in line with their own ideology". In other words, patrons make decisions about book selection, and professionals choose strategies for translating texts for children's and YA literature in the language, themes, and design in accordance with the ideologies inherent in the society in which they are located, while also focusing on that society's concept of childhood.

Tymoczko et al. (2002: xxi) continues to develop Lefevere's ideas, emphasizing that translators participate in powerful acts that create knowledge and shape culture. She connects translation with both the concepts of colonialism and imperialism, as well as movements of resistance to power and oppression. In addition, translation can contribute to nation-building. According to Venuti (2005: 180), translation can support the formation of national identities through both the selection of foreign texts and the development of discursive strategies in translation:

> A foreign text may be chosen because the social situation in which it was produced is seen as analogous to that of the translating culture, and thus as illuminating of the problems that a nation must confront in its emergence. A foreign text may also be chosen because its form and theme contribute to the creation of a specific discourse of nation in the translating culture. Similarly, a foreign text may be translated with a discursive strategy that has come to be regarded as a distinguishing characteristic of the nation because that strategy has long dominated translation traditions and practices in the

> translating culture. A translation strategy may also be affiliated with a national discourse because it employs a dialect that has gained acceptance as the standard dialect or the national language.

To comprehend these phenomena in translation, it is necessary to determine what cultural values society has regarding the spiritual formation of a child. Ideological manipulation is that which is adapted to adhere to adults' (parents', teachers', etc.) supposed sets of values (Alvstad 2010: 23). On the one hand, translators of literature for children and YA reflect the ideological values of a certain culture, such as their attitude to freedom, struggle, and colonization; on the other hand, they reproduce or avoid certain moral and ethical topics. Sex, violence, alcohol, and injustice are often challenging subjects, in particular. In fact, the norms of the source text may either forbid the translation, or it may be adapted to the norms of the target culture (O'Sullivan 2013: 452). Since the translation is often oriented towards the image of the reader of a certain target culture, the original is rewritten according to the ideological and cultural norms of the society. In the implementation of norms, in particular, the selection of books and topics for the translation of children's and YA literature, special place is given to institutions that select books for the implementation of certain ideologies. I will now discuss these institutions, some of which existed in the Ukrainian diaspora, while others were formed in the Soviet Union. I will also determine what place they assigned to translation and how it is related to the ideologies, in particular language ideologies that they promoted.

4. Colonial and National Strategies of the Patronage System

Literature for children and YA occupied a significant place in both the Diasporic-Ukrainian and in Soviet literary polysystems of the twentieth century. Like their sources, translations embodied opposite ideologies: nation-building and colonial. According to Marko Pavlyshyn (2014: 239), "the strategies of cultural colonialism include the exploitation of the cultural resources of the colonized (people, institutions, cultural objects, and historical memory); the control over the perception of cultural value, which provides the metropolis with prestige and an aura of universalism; the positioning of the colony as marginal, provincial, and able to gain meaning only through the mediation of the metropolis; and the regulation of cultural activities in the colony to minimize competition with the metropolis for visibility and prestige." In the Soviet empire, a cultural colonial strategy was used in censorship regarding the implementation of communist ideology into children's books, the selection of texts for translation, language ideology, and the invisibility of the Ukrainian translator.

It is worth mentioning that in the post-colonial Ukraine, recognizing Ukraine as a colony has been rejected. As Olena Yurchuk (2013: 19) suggests, it is connected with "a masked reluctance to perceive Russia as an empire, a misunderstanding of its actions as aggressive towards the Ukrainian nation." In fact, the Soviet Union used an imperial scheme: Russia is the center, Ukraine is the periphery; Russian culture is higher, which develops at a fast pace and dictates patterns; Ukrainian culture is lower, must be marginalized and assimilated into the culture of the colonizer. In this way, the Soviet Union promoted the myth of the common history of fraternal nations, as well as implemented the policy of Russification of Ukrainians, which occurred through the imposition of the Russian language and the appropriation of Ukrainian culture (Yurchuk 2013: 37). The imperial metropolis established a monopoly on high culture, which it equated with such language code as Russian, while its cultural institutions did not give the possibility for the development of other languages (Pavlyshyn 2014: 233). Instead, the Russian language and culture were imposed as the unifying force for creating a single nation through cultural assimilation in the USSR (Goodwin 2020: 37).

The idea of a new Soviet human (*homo soveticus*) and Soviet identity was total in all areas of society. Primarily, it manifested in the Sovietization of children's and YA literature, which aimed to "strengthen class, international, and labor education" (Goodwin 2020: 44). The Communist Party carried out the patronage of original and translated literature.

The state publishing house *Detskaia literatura*, established in 1933, was the official authority and was given full control over children's literature and selection of books. In 1955, *Detskaia literatura* opened a new section of foreign literature, which was to be responsible for the creation of corpora of books close to Soviet ideology. As Brian James Baer (2011: 9) claims, translation under communism created "the phenomena of extensive government-sponsored translation and strict censorship of translation." Thus, "the ideological context of the Soviet epoch laid the foundations for creating ideologically correct translations" (Goodwin 2020: 32).

In addition to the ideology of the literature itself and censorship in the selection of books, translations also had to embody a language ideology. Translations from various languages were to contribute to the creation of a global Socialist Realist canon, as well as a Soviet canon of representative expressions of national cultures from within the empire (Witt 2011: 151). At the same time, *realist translation* was approved by the official authorities as a new method of free translation. Although it condemned literal translation into Russian, for translations from Russian into minority languages, literalism was encouraged (Friedberg 1997 quoted in Witt 2011: 156).

Thus, Russification was connected with the official ideology of the Communist Party, which legitimized the colonization of Ukraine, in particular by means of language, thereby suppressing the national identity of Ukrainians. This political language ideology was forced onto translators, who were allowed to translate not from the original, but only through Russian as an intermediary language, i.e., from previous Russian translations, observing exact correlations between the source (Russian) translation and the target text. As Samantha Sherry (2015: 27) claims, "literal translation privileged the faithful reproduction of form and content in the transfer of the foreign text into the target language, muting the voice of the translator and allowing the source culture to come through." In this way, the Russian language, as well as Russian-Soviet ideologies, permeated the Ukrainian language and culture. According to Oksana Zabuzhko (2009), the implementation of this language ideology consisted of "demonstrating the optionality of the Ukrainian language." In this way, it was necessary to prove the impracticality and the lack of economy of using the Ukrainian language, which was to become absolutely non-independent, identical to Russian, and therefore, simply an extra language which one could do without (Zabuzhko 2009: 123).

The consequences of this policy of language ideology led to the total Russification of Ukrainian children and young adults, where the Ukrainian language remained only for home use. Likewise, the Ukrainian-Soviet translation operated within colonial discourse. According to Maksym Strikha (2020: 247), it aimed "not to affirm the self-worth of Ukrainian literature, but to fit it into the cruelly defined hierarchy of fraternal nations." Therefore, Ukrainian-Soviet translators were *invisible* (in Venuti's sense). They had to create an assimilation translation, imitate the expressions of the original Russian translations, raise the values of the dominant Russian culture, and were not allowed to challenge the colonial foundations of the regime.

At that time, the Ukrainian diaspora resisted this Russian colonial policy. "Ukraine is not Russia" was the rallying cry of the Ukrainian diaspora, which promoted the ideologies of nation-building through various channels, including through language, literature, and translation. Ukrainians abroad viewed Soviet Ukraine as a territory occupied by the Russian Bolsheviks since 1921. Therefore, the preservation of the Ukrainian language was of primary importance for them. In this way, they opposed Russification as a language ideology of the USSR and taught the Ukrainian language to their children, who were raised in a bilingual environment.

The ideology of the Ukrainian diaspora itself was based on the premise that language affiliation determines the self-sufficiency of Ukrainian culture, history, identity, and territory. The strategy for choosing translated books for publishing was one that would approve the path of Ukrainians to nation-building and self-sufficiency of the Ukrainian language. Therefore, Diasporic institutions were guided by the following principles in selection of literature for translation: first, the proximity of the original to the ideological and cultural values of Ukrainians, second, the popularity of the work and its translation into *cultural languages*. By *cultural languages*, they meant all the languages of prominent and ancient cultures. In this regard, the institutions aimed to raise the prestige of the Ukrainian language, to affirm the Ukrainian language as on par with other languages as an original one, and to draw the attention of young Ukrainians to books in their native language (Vardanian 2018: 335).

In the original and translated literature for children and YA, the Ukrainian diaspora mostly used the first academic all-Ukrainian spelling called *Kharkiv spelling*.[2] It was created in 1928 by Ukrainian linguists from different parts of Ukraine, uniting regional written traditions (Holodomor Museum 2022). In 1933, a new People's Commissar for Education of the UkrSSR approved a different spelling which contained significant changes and cancelled numerous norms seen as "nationalistic" and "intended to artificially separate the Ukrainian language from its great fraternal Russian" (Ukrainskyi pravopys 2019: 7). Only in 2018 did the modern edition of the Ukrainian spelling resurrect some features of the 1928 spelling. This update has a modern scientific basis and is part of the Ukrainian orthographic tradition (Ukrainskyi pravopys 2019: 8). The Ukrainian diaspora strove to preserve the first academic all-Ukrainian spelling in the twentieth century because it associated the three following aspects with the use of the Ukrainian language: national prestige, the soul of the Ukrainian nation, and belonging to the homeland (Horokhovych 1990: 152–153).

The selection of books for translation covered the classics of children's and YA literature, including Hans Christian Andersen, Daniel Defoe, Jules Verne, Aesop, the Brothers Jacob and Wilhelm Grimm, Charles Dickens, Miguel de Cervantes, Mark Twain, Rudyard Kipling, Victor Hugo, and others. The publishing repertoire of translations defined natural, religious-Christian, moral-ethical, patriotic, and ideological themes, as well as topics of colonization, war, and changes in the social system (Catalogue 1922, 1933, 1935, 1936, 1937, 1992, 1993). Books on patriotic themes were supposed to reflect Ukrainian analogies to nations who fought for their

---

2   Also called *Skrypnyk's spelling* from the surname of the People's Commissar for Education Mykola Skrypnyk who approved the spelling and *Holoskevich's spelling* from the name of the main ideologue of spelling, linguist Hryhoriy Holoskevych.

independence or resisted fascism during the Second World War. In addition to the national discourse, the Ukrainian diaspora promoted the Ukrainian language. These translated books were adapted to the ideological and cultural norms and models of the Ukrainian diaspora, which contributed to the establishment of Ukrainian identity, the reproduction of the durability of Ukrainian history and culture, and the preservation of the Ukrainian language. It is clear that translations for children and YA occupied a central place in the literary polysystem of the Ukrainian diaspora.

During the Interwar Years, translated books for children and YA were often published in the west of Ukraine, the home of much of the Ukrainian diaspora. However, they were republished under the patronage of numerous non-governmental institutions, in particular the Leonid Hlibov Association of Children's Literature, the International Educational Coordinating Council, youth unions and movements such as Plast (Пласт — *Ukrainian Scouting Organization*), CYM (СУМ, Сучасна Українська Молодь — *Ukrainian Youth Association*), educational institutions (Ukrainian Saturday Schools), scientific institutions, such as *Shevchenko Scientific Society*, and numerous publishing houses (*Svoboda, Hoverla*) (Vardanian 2020). Despite such a diversity of institutions, they were united by a common task: to unite for the preservation of the Ukrainian identity, national idea, and the Ukrainian language. These institutions brought together writers, translators, publishers, illustrators, researchers, and educators. Institutions had their own publishing houses which published books and magazines for children and YA.

The selection of published books was recorded in special catalogues. As evidenced by the catalogues of books published in the west of Ukraine and the Ukrainian diaspora (Catalogue 1922, 1933, 1935, 1936, 1937, 1977, 1992, 1993), books that were published in the Interwar Years in Ukraine were often republished in the diaspora either with or without the name of the original publishing house, of which there were over one hundred in the west of Ukraine at the time. This created an image of strong publishing activity in Ukrainian diaspora. The Ukrainian translation of Louis Boussenard's book *Le Capitaine Casse-Cou* translated as *Bortsi za Voliu* (Fighters for Freedom) and reprinted in 1965 in New York by the publishing house

OKO was one of these books.[3] In the New York edition of Boussenard's translation, the writer's surname and the publisher's name are added, but the translator's surname is not indicated. Although the translator is unknown, he is visible in the translation as it was fashioned according to the major Ukrainian theme of the independent Ukrainian state and resistance to the Russian Empire.

While many of Boussenard's books were published in Russian translations, only *Le Capitaine Casse-Cou* was translated into Ukrainian twice. I define these Ukrainian translations as Soviet-Ukrainian, or Russian assimilation (Boussenard 1957), and Diasporic-Ukrainian adaptation (Boussenard 1965). I suggest that the Ukrainian reprinted translation may be a response to the colonial assimilated translation of Yevhen Drobiazko. A connection between translations is evidenced not only by the time of the reprinting of the Diasporic-Ukrainian translation, but also using the same illustration by the French illustrator Charles Clerice in both the Ukrainian translations (1865–1912), these translations are dealt with in the next section.

---

3   *OKO* publishing house was founded in the former Halychyna in the west of Ukraine in 1921. According to the memoirs of Anatolii Kurdydyka (1988: 323), "the publishing house was liquidated by the war and the Bolshevik occupation of Ukraine in 1939". The publishing house was established by Osyp and Olena Kuzma. They published three types of books: (1) original books of patriotic Ukrainian content, (2) translations, and (3) a periodical series "library for all" called *Riast*, published monthly for mass distribution (Kurdydyka 1988: 323). At that time, most publishing houses independently determined the topics of books to be printed. So, *OKO* aimed at "forming the national self-awareness of the young generation in conditions of statelessness" (Pirko 2017: 544). The release about the Ukrainian translation of *Le Capitaine Casse-Cou* under the title *Bortsi za Voliu* is contained in the Polish catalogues for 1901–1939 (Dobrzyńska et al. 1993) and the Lviv catalogues (Catalogue 1935, 1936) for 1933–1936 and the catalogue (1937) of books published by Mykola Matviichuk for 1937. In the Ukrainian catalogues (Catalogue 1935, 1936), the translation is given without the writer's surname and the name of the publishing house, but with the translator's initials O. P. and number of pages.

5. One Original — Two Translation Strategies — Opposite Ideologies

5.1. Boussenard's *Le Capitaine Casse-Cou* in the original and its ideology

The adventure novel *Le Capitaine Casse-Cou* (1901) by French writer Louis Henri Boussenard (1847–1910) remains a highly influential writing of the early twentieth century. Although it is classified as an adventure novel, it is based on historical events of the Boer War. Between 1899–1902, Great Britain fought a bitter colonial war against the Boers[4] in South Africa, where it sought to expand British colonial possessions (Dumenko 2012). Boussenard portrays this war with historical accuracy, naming military and political figures, and describes in detail the geographical space of Africa, its toponyms and hydronyms. In addition, the novel contains autobiographical elements, as Boussenard also described his war experience in the Franco-Prussian War. Boussenard paints the Boer War as a bloody and cruel phenomenon with episodes of murder, cruel treatment, and torture of prisoners of war, war crimes against civilians, mass executions, and the use of the scorched-earth policy militarily, and looting by soldiers (Boussenard 1925). Boussenard evaluates military events and images of other nations. He is particularly negative in his description of the British, who are represented as the devious colonizers of Africa. However, he describes with sympathy the French and French-speaking Canadians who fought on the side of Great Britain as its subjects at that time.

Historical and autobiographical elements are included in the adventure plot. The young Frenchman Jean Grandier adds to the dynamism and adventurousness of the novel. He gathers an international battalion of volunteers from among other fourteen and sixteen-year-old boys like himself for the war against Great Britain in Africa, where the two republics of Transvaal and the Orange Free State seek to defend their independence. Jean Grandier, nicknamed

---

4   Boers or Afrikaners are the South African ethnic group from Dutch, French, and German settlers who arrived in Africa in the seventeenth and eighteenth centuries.

capitaine Casse-Cou (Captain Daredevil), and his comrades get into various dangerous situations, from which they always find a way out, and the war thus acquires the features of romance and adventurism. Therefore, the novel not only has vivid ideological features in the evaluations of the metropolis and colony of war values, but also a powerful didactic role in the upbringing of patriotic young adults.

Despite Boussenard's sharp criticism of Britain for the Boer War and their colonization policy, and his portrayal of the French as people with the best virtues who helped smaller nations fight for their independence, France itself had colonies in Africa, and between 1871 and 1931 developed a project of cultural colonialism. Such colonialism took various forms and spread through a diverse range of channels, including adventure literature (Cornick 2006: 137). A new literary genre, combining pedagogy with enthralling stories of "derring-do", was wildly supported by Jules Verne and his followers, such as Alfred Assollant, Paul D'Ivoi, Louis Boussenard, and Colonel Driant, who "were not exclusively vehicles for imperialist ideology:" "They were also read for the thrills, the violence, and the escapist exoticism, all of which were broadly considered constituting a beneficial experience" (Cornick 2006: 141). In this regard, Boussenard's adventure novel as an ideology can be interpreted from two views: (1) how the metropolis perceives the colony, determining national policy towards the colony, and (2) how the colony resisted the empire in pursuit of self-assertion and nation-building. This novel resonated both in the metropolis and colony, evoking a range of emotions from excitement to complete apathy.

5.2. The original rendered via two ideologies

At this time, the Boer War was a popular topic for European authors. Peoples who had no independent states interpreted this war as a call to fight for their identity against empires. Boussenard's book influenced Poles and Ukrainians because neither were independent at that time. The Polish translation was published immediately after the original in 1902 (Catalogue 1903). As Pawel Zajas

(2012: 30) points out, "writing about the fighting Boers was a way to bypass censorship and bring the forbidden political context to the Polish reader." During the Anglo-Boer War, "the Poles quite strongly saw their collective image in the Boers" (Zajas 2012: 48). In the presentation of this topic, as Pawel Zajas (2012: 48) emphasizes, the Polish writers ask: "what can a small nation, which has just become acutely aware of its smallness, do to physically survive and preserve its identity?". I suggest that the first Ukrainian translation of Boussenard's novel appeared under Polish influence due to the historical and cultural circumstances in which Poles and Ukrainians found themselves at the time. That is why the mention of the Ukrainian translation appears in Polish catalogues for 1901–1939 (Dobrzyńska et al. 1993: 117). Ukrainians were familiar with the Boer War, which they, like Poles, perceived in the same light as the struggle of the Ukrainian nation for their state independence against various types of colonization.

Those within the boundaries of early twentieth-century empires, however, perceived the South African War differently. The adventure novel, like other Boussenard's books, has never been translated into English, and references to the writer in English- and French-language studies on French literature are rare, too. However, Boussenard's books were actively published in Russian Empire (1721–1917) in 1911. *Literary Soviet Encyclopedia* explains why Boussenard's books were republished after the collapse of Russian Empire in the USSR. First, Boussenard's writings are "acceptable ideologically and artistically," the criteria for selecting books for translation by the Soviet censorship. Second, Boussenard was favorably received in the Soviet Union for his views on European conquerors. According to *Literary Soviet Encyclopedia,* he "condemned the cruel European conquerors, who by fire and sword planted their power in the colonies" (Friche et al. 1929–1939). It also corresponded to the ideological norms of Soviet culture, portraying itself to the West as the most noble of countries with class equality and equality of the nations of the socialist republics, while forming young communists.

To conform to these norms, in 1955 a new Russian translation by Konstantin Polevoi was written under the title *Kapitan Sorvi-*

holova (Captain Daredevil), which was published under the patronage of the state publishing house *Detskaia literatura* (Boussenard 1955). This edition was republished in 1956, and Yevhen Drobiazko's *Kapitan Zirvyholova* (Captain Daredevil) and a Ukrainian translation was published in 1957 (Boussenard 1957). *Kapitan Sorvi-holova* was repeatedly published in the USSR, and adapted to film where the story about the young avengers formed the basis of the popular Soviet film *Neulovimyie mstiteli* (The Elusive Avengers). Like Jules Verne's book, *A Captain at Fifteen*, the novel about *Captain Daredevil* was a classic of adventure literature in the polysystem of Soviet culture. It not only ideologically blended well with the norms of Soviet society, but it also played an important educational role in the formation of the new Soviet human. The concept of childhood develops through the formation of the image of a fully militarized young adult, ready for all bloody and cruel atrocities of the war, capable of fighting to the end while fully satisfying his international debt by helping the so-called young republics to gain independence. A few generations of young adults born in the USSR, as well as those who continued the traditions of the Soviet colonization culture, grew up on this ideology.

5.3. Translation as colonization

The Russian translation *Le Capitaine Casse-Cou* (1955) follows the strategy of foreignization and fidelity as the norm of the realist translation. Both the Russian translation and the Ukrainian indirect translation, i.e., translation from the previous Russian translation, preserve the storyline, reproducing exactly the original main character and cultural realities (e.g., geographical names, characters' names and surnames, national clothes, and coins). However, the ideological Soviet component is adapted at different levels.

The Russian translator Polevoi clearly defines it in the afterword to his Russian translation: "Readers love Boussenard's heroes for their indomitable courage; they have the most valuable quality of youth — to fight to the end for a righteous cause" (Boussenard 1955: 294). The translator emphasizes education in the spirit of internationalism, condemns the British colonial policy, and promotes the readiness to die at the behest of the authorities. To this end, the translator sometimes rewrites historical events, and discusses specific events with the author, in particular the battle of the Russian troops with the army of Frederick the Second. He deletes the prayer of the Boers, comments on the military tactics of the Boers, and adds his evaluations to the actions of the British military, which he calls civilized barbarians (Boussenard 1955: 15). This opinion is seen in the Soviet-Ukrainian assimilation, where we can read the translator's comments:

> Гнатися за людиною, бачити її агонію, — яка насолода для цивілізованих варварів.To pursue a human being, seeing their agony, what a pleasure for civilized barbarians (Boussenard 1956: 15).

In the original text, there is nothing similar to this comment.

Boussenard's mention of England as a great nation that was admired did not correspond to the Soviet ideology, so the translator deleted that part. Moreover, the translator constantly employed ideological images to form certain stereotypes. In particular, Polevoi changes, and Drobiazko transfers this into the Ukrainian translation, the name of a gang of people searching for gold from *de l'Étoile rouge* (Червона зірка — *Red Star*) to Коричнева зірка (*Brown Star*). *Red Star* is the ideological symbol of the USSR, the state emblem on the flags and the highest award for services to the USSR. Censorship would not allow a sacred Soviet symbol to stand for bandits or thieves in the translation. Instead, another image *Brown Star* became a suitable ideological substitution. It became an allusion to the brown plague which was used to denote the National Socialist movement in Germany in the first half of the twentieth century. While the memory of the Second World War (or for the USSR — the Great Patriotic War) was still quite fresh at that time, this substitution strategy emphasized the negativity of the image. To enhance the effect, the translator often added to the target text the following propaganda slogans which were often promoted by the Soviet authorities: *священний обов'язок перед вітчизною* (sacred duty to the country), *захисники нашої батьківщини* (defenders of our country), *священна справа боротьби* (sacred cause of struggle). They were intended to evoke a wave of patriotic feelings in those who had recently survived the onslaught of Nazi Germany and imbue a sense of support for those facing a powerful opponent.

Another image, that of *Гаврош* (Gavroche), played a similar manipulative meaning. For comparison, in the original, this is the general term for any homeless Parisian boy; in the translation, attention is focused on this image by the capitalization of the word and the translator's comments about the little boy of Victor Hugo's novel *Les Misérables*. The translator's manipulation of the theme of destitution can be seen through the distortion of information about *Kapitan Zirvyholova*'s wealth. In the original, he has millions in bank deposits, but in the Russian translation and Soviet-Ukrainian assimilation, only a few thousand pounds.

This is also an important ideological purification: a wealthy young man did not fit into the concept of an impoverished people. For the same reason, the translator sympathizes with another character — Fanfan, nicknamed *Тюльпан* (Fanfan the Tulip; fr. *La Tulipe*). In the comments, the translator characterizes him in the following way: "the image of a soldier created in French folklore as a brave and cheerful adventurer, always ready to defend a cause that he considers as a rightful one" (Boussenard 1955: 39). If these characters in the original are ordinary names or images, in the translation they acquire an ideological status.

In addition, Polevoi freely adds or deletes information about the Boers and the British to encourage the reader to make an ideologically correct choice. He even rewrites Boussenard's thoughts on colonization. The translator leaves intact information about British colonization policy but deletes general thoughts on colonization as a phenomenon:

> N'est-ce point là l'éternel recommencement de cette loi fatale de la nature qui livre les petits et les faibles à la voracité des plus gros et des plus forts! Is this not the eternal recommencement of this fatal law, which gives the small and weak to the slaughter of the largest and strongest! (Boussenard 1925: 152).

Thereby, the Russian translator links this phenomenon only to Great Britain. Through this strategy of omission, we see that the Soviet ideology did not recognize itself as a colonizer of other Soviet

82   MARYNA VARDANIAN

nations and the imperial narratives were hidden from other Soviet republics, in particular through linguistic colonization.

Drobiazko's assimilative translation follows this imperial ideology. In his translation, literal strategy is the initial norm (according to Toury), putting the translator's decision in compliance with the norm of the Russian source text. In the Soviet-Ukrainian translation, Drobiazko uses the Russian language culture of Polevoi's text as the original. At the lexical level, Drobiazko adheres to operational norms (according to Toury) that required Russian to be the original culture by often resorting to direct translation and calque(s) from Russian as a way of erasing and eradicating Ukrainianness. For comparison (Table 1):

Table 1.   Examples of calque from Russian into Ukrainian

Russian translation	Russian calque in Ukrainian translation	Standard Ukrainian form	English translation
"позарез нужна помощь" [pozarez nuzhna pomoshch]	"до зарізу потрібна допомога" [do zarizu potribna dopomoha]	"украй потрібна допомога" [ukrai potribna dopomoha]	really need help
"стать на защиту дела" [stat na zashchitu dela]	"стати на захист діла" [staty na zakhyst dila]	"стати на захист справи" [staty na zakhyst spravy]	stand up for the cause
"200 тысяч человек" [200 tysiach chelovek]	"200 тисяч чоловік" [200 tysiach cholovik]	"200 тисяч осіб" [200 tysiach osib]	200 thousand people
"товарищи-солдаты" [tovarishchi-soldaty]	"товариши-солдати" [tovaryshy-soldaty]	"бойові побратими" [boiovi pobratymy]	comrades in arms

Drobiazko also uses the Russian calque "превосходительство" ("Your Excellency"), which was used in Russia until 1917 to address titled persons. Similarly, Drobiazko borrows paratextual material, in particular Polevoi's comments, but does not add the afterword because he must be invisible, the voice of the colony — inaudible, the translation — Sovietized, the language — assimilated. The Ukrainian language in this translation then acts as a record of the subordination of culture, its use in accordance with the prevailing Russian norms and values.

5.4. Translation as nation-building

By contrast, Diasporic-Ukrainian translation (Boussenard 1965) acquired a rather distinct Ukrainian cultural color. The translator chose his strategy for the following reasons: (1) as an opposition to Drobiazko's assimilative translation; (2) to promote Ukrainian culture, language, and national ideas; and (3) to comply with publishing requirements regarding volumes of children's and YA books. As Oittinen (2014: 43) emphasizes, "anything can be domesticated: names, the setting, genres, historical events, cultural or religious rites and beliefs."

In the Diasporic-Ukrainian translation, the first technique of domestication is the reduction of Boussenard's novel to the genre of a short story. This genre was quite widespread in the literary polysystem of Ukrainian diaspora. It is easier perceived by children and YA due to its format. Moreover, it contributes to the brief transmission of certain values. The second technique is rewriting the plot through the use of a purification strategy. This technique deletes everything that is considered inappropriate in order to emphasize the patriotic model of education for the struggle for Ukrainian freedom. The translator omits and deletes from Boussenard's book many scenes about violence, racism, smoking, and alcohol — all things that are challenging and frequent themes in children's and YA literature. The language of translation is purified, too. The translator uses Ukrainian cultural realities *козак* (Cossack), *хлоп* (farmer, peasant), *сотник* (captain, centurion), *побратими* (brothers), *степовий* (steppe) and domesticates names *Павло* (Pavlo). In addition, he uses the Ukrainian letter Ґ ([G]) for geographical names (*Ґвінейська затока* — Gulf of Guinea), defined by the norms of the Kharkiv spelling (1928), as well as various expressions or words used in a dialect of Ukrainian spoken in the west of Ukraine. The third technique is explication through paratextual explanations in the form of the title and subtitle, footnotes, preface, afterword, illustrations, and a map of Africa.

As Taras Shmiher (2009: 185) emphasizes, "translation of the title by itself already creates certain conceptual guidelines for the translation of the full text." Unlike the Soviet translations, the Diasporic-Ukrainian translation changes the title to *Bortsi za voliu* (Fighters for Freedom) to emphasize the unity of the people to fight, and adds a subtitle: "A short story about the Anglo-Boer War." This emphasizes the ideological center of the translation, in particular the opposition of the colony to the metropolis. A similar national struggle for Ukrainian independence occurred in 1917–1921. Therefore, this idea was the most important for the Ukrainian diaspora (Vardanian 2020: 5). Unlike the original and Drobiazko's assimilated translation, the translator makes his protagonist not a Frenchman, but a Boer. Obviously, the translator believed that only natives of a territory or homeland should protect it. He emphasizes this opinion in his comment about the distinctions between mercenaries and protectors (Boussenard 1965: 26–27):

> Англійська армія була далеко від свого рідного краю і не знала терену. Це були наємні вояки, які служили не для ідеї, а за гроші. Зате Бури горіли запалом оборони свого рідного краю перед захланим ворогом, світовим грабіжником, якому ще було замало чужих країн і кольоній.
> The British army was far from its native land and did not know the new country. They were mercenaries who fought not for an idea, but for money. By contrast, the Boers were burning with the fervor of defending their native land against a greedy enemy, robbers of the world, ever looking for more countries and colonies.

To emphasize the defender's connection with his native land, the translator changes the image of the sister to the image of the mother, to whom the son is writing a letter. This is not accidental. The image of the son and mother is a critical cultural code in Ukrainian culture. A son is a defender of his native land; a mother is not only a woman, but also a symbol of Ukraine. If we compare the conclusion of the protagonist's letter in the assimilated Soviet translation and the translation published in the Ukrainian diaspora, we can identify certain elements of the model of education promoted through translated literature. In the Diasporic version, the idea of love for the land and mother is openly professed; in the

Soviet version, the young adult is not rooted in the land, he has other values for which he is ready to fight. For comparison:

> *Original*: "Il est impossible, vois-tu, chère soeur aimée, que ton Jean ferme si prématurément le livre de ses aventures. Ou je me trompe fort, ou tu entendras bientôt parler de ton frère qui, plus que jamais, demeure et signe: *Capitaine Casse-Cou*" (It is impossible, you see, dear sister, for your Jean to close the book of his adventures so prematurely. Either I am very wrong, or you will soon hear about your brother who, more than ever, remains and signs: *Captain Daredevil*) (Boussenard 1925: 224).
> *Soviet translation*: "Якщо передчуття не обманює мене, люба сестро, ти ще почуєш дещо про свого брата, який більше, ніж будь-коли, палає бажанням виправдати своє прізвисько — *капітан Зірвиголова*" (If my premonition does not deceive me, dear sister, you will hear something about your brother, who is more than ever burning with the desire to live up to his nickname — *Captain Daredevil*) (Boussenard 1957: 293).
> *Diasporic translation*: "Я сподіваюся, що наш народ оборонить свій край і я побачу тебе ще, мамо. І ти, і я будемо тоді щасливі. *Твій Жан*" (I hope that our nation will defend their land and I will see you again, mummy. Both you and I will be happy then. *Your Jean*) (Boussenard 1965: 32).

The paratext of the Diasporic translation also talks about the implementation of the educational model to defend a homeland. At the beginning of the translation, the translator addresses the reader through a map of Africa with the following comments:

> Нині ціла Південна Африка є під владою Англії, хоч має свій парлямент і самоуправу. — А тепер гляньте ген-ген вгору! Там побачите наше Чорне Море і кінчик нашого краю — України! Читаючи цю книжку, вгадуйте свою Україну!
> Today South Africa is colonized by Great Britain, though it has its parliament and self-government. Now look up! There you will see our Black Sea and a strip of our motherland. It is Ukraine! Reading this book, see in it your Ukraine! (Boussenard 1965: 2).

In this way, the translator not only actualizes the issues of writing for young Ukrainians, but also draws parallels about the struggle of the Ukrainian people for their independence with various forms of colonization through the description of the South African War. He calls the Boers a nation of peasants who lead a peaceful agricultural life. In his victory over the greedy enemy, the translator compares the Boers to Cossacks — a cultural reality for Ukrainians (Vardanian 2018: 338–339). According to the Ukrainian diaspora, as

Ukraine did not have its independence at that time, the struggle for its freedom had to continue. In the afterword, the translator draws more parallels to the Anglo-Boer War.

Boussenard's original describes that the Boers were defeated by the British. However, the Diasporic translator rewrites the ending and presents his own understanding of the victory:

> Війна обернулась на користь Бурів (…) Хоч Бури мусіли визнати над собою зверхність Англії, то дістали автономію (самоуправу).
> The war turned in favor of the Boers (…) Although Boers had to recognize the supremacy of Great Britain over them, they gained autonomy, self-government. (Boussenard 1965: 32).

The translator substantiates these considerations with the didactic purpose of encouraging the Ukrainian reader to fight for the liberty of their land:

> Англія пішла Бурам на великі уступки, бо знала їх завзяття і їх геройську постанову: що доки живий хоч один Бур, не бачити ворогам поневоленого Трансвалю!
> Great Britain made great concessions to the Boers because it knew their bravery and their heroic attitude: as long as there was at least one Boer alive, the enemies would not see the Transvaal colonized! (Boussenard 1965: 32).

The translator leads the Ukrainian reader to this idea throughout the text, via the map, comments, afterword, and illustrations. Like Drobiazko, the Diasporic translator used the picture by the French illustrator Charles Clerice on the cover of the book. However, the Soviet-Ukrainian translation used an illustration with the Boers only (Fig. 1), while the Ukrainian-Diasporic translation showed both the parties to the war (the Boer on horseback and the British people) (Fig. 2). Since, in the story, the British people appeared in the negative light, the censorship did not allow them to be depicted on the cover of the Soviet translation. By contrast, the Diasporic translation uses illustrations to convey the images of British soldiers surrendering to the Boers because this would have corresponded to the translator's idea of positive prospects for the end of the Boer War as a hope for the future of Ukrainians.

TRANSLATION AS IDEOLOGY   87

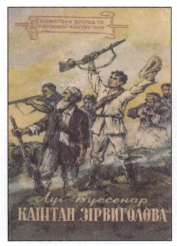 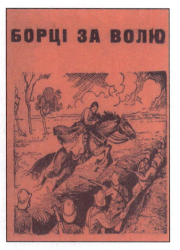

Figure. 1.
The cover of the Soviet-Ukrainian translation *Kapitan Zirvyholova* (Captain Daredevil) by Yevhen Drobiazko.
(Source: Chtyvo.org.ua)

Figure. 2.
The cover of the Diasporic-Ukrainian translation *Bortsi za voliu* (Fighters for Freedom).
(Source: Diasporiana.org.ua)

Figure. 3.   The Russian-Soviet translation *Kapitan Sorvi-holova* (Captain Daredevil) by Konstantin Polevoi (Source: Boussenard 1955)

Figure. 4. The Soviet-Ukrainian translation *Kapitan Zirvyholova* (Captain Daredevil) by Yevhen Drobiazko. (Source: Chtyvo.org.ua)

Figure. 5. The Ukrainian-Diasporic translation *Bortsi za voliu* (Fighters for Freedom). (Source: Diasporiana.org.ua)

Through the illustrations, the narrative of the translations, as well as their implicit ideology, is embodied in different ways: in the Russian translation, the image of the horseman Zirvyholova is presented as a model of the militarization of youth (Fig. 3); Drobiazko's Soviet-Ukrainian translation uses a picture with weapons laid down as a manifestation of the subjugation of Ukrainians (Fig. 4); and the Ukrainian-Diasporic translation depicts a ship with the comment "Кінець. Англійський корабель" (The end. A British ship) (Fig. 5), which, for today's reader, alludes to the well-known phrase by a Ukrainian soldier addressed to the Russian warship near the Ukrainian Zmiinyi (Snake) Island.

6. Conclusion

The ideological undercurrent in children's literature is a deep, broad, and complex concept that includes the ideological norms of a certain group or power, as well as the socio-cultural values of a certain society, which a writer shares in their works in three ways: explicitly, implicitly, and as an ideology of language as an intermediary. Since the ideological norms and the socio-cultural values of certain societies are implemented through various channels, translations for children and young adults also embody these norms. Ideology in translation necessitates selecting and rewriting the original text according to the norms and values of the target culture. As a foreign text is selected by different groups in a certain society, it creates colonial and nation-building discourses in the target culture through the development of foreignization and domestication translation strategies. In this way, colonial ideology implements the subjugation of one culture and language by another, whereas nation-building ideology develops a national identity through the promotion of a national history, culture, and language.

The Soviet-Ukrainian and the Ukrainian-Diasporic translations of Boussenard's French adventure novel *Le Capitaine Casse-Cou* describe the respective ideological norms of their societies. Both translations are ideological, but they embody different ideologies: the Soviet-Ukrainian translation, which I call Russian assimilation, embodies the colonial ideology; the Ukrainian-Diasporic translation, or cultural adaptation, expresses the ideology of nation-building. These opposing ideologies are realized through the selection of Boussenard's novel for translation, the embodiment of concepts of childhood, and the use of different ideologies of language. In the Soviet language ideology, the Russian language permeated the Ukrainian language in order to demonstrate that the Ukrainian language was optional and almost identical to the Russian language. Instead, Ukrainian-Diasporic language ideology promotes the Ukrainian language according to the first academic all-

Ukrainian spelling, which was banned by the Soviet authority, because of its association with national prestige, the originality and independence of the Ukrainian language, and the uniqueness of Ukrainian culture and history.

The colonial ideology of the Soviet-Ukrainian translation can be seen in the fact that Yevhen Drobiazko's translation into Ukrainian was carried out not through the French original but through the Russian language, in particular from the Russian-Soviet translation by Konstantin Polevoi. Since the Ukrainian language was considered an optional language, the literal translation and borrowings from Russian can be traced in the translation into Ukrainian. In the Soviet-Ukrainian translation, such symbolic substitutions occur, as the *Red Star* (the sacred symbol of the USSR) is replaced by the *Brown Star* (as an allusion to the brown plague). However, the most important ideological shift in the Soviet translations is the emphasis on the international debt in a war as an aim for young adults.

By contrast, the Ukrainian-Diasporic translation promotes the ideology of nation-building. It can be traced in the language, the content of the text, and the paratextual material (maps, pictures, etc.). The translator not only reduces the novel to a short story and changes the title to *Bortsi za voliu* (Fighters for Freedom), but also changes the main character's nationality, who, in the translation, becomes a Boer, not a Frenchman. All these shifts are designed to achieve one goal: to instill in the young generation a desire to learn the Ukrainian language, culture, and history and to fight for their own independence.

The ideological approach is a promising venue for research in critical translation studies, which examines translation as one of the channels for promoting ideologies in a society. It includes the concepts of rewriting in translation, the translator's (in)visibility, as well as the concept of norms framed within the postcolonial theory of translation. In this way, ideologies in translation are realized through the system of patronage and rewriting, and via the strategies of domestication and foreignization which can shape colonial and national cultures. The ideological approach considers colonized cultures from the perspective of metropolis and colony, while at the same time revealing the ideological and socio-cultural norms that should be recognized and critically interpreted. Translation studies of children's literature are not only based on these ideological concepts and theories, but also on an understanding of the specificities and levels of ideologies in children's literature; cultural specificities in translated literature for children and young adults; and ideological manipulations in children's literature. The ideological approach is, therefore, a productive way of developing a critical tradition in translation studies of literature for children and young adults.

Bibliography:

Aksoy, Nüzhet Berrin. (2010). The relation between translation and ideology as an instrument for the establishment of a national literature. *Meta* 55(3): 438–455.

Alvstad, Cecilia. (2010). Children's literature and translation. In *Handbook of translation studies*, Gambier, Yves & van Doorslaer, Luc (eds). Amsterdam & Philadelphia: John Benjamins Publishing Company. Vol. 1, 22–27.

Baer, Brian James. (2011). Cultures of translation. In *Contexts, subtexts and pretexts*, Baer, Brian James (ed). Amsterdam & Philadelphia: John Benjamins Publishing Company, 1–15.

Boussenard, Louis. (1925). *Le Capitaine Casse-Cou*. Roman d'aventures. Paris: Tallandier.

Boussenard, Louis. (1955). *Kapitan Sorvi-holova* [from Rus.: Captain Daredevil], translated from French into Russian by Konstantin Polevoi. Moscow: The State Publishing House of Detskaia literatura of the Ministry of Education of the RSFSR.

Boussenard, Louis. (1957). *Kapitan Zirvyholova* [from Ukr.: Captain Daredevil], translated from Russian into Ukrainian by Yevhen Drobiazko. Kyiv: Publishing House of the Central Committee of LKSMU "Molod". Accessed June 18, 2023. https://chtyvo.org.ua/authors/Louis_Boussenard/Kapitan_Zirvyholova/

Boussenard, Louis. (1965). *Bortsi za voliu. Opovidannia z bursko-anhliiskoi viiny* [from Ukr.: Fighters for freedom. A short story about the Anglo-Boer War]. New York: OKO. Accessed June 18, 2023. https://diasporiana.org.ua/dityacha-literatura/2437-bussenar-l-bortsi-za-volyu/

Catalogue. (1903). *Katalog Czytelni W. Makowskiego W Wilnie* [from Pol.: Catalogue of W. Makowski's reading room in Vilnius]. Warsaw: W drukarni synow St. Niemiry.

92   MARYNA VARDANIAN

Catalogue. (1922). *Kataloh Knyharni Naukovoho tovarystva imeni Shevchenka* [from Ukr.: Catalogue of the bookstore of the Shevchenko Scientific Society]. Lviv: Shevchenko Scientific Society.

Catalogue. (1933). *Iliustrovanyi kataloh knyzhok dlia ditei, molodi y samoosvitnikh hurtkiv* [from Ukr.: Illustrated catalogue of books for children, youth, and self-education groups]. Lviv: M. Matviichuk's publishing house.

Catalogue. (1935). *Kataloh novostei, vydanyi u 1933, 1934 i 1935* [from Ukr.: Catalogue of new books published in 1933, 1934, and 1935]. Lviv: Shevchenko Scientific Society.

Catalogue. (1936). *Kataloh novostei za 1933, 1934, 1935, 1936* [from Ukr.: Catalogue of new books published in 1933, 1934, 1935, and 1936]. Lviv: Shevchenko Scientific Society.

Catalogue. (1937). *M. Matviichuk's publishing house catalogue.* Lviv.

Catalogue. (1977). *Howerla books catalogue (1976–1977).* New York: Howerla.

Catalogue. (1992). *Vystavka dytiachoi literatury diaspory* [from Ukr.: An exhibition of children's literature of the diaspora]. Lviv & Kyiv: Ukrainian National Women's League of America.

Catalogue. (1993). *My i nashi dity. Biuleten-kataloh Ukrainskykh pratsinykiv literatury dlia litei i molodi* [from Ukr.: We and our children. Bulletin-catalog of Ukrainian literature for children and young adults]. Toronto: U.P.L.D.M.

Cornick, Martyn. (2006). Representations of Britain and British colonialism in French adventure fiction, 1870–1914. *French Cultural Studies,* 17(2): 137–154.

Dobrzyńska, Bożena & Olszewska, Irena (eds). (1993). *Bibliografia Polska 1901–1939* [from Pol.: Polish bibliography 1901–1939]. Tom 3. Bol–Ce. Warsaw: Biblioteka Narodowa.

Dumenko, Serhii. (2012). Druha anhlo-burska viina [from Ukr.: The Second Anglo-Boer War]. *Tsei den v istorii* [from Ukr.: This day in history], 11 September, https://www.jnsm.com.ua/h/1011M/ (accessed 20 August 2022).

Even-Zohar, Itamar. (2000). The position of translated literature within the literary polysystem. In *The translation studies reader,* Venuti, Lawrence (ed). London & New York: Routledge, 192–197.

Friche, V. M. & Lunacharskii, A. V. (eds). (1929 — 1939). Bussenar. In *Literaturnaia entsyklopediia. 1929 — 1939* [from Rus.: Literary Soviet encyclopedia. 1929—1939]. Moskow: Communist Academy Publishing, https://rus-literature-enc.slovaronline.com/1077-%D0%91%D1%83%D1%81%D1%81%D0%B5%D0%BD%D0%B0%D1%80 (accessed 20 August 2022).

Goodwin, Elena. (2020). *Translating England into Russian: The politics of children's literature in the Soviet Union and modern Russia.* London: Bloomsbury Academic.

Hollindale, Peter. (1988). Ideology and the children's book. *Signal* 55: 3–22.

Horokhovych, Antonina. (1990). *Batky ta dity* [from Ukr.: Parents and children]. Winnipeg & Toronto: World Coordination Educational Council.

Irvine, Judith T. & Gal, Susan. (2000). Language ideology and linguistic differentiation. In *Regimes of language: Ideologies, polities, and identities,* Kroskrity, Paul V. (ed). Santa Fe: School of American Research Press, 35–84.

Holodomor Museum. (2022). "Kharkiv spelling" as one of the successes of Ukrainization. *Holodomor Museum,* 14 July, https://holodomormuse um.org.ua/en/news-museji/13339/ (accessed 28 August 2022).

Khotyn, Rostyslav. (2022). "Russkyi myr", "pobiedobiesiie", "rashyzm". Za yaki ideolohii Kreml voiuie v Ukraini? [from Ukr.: *Russian world, pobedobesiye, rashyzm*: What ideologies does the Kremlin fight for in Ukraine?]. *Radio Liberty,* 5 May, https://www.radiosvoboda.org/a/r osiya-ukrayina-viyna-ruskiy-mir-pobedobesiye-rashyzm/31835603. html (accessed 20 August 2022).

Kurdydyka, Anatolii. (1988). Drukovane slovo v Kolomyi [from Ukr.: The printed word in Kolomyia]. In *Kolomyia and its region. Almanac of memoirs and articles about its recent past,* Romanenchuk, Bohdan (ed). Philadelphia: Publisher Committee of the Kolomyians, 313–324.

Lefevere, Andre. (1992). *Translation, rewriting, and the manipulation of literary fame.* London & New York: Routledge.

Leonardi, Vanessa. (2020). *Ideological manipulation of children's literature through translation and rewriting. Travelling across times and places.* London: Palgrave Macmillan.

Neskorozhana, Dina. (2022). Cultural destruction in Ukraine by Russian forces will reverberate for years, UN rights expert warns. *UN News,* 25 May, https://news.un.org/en/story/2022/05/1119052 (accessed 20 August 2022).

Oittinen, Riitta. (2014). No innocent act: On the ethics of translating for children. In *Children's literature in translation. Challenges and strategies,* Coillie, Jan Van & Verschueren, Walter P. (eds). London & New York: Routledge, 35–45.

O'Sullivan, Emer. (2013). Children's literature and translation studies. In *The Routledge handbook of translation studies,* Millán, Carmen & Bartrina, Francesca (eds). London & New York: Routledge, 451–463.

94 MARYNA VARDANIAN

Pavlyshyn, Marko. (2014). Pro koryst i shkodu postkolonializmu dlia zhyttia [from Ukr.: About the benefits and harms of postcolonialism for life]. *Vsesvit* 3–4: 229–240.

Pérez, María Calzada (ed). (2014). *Translation studies on ideology*. London & New York: Routledge.

Pirko, Mariia. (2017). Retrospektyva ukrainskoho knyhovydannia u mizhvoiennii Halychyni (za materialamy literaturno-naukovoho zhurnalu «Dzvony») [from Ukr.: Ukrainian book publishing in eastern Galicia through the retrospective of "Dzvony" the literary and scientific journal]. *Visnyk of the Lviv University*. Series History. Special Issue: 541–556.

Sarland, Charles. (1996). Ideology. In *International companion encyclopedia of children's literature*, Hunt, Peter (ed). London & New York: Routledge, 39–55.

Shavit, Zohar. (1981). Translation of children's literature as a function of its position in the literary polysystem. *Poetic Today* 2 (4): 171–179.

Sherry, Samantha. (2015). *Discourses of regulation and resistance censoring translation in the Stalin and Khrushchev era Soviet Union*. Edinburgh: Edinburgh University Press.

Shmiher, Taras. (2009). *Istoriia ukrainskoho perekladoznavstva XX stolittia* [from Ukr.: The history of Ukrainian translation studies of the twentieth century]. Kyiv: Smoloskyp.

Stephens, John. (1992). *Language and ideology in children's fiction*. London & New York: Longman.

Strikha, Maksym. (2020). *Ukrainskyi pereklad i perekladachi: mizh literaturoiu i natsiietvorenniam* [from Ukr.: Ukrainian translation and translators: between literature and nation-building]. Kyiv: Dukh i Litera.

Toury, Gideon. (2000). The nature and role of norm in translation. In *The translation studies reader*, Venuti, Lawrence (ed). London & New York: Routledge, 198–211.

Tymoczko, Maria & Edwin, Gentzler (eds). (2002). *Translation and power*. Amherst & Boston: University of Massachusetts Press.

Ukrainskyi pravopys. (2019). *Ukrainskyi pravopys* [from Ukr.: Ukrainian spelling]. Kyiv: Naukova dumka.

Vardanian, Maryna. (2018). *Svii – chuzhyi v ukrainskii diaspornii literaturi dlia ditei ta yunatstva. Natsionalna kontseptosfera, imaholohichni modeli* [from Ukr.: The Self — The Other in the children's literature of the Ukrainian diaspora: National sphere of concepts, imagological models]. Kryvyi Rih: Dionat. DOI: https://doi.org/10.31812/123456789/3017 (accessed 20 August 2022).

Vardanian, Maryna. (2020). Translating children's literature of Ukrainian diaspora as an implementation of the educational ideal of Ukrainian abroad. *SHS Web Conferences. The International Conference on History, Theory and Methodology of Learning (ICHTML 2020)* 75: 1–7. DOI: https://doi.org/10.1051/shsconf/20207501002 (accessed 28 August 2022).

Venuti, Lawrence. (2000). Translation, community, utopia. In *The translation studies reader*, Venuti, Lawrence (ed). London & New York: Routledge, 468–488.

Venuti, Lawrence. (2005). Local contingencies: Translation and national identities. In *Nation, language, and the ethics of translation*, Bermann, Sandra & Wood, Michael (eds). Princeton & Oxford: Princeton University Press, 177–202.

Woolard, Kathryn A. (2021). Language ideology. In *The international encyclopedia of linguistic anthropology*, Stanlaw, James (ed). New York: John Wiley & Sons, 1–21. DOI: https://doi.org/10.1002/9781118786093.ie la0217 (accessed 20 August 2022).

Witt, Susanna. (2011). Between the lines: Totalitarianism and translation in the USSR. In *Contexts, subtexts and pretexts*, Baer, Brian James (ed). Amsterdam & Philadelphia: John Benjamins Publishing Company, 149–170.

Yurchuk, Olena. (2013). *U tini imperii. Ukrainska literatura u svitli postkolonialnoi teorii* [from Ukr.: In the shadow of the empire. Ukrainian literature within postcolonial theory]. Kyiv: Akademiia.

Zabuzhko, Oksana. (2009). *Khroniky vid Fortinbrasa* [from Ukr.: Chronicles from Fortinbras]. Kyiv: Fakt.

Zajas, Pawel. (2012). Polacy jako Burowie. Imagologia pomiędzy auto- i Heterostereotypem [from Pol.: Poles like Boers. Imagology between auto- and heterostereotype]. In *Wokół "W pustyni i w puszczy". W stulecie pierwodruku powieści* [from Pol.: Around "In the desert and in the wilderness." On the centenary of the novel's first edition], Axer, Jerzy & Bujnicki, Tadeusz (eds). Kraków: Universitas, 29–53.

Language and Social Inequalities in Ukraine
Monolingual and Bilingual Practices[1]

Yuliia Soroka[2], Natalia Kudriavtseva[3], Igor Danylenko

Abstract: *Drawing from Bourdieu's idea of language as a factor of social inequality and distinction, we examine the symbolic power of monolingual (Ukrainian and Russian) and bilingual (Ukrainian-Russian) linguistic practices as captured before the 2022 full-scale Russian invasion of Ukraine. To account for the legitimacy of both Ukrainian and Russian, we follow the extended version of Bourdieu's concept of the legitimate language (Søvik 2010) and overview the language ideologies that legitimate each of them. The data for this study comes from the survey "Social inequalities: perception by Ukrainian society" conducted in 2017–2018 by the Sociological Association of Ukraine. The novelty of our analysis is the introduction of an additional variable for Ukrainian-Russian bilinguals, which allowed us to add practices where both Ukrainian and Russian are reportedly used by the respondents.*

The analysis shows the quantitative results for the three identified groups (Ukrainian speakers, Russian speakers, Ukrainian-Russian bilinguals) in terms of language-related social inequalities and distinctions. To track social distinctions, we analyzed responses to questions on identification and perceived support of the Ukrainian state. In terms of social inequalities, we compared the three groups in their self-assessments of English language proficiency; social status; material welfare; sectors of the economy where they are employed; and their levels of mobility. We find that there are no significant social inequalities and distinctions as related

---

1   The authors express their deep gratitude to the Sociological Association of Ukraine and personally to Lyudmila Sokuryanskaya for providing access to the primary data of the "Social inequalities: perception by Ukrainian society" research. We are also grateful to Nicholas Baer for his useful comments on the contents and style of the chapter.

2   This chapter was prepared for publication by Yuliia Soroka with the support of Scholars-at-risk programme, University of Fribourg, Switzerland.

3   This chapter was prepared for publication by Natalia Kudriavtseva with the support of Alfried Krupp Junior Fellowship at the Alfried Krupp Institute for Advanced Study, Greifswald, Germany.

to the use of either Ukrainian or Russian in Ukraine, with indirect evidence for greater symbolic power linked to the Ukrainian-Russian bilingual practice. Comparing the potential of monolingual and bilingual practices to become a factor of social tension, we state the absence of reasons for linguistic discrimination as measured before the start of the full-blown Russian war on Ukraine.

Key words: *legitimate language, social inequality, monolingual practices, bilingual practices, language ideology, Ukraine.*

1. Introduction

Relations of communication are always, inevitably, power relations where natural language constitutes a basis for social inequality and distinction. According to Pierre Bourdieu (1991), the relations of power are not inherent in symbolic systems as such but derive from the social positions of those who use them. Capable of producing real effects like physical or economic power, symbolic power can be exercised only if it is disguised as something else, that is exercised "only with the complicity of those who do not want to know that they are subject to it or even that they themselves exercise it" (Bourdieu 1991: 164). Disguised as culturedness, prestige or good taste, symbolic power is the power to make people see and believe a particular view of the world and agree to what is "correct" and "appropriate" in it. Via this worldview, the domination of certain groups in society is legitimized while their cultures and modes of expression are privileged over others. Symbolic power is a "misrecognizable and legitimated" form of the other forms of power, says Bourdieu (1991: 170), and language is among the ways to exercise it legitimately.

A language variety endowed with symbolic power is the "legitimate language" (Bourdieu 1991) and linguistic skill in this language constitutes a person's linguistic capital, which translates to social mobility and material welfare. Individuals lacking competence in this variety, the "legitimate competence" (Bourdieu 1991: 55), are excluded from interaction in those domains which can be accessed via the legitimate language. According to Bourdieu, who conceived of the linguistic market as unified, the mode of expression imposed as legitimate is the standard language since it is the variety linked to elites, promoted in education and backed by the state institutions. Hence, language does not only relate to communicating but, as Bourdieu (1991: 167) says, also contributes to social division: concealed beneath the function of communication is always the function of separation, since in legitimate situations, that is on the appropriate market, only those competent in the legitimate language are privileged to communicate (Bourdieu 1977: 650).

Despite being one of the most comprehensive accounts of the production of legitimate language, Bourdieu's theoretical framework fails to explain how some languages can still dominate in situations where other languages are promoted by school and supported by state institutions. Kathryn A. Woolard (1985) showed that the privileged position of the Catalan language in Spain, in the context where the government has been supporting Castilian, has its basis in "primary economic relations on arrangements for everyday living" (Woolard 1985: 742) rather than the support of the state. It is this economic basis that gives authority to the Catalan language and grants it "covert prestige," which inverts the hierarchy of dominant values. Christopher Stroud's (2002) study of the linguistic market in Mozambique illustrates the hegemony of standard European Portuguese in a context where cultural institutions, political and economic processes lending support to legitimate language are absent. "Standard European Portuguese provides the means whereby social identities and moral stances are represented" (Stroud 2002: 271) and therefore holds a strong hegemonic position against vernacular Portuguese and African languages in Mozambique. In her study of French-medium education in Ontario, Canada, Monica Heller (1996) describes how French is constructed as the legitimate language in advanced French-language classes while English, the dominant language of the province Ontario, is strongly suppressed. The legitimacy of English could, however, be recognized in general-level French-language classes and other subjects where English, but not any of the students' other first languages, was seen as an appropriate counterpart to be used. Stroud (2002) argues that an "alternative legitimacy" of another language could be explained by the emergence of a new ideology on which the authority of this language would rest.

Margrethe Søvik (2010) extends the definition of Bourdieu's concept of the legitimate language to make it applicable in cases where the language situation is dynamic or changing and the linguistic market is not unified. She agrees that "several languages may coexist as legitimate languages, and there may be several ideologies which account for an alternative legitimacy" (Søvik 2010: 6). Søvik considers legitimate not only the language endorsed by state institutions, but also the language "which one is expected to use in certain settings" where this language constitutes the norm (Søvik 2010: 8-9). In her study of Kharkiv, Ukraine, where both Ukrainian and Russian can be seen as legitimate languages, Søvik (2002) links the legitimacy of Ukrainian to the support of the state while Russian is legitimated by its use as an accustomed means of communication.

In this chapter, we will look at the Ukrainian situation in general. Rather than examining language use in a separate city or region, we will analyze the results of a nationwide survey conducted in 2017–2018 to measure the perception of social inequality as related to language choices. The data analyzed in this chapter were collected prior to the 2022 full-scale Russian invasion of Ukraine, so the results of the analysis should be perceived as reflecting the then state of affairs. The full-scale invasion may have substantially changed the situation since then, which requires conducting a new investigation. In this chapter, we intend to explore if there were any significant inequalities and social distinctions related to the use of either Ukrainian or Russian in Ukraine before the full-scale invasion.

Besides the two monolingual groups of Ukrainian speakers and Russian speakers singled out in the nationwide survey, we also take into account existing bilingual practices and include a third group of Ukrainian-Russian bilinguals in the analysis of the survey results. Alongside the identified language practices, we consider respondents' self-reported proficiency in English which is treated here as an indicator accompanying material status and social prestige. Thus, we seek to examine the linguistic capital related to each monolingual practice (Ukrainian or Russian), and also aim to detect bilingual (Ukrainian and Russian) linguistic practices and the symbolic power that is accorded to them. We set out to answer the following questions: does linguistic competence define significant social distinctions? Which linguistic competence relates to greater social mobility and an increase in material welfare? Which linguistic practices demonstrate a potential to become a factor of social tension? And is there any linguistic capital related to Ukrainian-Russian bilingualism in Ukraine?

In the following section, we will take a closer look at the ideologies legitimating each language since it is within this theoretical framework that the survey data will be discussed. After that, we will provide the details of the design of the survey and the method of collecting the data, and we will present the analysis of the survey results. We will then discuss the results and argue that, despite the different ideologies legitimating each language, neither linguistic competence (neither Ukrainian nor Russian) is perceived to be linked to greater success. Instead, a certain relation between linguistic competence and the respondents' material welfare can be detected in the case of foreign languages such as English, which is viewed in this study as an attribute accompanying social status and material welfare. The level of English proficiency rises within the group of Ukrainian-Russian bilinguals, which suggests that there is more access to valuable economic resources for them. We will also compare the potential of monolingual and bilingual practices to become a factor of social tension and conclude by affirming the absence of language-related reasons for the increase of social collision in Ukraine.

2. Ideologies of the Legitimate Language

In this section, we will overview ideologies which can account for the legitimacy of a particular language. These are commonly held beliefs used to justify the authority of a language, or its particular variety, to be respected and widely used. Within a critical approach, a language ideology is defined as "the cultural (or subcultural) system of ideas about social and linguistic relationships, together with their loading of moral and political interests" (Irvine 1989: 255; see also Woolard & Schieffelin 1994; Woolard, Schieffelin & Kroskrity 1998; Kroskrity 2004; Woolard 2021). The concept of language ideology, thus, captures what Bourdieu meant by saying that language is not only about communication, but is also about social separation and material concerns.

The view of language as a neutral means of communication arose in the process of the standardization of modern French and is associated with the eighteenth-century Enlightenment (Geeraerts 2003). This view is also known as "anonymity" within language ideology research (Woolard 2016). This is the ideology on which dominant languages often rest as they are presented as open to all and universally available. Woolard (2008) gives an example of Standard English in North America which is perceived to be a neutral medium of communication, participation and inclusion in wider social and political domains. However, she remarks that Standard English is, in fact, not everybody's language since it does belong to specific "someones" and always functions in the interests of specific groups (e.g. Standard English in America is coded as "white") (Woolard 2008).

A language can be legitimated by yet another view, or an ideology, of language. Opposing the vision of language as a neutral communication tool is the view of language as a marker of identity. This view contrasts with the participatory ideal of the communication ideology by emphasizing a unique identity of those who speak the language and a particular conception of the world contained within it. Instead of stressing uniformity, the language-as-identity-marker view values diversity as it prioritizes the expressive function of language over the communicative function.

This ideology originated in the nineteenth-century Romanticism and is also referred to as "authenticity" whereby the value of a language is derived from its relationship to a particular community and culture (Woolard 2016). The function of the standard language is to emphasize a distinct identity of its speakers and in this way to separate them from the other groups. A clear example of standardization based on this ideology is the initial period of the formation of Standard Ukrainian which was conceived of as a living vernacular used primarily in the village and opposed to Russian as the language of communication of urban elites (Yavorska 2010). However, the Standard was, in fact, modelled on the language used in literary works of some Ukrainian writers (e.g., Ivan Kotliarevskyi, Hryhorii Kvitka-Osnovianenko, Marko Vovchok) and not on the actual folk speech.

In multilingual contexts, several languages may be held legitimate because the situation is dynamic and the linguistic market is not unified. This can be evident in domains prioritizing formal rather than informal use, or in situations where the desire for uniformity in communication confronts identity issues in the multinational dimension. These are the sites of the formation of language hierarchies which are beliefs in the unequal value of different languages not necessarily conforming with their officially designated roles. An illustration of language hierarchies enacting social hierarchies on the basis of linguistic differentiation is the film industry in Bollywood (Ganti 2016), where English has become a lingua franca in the process of filmmaking, prioritizing those possessing the linguistic skill for respective jobs. Against the dominance of English as "the unmarked, naturalized language of production," it is possible for Hindi to be valued on camera only, that is when spoken by actors, as a specific feature of Indian films (Ganti 2016: 128). Similarly, in a Finnish-Swedish corporation, English was perceived as "the most natural and legitimate choice" for official communication since it was not seen as belonging to either Finns or Swedes (Vaara et al. 2005: 617). At the same time, however, this choice could be utilized only by those who possessed the necessary linguistic competence, leaving others with no opportunities for professional success.

In Ukraine, the linguistic market has been defined by the dynamic use of two major languages—Ukrainian and Russian. From the end of the eighteenth through to the beginning of the twentieth century, the majority of modern Ukraine was subsumed by the Russian Empire with only a minor territory in the west, comprising Bukovyna, Zakarpattia and eastern Halychyna, belonging to Austro-Hungary at the time. The use of Ukrainian was restricted both in the part of Ukraine under Austro-Hungary and in the part under the Russian Empire, where the public use of the language was forbidden by official decrees. This policy, referred to as "Russification," continued throughout the Soviet time with the aim of converging Ukrainian and Russian in structure and entirely marginalizing Ukrainian to a language of limited use. By the time of Ukraine's independence in 1991, the Ukrainian language had been considerably forced out of use by the former common imperial language — Russian — primarily in the south-eastern parts, as well as in large industrial centers all over Ukraine. However, Ukrainian was not completely superseded by Russian even in the southeast, where the rural areas still remained Ukrainian-speaking (Masenko 2010: 97). In the early years of independence, Russian enjoyed higher prestige, still dominating the southeast, despite the language planning prioritizing the use of Ukrainian (Ivanova 2013: 264; Kulyk 2015: 287). Additionally, while surveys revealed that the prestige of speaking Russian had been surpassed by that of speaking Ukrainian and English already by 2008 (Masenko 2010: 110), younger generations continued relying on Russian, which was seen as more prestigious (Kulyk 2015: 287) and perceived as a normative practice by them (Friedman 2016: 173). The shift toward Russian ended around 2012; however, the language remained a major means of transnational communication and globalized job markets (Kulyk 2015: 297-298).

For these reasons, in the Ukrainian context, where Ukrainian and Russian are widely used, both languages may be considered legitimate. The legitimacy of the Ukrainian language derives from its status as the state language, whereby it is promoted in education and supported by the state, as well as from its symbolic significance as the language of the Ukrainian nation. Søvik (2010) suggests that the legitimacy of Ukrainian is, thus, primarily constructed within the "identification" dimension, while it can also be used as a communication tool. The legitimacy of Russian is secured by its being a habitual means of communication normally used in certain domains. The legitimacy of Russian is thus defined in terms of its "utility" related to economic capital as it facilitates access to certain sectors of the labor market (Sovik 2010). Recent research shows a relative stability in language attitudes towards Ukrainian and Russian over time: while Russian is still primarily valued as a means of communication, the importance of Ukrainian is both communicative and symbolic (Kulyk 2017). In view of the dynamism of the linguistic market and growing support for Ukrainian on the part of the state, the legitimacy of this language is increasingly being constructed within both the identification and the utility dimensions, the latter attitude now also evident in younger generations (Kudriavtseva 2021).

Though changes in the linguistic market may dictate a more widespread acceptance of the attitude that Ukrainian-Russian bilingualism is beneficial in terms of the linguistic and economic capital that it provides, the hegemonic ideologies legitimating the standard varieties of Ukrainian and Russian significantly overshadow the value of bilingual practice. The ideology of standard language is built upon the construct of an ideal discrete language which entails heightened concerns for linguistic purism and deprecation of language mixing of all kinds. Under this view, the Ukrainian-Russian mixed variety *surzhyk* is considered illegitimate (Bilaniuk 2005; Friedman 2021) while Ukrainian-Russian bilingualism is also delegitimized in public discourse shaped by Ukraine's postcolonial narrative.

The postcolonial narrative frames the Russian language as the "tragic colonial legacy" in Ukraine; the result of Russification policy which lasted for about three hundred years (Pavlenko 2011: 48). Consequently, Russian is perceived as alien to Ukrainians in Ukraine, "the language of the former empire" linked to a Eurasian identity and "authoritarian Eurasian values" (Pavlenko 2011: 49). Ukrainian arises as the only language that "belongs" to Ukraine and relates to a European identity, the ideology encoded in the expression *nasha ridna mova* prominent in hegemonic discourse (Friedman 2016: 168). Its basic tenets proclaim the necessity "to undo the Russification of the Ukrainian population" since Ukrainian-Russian bilingualism is a "distorted" and "anomalous situation" and monolingualism is the only "normal" state of affairs (Pavlenko 2011: 48, 52) [cf. the "normalization" debates in Catalonia (Woolard 2020)]. This brings about the so-called "split-identity framework" (Kudriavtseva 2021: 155) which discursively frames societal bilingualism in Ukraine [cf. the "divided identity" view that frames bilingualism in Catalonia (Woolard 2020: 265-266)]. The split-identity stance nurtures the "subtractive bilingual" model of language acquisition (see Riley 2011: 500) whereby the acquisition of Ukrainian implies a total erasure of the use of Russian.

Ukrainian-Russian bilingualism is a widespread phenomenon in Ukraine (Shevchuk-Kliuzheva 2020), however, often speakers are not willing to recognize their being bilingual either because bilingualism is stigmatized (Csernicskó 2017) or because of the major perception that only active and/or balanced bilingualism, where competency is equally strong in both languages, is deemed valuable as part of one's cultural capital (Lakhtikova 2017: 147). Moreover, the term "bilingualism" is compromised in western Ukraine where it has been traditionally identified with aggressive Russification (Lakhtikova 2017: 153).

Concerns for the protection of Ukraine's Russian-speaking population have become for Russia "a justification" for aggression since the invasion of Donbas and the annexation of Crimea in 2014 (Stepanenko 2017). The fact that the Russian language has been used to justify Russia's military aggression against Ukraine highlights the symbolic value of Ukrainian and correspondently diminishes the practical significance of Russian as a neutral medium of communication. The 2013–2014 Euromaidan and the Russian annexation of Crimea and parts of Donbas gave rise to the idea that speaking Russian "can undermine Ukraine's peace and security" (Bilaniuk 2016: 147) while speaking Ukrainian is a sign of belonging to Ukraine (Seals 2019: 114).

Though the war has significantly politicized language choice, a counter ideology, which sees this choice as transparent and politically neutral, has not lost its power, since "many people's deeds show that being Russophone often goes along with being a Ukrainian patriot" (Bilaniuk 2016: 142). There are also indications of a more positive appreciation of bi-/multilingualism within the recent developments in the language pedagogy for Ukrainian as a second language, which has been part of language activism since the Euromaidan (Kudriavtseva 2023).

Against the backdrop of this complex set of conflicting and contesting ideologies, it is hard to predict which linguistic competence can be perceived as more valuable in the linguistic market of Ukraine. Among the factors defining the social inequality of different groups, there are not only long-term and gradual processes such as state support and promotion via education, but also the effects of influential discourses shaped by the war as well as the overall politicization of symbolic spaces.

Such a perspective foregrounds monolingual practices in the first place. For instance, the Ukrainian legislation as well as the hegemonic discourses of education and civil service legitimize the use of Ukrainian in these domains. The discourse of cultural heritage legitimizes the linguistic practices of ancestors, particularly parents, and this supports the monolingual practices of family communication. The discourse of ethnic identity and the "identification" ideology link language to a particular ethnicity and justify the use of one respective language as legitimate for that group. The link of language to ethnic identity has also characterized Ukrainian legislation: for instance, from the 1990s until specific laws on education were passed,[4] local authorities would determine the number of schools operating in particular languages on the basis of the ethnic composition of the population (Kulyk 2009: 19).

The practice of bilingualism is a separate phenomenon relevant for the study of the relationship between linguistic practices and social inequalities. Of special interest is the bilingual competence in the case of Ukraine since here it has hardly been legitimated by influential discourses. Here, bilingual practices are called forth by practical reasons and grounded in urgent needs, rather than sanctioned by specific ideologies. In this respect, self-reported linguistic practices in various communicative situations should be considered too, since these may differ from those explicitly recognized in terms of deliberate language choices (i.e. as responses to general questions on language spoken in everyday life).

---

4   The 2017 Law of Ukraine "On Education" and the 2020 Law of Ukraine "On Complete General Secondary Education" provide for Ukrainian as the only means of instruction in post-primary school education in all of Ukraine's state-funded schools.

3. Data and Method

Empirical data presented and analyzed in this chapter was obtained within the framework of the project "Social inequalities: perception by Ukrainian society" carried out in 2017–2018 by the Sociological Association of Ukraine with the financial support of the "Renaissance" International Foundation. The main objective of the project was to determine the types of social inequality that significantly increase the level of social tension within Ukrainian society. The aspects surveyed in the project included inequalities in access to education, professional self-realization, the labor market, opportunities to start one's own business, power and political participation, the consumer market, quality medical services, means of personal safety, information technology and the Internet, cultural resources, as well as opportunities related to linguistic competence.

The data of the "Social inequalities: perception by Ukrainian society" research, analyzed in this chapter, were collected by the method of mass survey. The primary data collecting was carried out by Oleksandr Yaremenko Ukrainian Institute of Social Research between August 28 and September 8, 2017. The subject of the survey was the adult population of Ukraine over age 18 residing in all regions, except for the temporarily occupied territories of Crimea and Donbas. The sample is representative in terms of age, gender and place of residence (e.g., urban, suburban, rural). The sample population is 2046 respondents, comprising 1107 women and 939 men. The mass survey was conducted in 25 territorial and administrative units of Ukraine: the Ukraine's 24 oblasts (Vinnytsia, Volyn, Dnipropetrovsk, Donetsk, Zhytomyr, Zakarpattia, Zaporizhzhia, Ivano-Frankivsk, Kyiv, Kirovohrad, Luhansk, Lviv, Mykolaiv, Odesa, Poltava, Rivne, Sumy, Ternopil, Kharkiv, Kherson, Khmelnytskyi, Cherkasy, Chernivtsi, Chernihiv) and the city of Kyiv.

The respondents' distribution by age is as follows: 421 respondents aged between 18-29, 388 respondents between 30-39, 350 respondents between 40-49, 360 respondents between 50-59 and 527 respondents aged 60 and older. According to the survey results, the age of Ukrainians does not affect their language practices. A z-test reveals slightly more Ukrainian speakers among respondents aged over 40. Variation in the number of bilinguals and Russian speakers in different age groups is not statistically significant. In general, there is no relationship between the variables "age" and "language practices:" the chi-square test is insignificant (Chi-Square Tests: Pearson Chi-Square -10.014, df -8, Asymptotic Significance (2-sided) -0.264; N of Valid Cases -2047).

The data analyzed in this chapter covers the issue of language practices as related to the kinds of inequalities mentioned above. The data were obtained using individual standardized face-to-face interviews conducted at the respondents' place of residence. All the respondents had to answer the same questions from the suggested list (available both in Ukrainian and Russian; the language of the interview was chosen by respondents). Answers to the questions on language practices, foreign-language proficiency and personal material welfare were recorded as reported by the respondents. This means that to obtain the data on the use of languages, language proficiency and income, we did not use any specific language tests, but accepted the respondents' self-assessments.

The analysis of the data presented in this chapter is given in five subsections. First, we focus on the questions of the part of the survey devoted to language issues. These questions were aimed at collecting information on actual language use as well as the opinions of respondents on potential tensions between various linguistic groups. The questions were formulated taking into account previous studies on language practices in Ukraine (Vyshniak 2009; Skokova 2018). The list of questions is as follows:

> In which language do you usually communicate... (at home, at work or educational institutions, in public places, with friends and acquaintances)?
> Which foreign languages do you speak and how fluently?
> In your opinion, is the following statement correct: the successes and achievements of Ukrainian citizens do not depend on the language they speak?
> Are relations between Ukrainian-speaking and Russian-speaking citizens tense in Ukraine?

The analysis of the responses to the first question on language choice in various communicative situations allowed us to introduce an additional variable for the Ukrainian-Russian bilinguals. This means that we treat "bilingualism" as a variable in this study. The group of respondents seen as bilingual in practice comprises all the respondents who reported using more than one language in different communicative settings (e.g., those who chose the option "Ukrainian" for communication at work and the option "Russian" for communication with family at home) while not necessarily explicitly recognizing their own bilingualism (i.e. choosing the option "Ukrainian and Russian" for various communication situations). We merged these respondents into one group of Ukrainian-Russian bilinguals since they reported on the use of more than one language in different contexts. Ukrainian-Russian bilingual practices, as we understand them here, do not refer to *surzhyk*, but include the ability to communicate in Ukrainian and Russian, regularly switching between them.

The following subsections present the results of statistical analysis (z-test — to confirm the statistical significance of the differences in percentages; the construction of an additional variable; xi-square test — to define the correlation of indicators; ANOVA — to estimate the difference between the mean values of self-assessed social status on the seven-point scale (the imaginary ladder) among the respondents with different levels of English proficiency) carried out in order to answer our research questions. At the core of our analysis is the data for the three linguistic groups (Ukrainian speakers, Russian speakers and Ukrainian-Russian bilinguals) and their comparison in terms of social inequalities and distinctions. In order to track social distinctions, we posed questions on identification (i.e. nationality — *національність*) and the perceived support of all ethnic groups by the state. The exact wording of these survey questions is as follows:

> *What nationality do you consider yourself to be?*
> *In your opinion, is the following statement correct: The Ukrainian state provides equal opportunities and creates equal living conditions for all ethnic groups?*

To elucidate social inequalities as related to linguistic choices, we compared the three identified groups (Ukrainian speakers, Russian speakers and Ukrainian-Russian bilinguals) in terms of their foreign-language proficiency; social status (using an imaginary ladder locating people at different points); material welfare (using a five-point scale where 1 is "very low", 2 is "low", 3 is "below average", 4 is "average", and 5 is "above average"); sectors of the economy where they are engaged in jobs (agrarian, industrial, industrial services, education and health, postindustrial services); and levels of mobility (visits to other countries for any purpose in the three years before the survey). The statistical use of these indicators allowed us to test the hypothesis about the impact of language practices on social inequalities in Ukraine.

4. Results

In this section, we present the results of the nationwide survey. To allow an examination of Ukrainian society's perception of social inequality as related to language use, we first measure self-reported linguistic practices and competence and show the responses to the questions on the language of communication (Ukrainian, Russian, other) in different settings. Then we show the data on ethnic identification in relation to the linguistic practices that we detected, followed by the respondents' evaluation of the state support for various ethnic groups in Ukraine. After that, we present the results on the perceived relation of Ukrainian citizens' successes and achievements to their language of communication as well as on their perceptions of existing tensions among various ethnic and linguistic groups in Ukraine. Then, we give details of the respondents' self-reported foreign-language proficiency and draw correlations between the levels of proficiency and the monolingual and bilingual language practices. Finally, we compare the three linguistic groups in terms of social inequalities understood as varying social status, material welfare, external mobility (travels abroad) and job prestige.

4.1. Linguistic practices: monolingualism and bilingualism in everyday communication

The distribution of responses to the questions on the language of communication in various communicative situations (at home, at work, in public places and with friends and acquaintances) is presented in Table 1.

Table 1. Language of communication in various communicative situations (by percentage of those who answered the questions)

	With family at home	at work / in educational institutions	in public places	with friends and acquaintances
Ukrainian	**43.5**	40.9	39.9	39.0
Russian	**34.8**	31.7	32.8	33.3
Both Ukrainian and Russian	21.4	27.3	27.2	**27.5**
Other	0.3	0.1	0.1	0.2

Table 1 shows that the dominant languages of communication are Ukrainian and Russian. Other languages named by the respondents included Crimean Tatar, Moldavian, Azerbaijani, Polish and Slovak. The order of distribution of language use in the surveyed communicative situations is similar: in all types of communication, the Ukrainian language prevails, followed by Russian and then by bilingual practices. The use of the Russian language is lower than the use of Ukrainian: by 9.2% in communication at work and by 5.7% in communication with friends. The distribution of monolingual and bilingual practices in communication at work and in public places has no significant differences.

The analytical design, in particular the introduction of the additional variable, made it possible to reveal the number of respondents who are monolingual or bilingual in all the given communicative settings (Fig. 1). The use of the additional variable allows us to add to the bilingual competence claimed by the respondents those bilingual practices reported on in various communicative situations, that is, where both Ukrainian and Russian are used for different types of communication. The share of respondents who communicate in Ukrainian both privately and publicly is 36.6%, in Russian — 27.2%, while 17.6% of respondents use both languages in all the situations surveyed. Other variants of bilingualism make up 18.6% (Fig. 1), for example, respondents recognize that they are bilingual at home and speak Ukrainian in other situations. In general, the share of respondents who use both Ukrainian and Russian in various types of communication is 36.2 %.

Figure 1. Language practices in Ukraine (by percentage of those who answered the questions)

Table 2 is based on language practices reported in Figure 1 and shows the results of the regional distribution of monolingual and bilingual practices. Ukrainian-speaking practices prevail in the west and the center, while Russian-speaking practices dominate in the east and the south.[5] The level of bilingual practices rises from the west to the north. The highest prevalence of bilingual practices

---

5   The grouping of oblasts into larger regions is as follows. West: Volyn, Zakarpattia, Ivano-Frankivsk, Lviv, Rivne, Ternopil, Chernivtsi (N = 428); Center: Vinnytsia, Kirovohrad, Poltava, Khmelnytsky, Cherkasy (N = 315); North: Zhytomyr, Kyiv, Sumy, Chernihiv (N = 274); East: Dnipropetrovsk, Zaporizhzhya, Kharkiv (N = 462); Donbas: controlled areas of Donetsk and Luhansk oblasts; South: Mykolaiv, Odesa, Kherson (N = 221); the city of Kyiv (N = 158).

is found in the north (44.0%), Donbas (the controlled territories of Donetsk and Luhansk regions) (50.6%) and the capital Kyiv (62.8%) (Table 2).

Table 2. **Distribution of language practices by region (by percentage of those who answered the questions)**

	Survey region						
	West	Center	North	East	Donbas	South	city of Kyiv
Ukrainian speakers	**86.5**	**63.2**	40.8	6.9	1.7	8.7	10.3
Russian speakers	0.6	8.3	15.2	**51.3**	47.7	**48.7**	26.9
Ukrainian-Russian bilinguals	12.9	28.5	**44.0**	41.8	**50.6**	42.6	**62.8**

4.2. Identification and state support

In Table 3, we compare the results on self-reported identification of monolingual and bilingual respondents. The data show that there is no significant difference in self-reported nationality between Ukrainian-speaking and Russian-speaking respondents and those respondents who use both Ukrainian and Russian. Ukrainian identification prevails in all three of the groups, with only 5.1% of bilinguals and 18% of Russian speakers naming their nationality as Russian (Table 3). In terms of the whole survey, 91% of all respondents identify their nationality as Ukrainian and 6.9% as Russian. Table 3 shows self-identification by Ukrainian speakers, bilinguals and Russian speakers.

Table 3.   Self-reported identification in relation to linguistic practices (by percentage of those who answered the questions)

"What nationality do you consider yourself to be?"	Linguistic practices		
	Ukrainian speakers	Bilinguals	Russian speakers
Ukrainian	99,4	93,2	80,6
Russian	0,6	5,1	18
Other	0	1,7	1,4

The introduction of the additional variable for bilingual respondents diversifies the linguistic landscape of Ukraine and makes it possible to study the perceptions of monolingual and bilingual groups of respondents in terms of influences of their language use on their social positions. These perceptions include opinions on state support as well as ensuing tensions between different ethnolinguistic groups in Ukrainian society.

Table 4 shows a correlation between language practices and the perception of the activities of the state to ensure equal opportunities and living conditions for various ethnic groups in Ukraine (xi-square = 41.45, $p < 0.001$). The bilingual respondents' evaluations of state support are lower than those of the Ukrainian speakers, but do not differ from the evaluations reported by the Russian speakers both in terms of positive and negative responses to the respective question.

Table 4. **Answers to the question "In your opinion, is the following statement correct: "The Ukrainian state provides equal opportunities and creates equal living conditions for all ethnic groups" in relation to language practices (in percentages; [a,b] different letters indicate significant differences by *z-test* at the level of 0.05, and identical letters mean that such differences are absent)**

	Ukrainian speakers	Bilinguals	Russian speakers
Incorrect	28.9 [a]	39.3 [b]	45.4 [b]
Correct	63.7 [a]	54.0 [b]	47.4 [b]
Undecided	7.4	6.7	7.2

4.3. Linguistic practices, inequalities and social tension

Table 5 shows the responses to a general question on the perceived dependence of Ukrainian citizens' successes on their language of communication. Here there is no statistically significant difference between the positions of monolingual and bilingual respondents (xi-square = 3.24, p = 0.519). This result demonstrates that the language of communication is not generally perceived as a privilege conditioning success and advantage by the population in Ukraine.

Table 5. **Responses to the question "In your opinion, is the following statement correct: "Successes and achievements of Ukrainian citizens do not depend on the language they speak" in relation to language practices (in percentages)**

	Ukrainian speakers	Bilinguals	Russian speakers
Incorrect	18.5	19.9	20.9
Correct	75.1	74.2	74.7
Undecided	6.4	5.9	4.4

Table 6 summarizes the responses to questions on possible tensions among ethnic, regional and linguistic groups in Ukraine. The results show that all three linguistic groups perceive the tensions between Ukraine's various regions to be most salient (Table 6).

Table 6. Positive responses to the question on tensions in relation to language practices (by percentage of those who answered the questions)

Are there tensions in Ukraine between...	Ukrainian speakers	Bilinguals	Russian speakers	xi-square	p-level
...ethnic Ukrainians and the other national and ethnic groups	15.8	18.2	21.0	8.176	0.085
...residents of the country's different regions	22.2	34.8	32.9	33.658	< 0.001
...the inhabitants of the west and the southeast	28.4	37.9	38.0	24.267	< 0.001
...Ukrainian speakers and Russian speakers	21.8	17.2	18.4	7.327	0.120

4.4. Inequalities and foreign-language proficiency

The questions reported on in Table 7 asked the respondents to assess their own level of foreign-language proficiency. The results show that the most common foreign language mastered by the respondents is English. About half of the respondents (45.1%) reported some level of English-language proficiency; for German this figure is 13.5%, for Polish it is 9.2%, and for French it is 4.5% (Table 7).

LANGUAGE AND SOCIAL INEQUALITIES   119

Table 7. The level of foreign-language proficiency (by percentage of those who answered the questions)

	Not proficient	Initial level	Average level	Sufficient level	Very high level
in English	54.9	25.0	15.0	4.3	0.8
in German	86.5	10.6	2.5	0.4	0.0
in Polish	90.8	6.5	1.9	0.6	0.2
in French	95.5	3.4	0.8	0.3	0.0

The results of the survey show that there is a correlation between the self-assessed level of English-language proficiency and self-assessed social status (the xi-square test is significant: xi-square = 164.664, $p < 0.001$) (Fig. 2). Figure 2 depicts the steps of an imaginary ladder. The lowest step 1 locates those who assess their social status as the lowest, and the highest step 7 locates those who assess their status as high. The percentage of those who see themselves as not proficient in English decreases from the first to the fourth step (45%), while it remains almost the same at steps five, six and seven: about half (from 58% to 54%) of those respondents who assess their social status as average and above are to a certain extent proficient in English. However, this proficiency is not an exclusive sign of middle or high social status: advanced proficiency in English increases from 2% at the first step to 17% at the seventh, that is the highest step of the ladder. This means that there are people with high level proficiency in English not only at the higher steps of the social status ladder, but also on the lower steps.

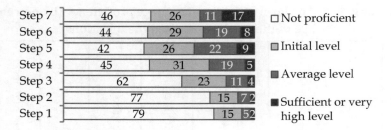

Figure 2. English-language proficiency on the steps of an imaginary ladder locating people of different social status (by percentage of those who answered the questions)

The relationship between the level of English-language proficiency and social status is more clearly shown in Figure 3. The average self-assessment of one's social status on the seven-point scale (the imaginary ladder) by the respondents with different levels of English proficiency has significant differences (ANOVA, F = 42.264, p < 0.001). In particular, the scores of those who do not speak English at all differ at the 0.05 level (3.37) from those who have an initial (3.85) or average level (4.04). The average score of those who assess their English-language proficiency as sufficient and very high is significantly higher (4.23).

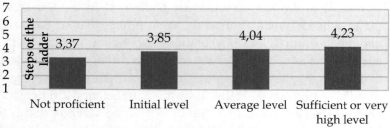

Figure 3. Average positions of people with different levels of English proficiency on the steps of an imaginary ladder which locates respondents with different social status: the lowest step 1 locates those who assess their social status as the lowest, and the highest step 7 locates those who assess their status as high (average values)

Figure 4 shows how an increase in the level of English proficiency is accompanied by an increase in the respondents' material welfare, which is depicted with the help of a scale diagram (Fig. 4). For groups with different levels of English proficiency, the average trend of assessing one's material welfare increases: from "below average" for the initial level of English proficiency to "above average" for the sufficient and high levels.

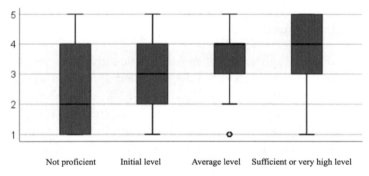

Figure 4. Comparison of the respondents' self-assessment of their material welfare* with their self-assessed levels of English proficiency (*material welfare: 1—"very low", 2—"low", 3—"below average", 4—"average", 5—"above average")

Figure 5 depicts the relationship between the respondents' English-language proficiency and occupation (xi-square test is significant: xi-square = 55.979, $p < 0.001$). The lowest English proficiency is found in the agrarian sector: there, only a quarter of the respondents assess their English to be of initial and average levels. In the industrial sector, the figure increases to 55.1%, of which 3.8% of respondents consider themselves to have sufficient and high levels of English proficiency. For the sectors of industrial and post-industrial services, as well as education and health care, more than 50% of respondents declare either initial or sufficient and very high levels of proficiency in English.

```
                        ☐ Not proficient           ☐ Initial level
             Agrarian │         75        │    18    │7│
           Industrial │     45      │   37    │  15  │
   Industrial services│     49      │   31    │  16  │
  Education and health│    42       │   30    │  18  │
Postindustrial services│   38       │   30    │  22  │
```

Figure 5. Level of English proficiency in different sectors of the economy (by percentage of those who answered the questions)

The level of English proficiency is significantly higher among those respondents who report to have travelled abroad (xi-square test = 168.177, p < 0.001) (Fig. 6). However, 30.3% of those who travelled for the purposes of temporary occupation, study, holidays and leisure, visiting relatives, medical treatment, or participation in conferences or business trips recognize no level of proficiency in English.

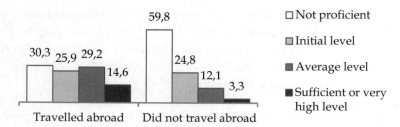

Figure 6. Levels of English-language proficiency for respondents with different levels of mobility (visits abroad for various purposes within the three years preceding the survey; in percentages)

Proficiency in foreign languages (especially English) can be seen as an accompanying indicator of material status and social prestige. The results of the survey depicted in Figures 2-6 suggest that the higher the respondents assess their material welfare and social position, the higher they evaluate their English language proficiency and the more probable it is for them to be engaged in jobs within more profitable sectors of the economy.

4.5. Inequality and linguistic practices

In our study, we also examined the relationship between the level of English-language proficiency and monolingual and bilingual practices. Table 8 shows the differences among the three studied groups of Ukrainian speakers, Russian speakers and Ukrainian-Russian bilinguals in relation to the level of English-language proficiency that they declare. While the Ukrainian speakers show the highest rate of no proficiency in English (64.8%) and the Russian speakers tend to have the highest rate at the initial level (31.7%), the bilingual respondents most often rate their English language proficiency as average, sufficient and very high (25%) (Table 8).

Table 8. **Levels of English-language proficiency in relation to language practices (by percentage of those who answered the questions)**

	Ukrainian speakers	Bilinguals	Russian speakers	In general
Not proficient	**64.8**	50.1	47.5	54.9
Initial level	20.3	24.9	**31.7**	25.0
Average level	11.5	**18.2**	15.3	15.0
Sufficient or very high level	3.4	**6.8**	5.5	5.1

At the same time, however, the statistical analysis shows the absence of significant differences between the monolingual and bilingual groups in terms of social inequality. The comparison of the average positions of the groups on the steps of the imaginary social ladder depicts the absence of significant differences (ANOVA, F = 1.452, p = 0.234) (Fig. 7).

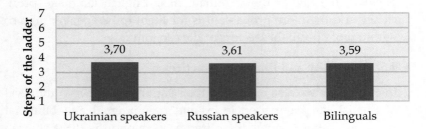

Figure 7. Average positions of respondents with different language practices on the steps of an imaginary ladder which locates respondents with different social status: the lowest step 1 locates those who assess their social status as the lowest, the highest step 7 locates those who assess their status as high (average values)

The comparison of the material welfare as reported by monolingual and bilingual respondents also shows no differences (Fig. 8).

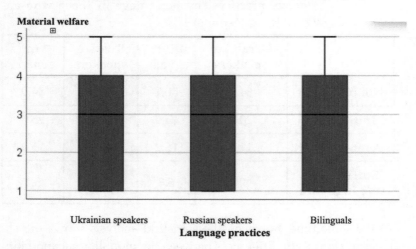

Figure 8. Comparison of material welfare* for respondents with different language practices (*Material welfare: 1—"very low", 2—"low", 3—"below average", 4—"average", 5—"above average")

The scale diagram shows that Ukrainian-speaking, Russian-speaking and bilingual respondents report the same level of material welfare. Among them, there are those who assess their material welfare as "higher than average," this being the highest level of self-assessment for the three groups. The average tendency for self-assessment of material welfare for the three linguistic groups is located at the level of "below average."

The comparison of the presence of monolinguals and bilinguals in different sectors of the economy also shows no significant differences (xi-square = 7.664, p = 0.264), except for the agrarian sector (Fig. 9). Here, the share of Ukrainian speakers significantly prevails and constitutes 60.8%, while the share of Russian speakers is only 6.3%.

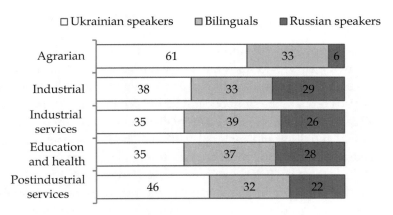

Figure 9. Language practices in different sectors of the economy (by percentage of those who answered the questions)

As for external mobility, that is travelling abroad, the share of Ukrainian speakers is higher among those who have never travelled abroad (Fig. 10). The share of bilingual respondents prevails among those who had visited other countries for various purposes within the three years preceding the survey. This is another characteristic which singles out bilinguals in terms of inequality, in addition to the already mentioned higher self-assessments of proficiency in English.

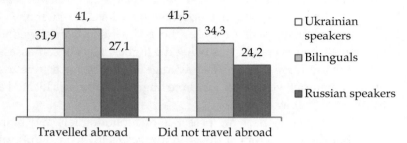

Figure 10. Language practices of respondents with different levels of mobility (travelling abroad for various purposes within the three years preceding the survey; in percentages)

5. Discussion and Conclusion

In this section, we will summarize the analysis of the results of the nationwide survey to trace the inequalities and social distinctions that can be seen as linked to particular languages in Ukraine. We will also compare the symbolic power of Ukrainian and Russian, as well as of Ukrainian-Russian bilingualism, in terms of their relation to social mobility and material welfare. Though the survey also asked respondents to report on their foreign language proficiency, and the level of proficiency in such foreign language as English was related to the monolingual and bilingual practices, it is important to bear in mind that we did not consider English language proficiency in terms of its symbolic power. Neither did we examine ideologies underpinning the perception of English, nor its legitimating discourse. The focus of our study is primarily on Ukrainian and Russian, as well as on Ukrainian-Russian bilingualism, and the symbolic power related to them. The English language proficiency is, therefore, considered here a stand in for measures of external mobility which can be available to different people in a varying degree.

The analysis of the survey results shows that Ukrainian is more often used in both private and public communication. Ukrainian is more often spoken at home (43.5% of all respondents), at work (40.9%), in public places (39.9%) and with acquaintances and friends (39.0%). Russian is less often used at home (34.8% of all respondents), at work (31.7%), in public places (32.8%) and with acquaintances and friends (33.3%). The data shows that, while communication with friends is the most common context for bilingual practices (27.5%), communication in the family shows the highest indicators of monolingual practice (43.5% for Ukrainian and 34.8% for Russian). These results mirror the idea of family communication as largely monocultural and, as a result, monolingual.

In terms of regional distribution, Ukrainian dominates western and central regions (86.5% and 63.2% respectively), while Russian is more often used in the east and south (51.3% and 48.7% respectively). The majority of Ukrainian-Russian bilinguals reside in the north (44.0%), the controlled territories of Donbas (50.6%) and the capital Kyiv (62.8%). It should be stressed that the share of bilinguals in the east and south is also rather high: 41.8% in the east and 42.6% in the southern regions. These results testify to the growing significance of the Ukrainian language all over Ukraine and especially in the northern and southeastern regions; that is, the share of bilinguals has increased there because of a wider spread of the Ukrainian language. In line with earlier surveys relating the importance of Ukrainian to both the communicative and symbolic dimensions (Kulyk 2017), the language is increasingly perceived as a valuable resource in the north and southeast of Ukraine which was traditionally seen as largely Russian-speaking.

This tendency continues the trend of the so-called "bilingualization" — a major disposition of the speakers to use both Ukrainian and Russian in communication — characteristic of the central and northern regions and the capital Kyiv around 2008 (Ivanova 2013). A new finding is that the bilingualization has since also spread to the eastern and southern regions, with a remarkable figure of more than half of bilingual respondents residing in the controlled territories of Donbas in 2018. This can be seen as a natural development of the sociolinguistic situation there, taking into account the suggestion that Russian speakers in Ukraine are, in fact, passive bilinguals; that is, they have a passive competency in Ukrainian in addition to their fluency in Russian (Lakhtikova 2017). Another new result of our survey is that the central region was found to have now become predominantly Ukrainian-speaking, the regional sociolinguistic dynamics suggesting a view that Ukrainian-Russian bilingualism may be a transitional stage in the process of public Ukrainianization.

It is our focus on the dynamics of the language situation in Ukraine that draws attention to bilingual practice. The introduction of an additional variable for bilingual respondents allows us to single out the share of bilinguals equaling 36.2% in the whole sample, with 36.6% of Ukrainian speakers and 27.2% of Russian speakers. The share of Ukrainian-Russian bilinguals turns out to be significant enough to be tested for relevant social distinctions. In terms of self-reported nationality, there is no difference between Ukrainian-speaking respondents and bilinguals, where the majority identify as Ukrainians (99.4% and 93.2% respectively). However, in the group of Russian speakers, the share of those who recognized their nationality as Russian (18%) is significantly higher. The question on nationality links to the next question on equal support of ethnic groups by the Ukrainian state as it is perceived by groups of monolingual and bilingual respondents. Since language is often linked to ethnic identity in hegemonic discourse, the responses to this question on state support can be interpreted as the respondents' perceptions of the support not only for ethnic groups, but also for their respective languages. The difference here is significant: a higher share of Ukrainian-speaking respondents (63.7%) agrees with the statement that the state equally supports all ethnic groups in Ukraine; among bilinguals and Russian speakers, the share of positive responses is significantly lower (54.0% and 47.4% respectively). Taking into account the fact that the overwhelming majority of each group identifies as Ukrainians, and that the Ukrainian language is legitimated by the state, the smaller number of positive responses on the part of Russian-speaking and bilingual respondents can be interpreted as their perception of unequal support for languages. The ideology of "identification" legitimates support for the Ukrainian language and for Ukrainian ethnic identity since this ideological framework conflates the two. Hence, there are more Ukrainian-speaking Ukrainians who agree with the statement while those who can draw from the experiences of using another language (bilinguals and Russian speakers) more often disagree.

At the same time, however, neither of the monolingual groups, nor the bilingual respondents, tend to see the successes of Ukrainian citizens as dependent on their language use: around 75% in each group agree on the absence of such a dependence, while only around 20% of the respondents disagree. Likewise, the majority within the three groups report the absence of any tensions between ethnic Ukrainians and the other ethnic groups in Ukraine: the number of those who perceive the interethnic relationships to be tense is lowest among the Ukrainian-speaking respondents (15.8%) and slightly increases within the two other groups (18.2% of bilinguals and 21.0% of Russian speakers). Any tensions between Ukrainian-speaking and Russian-speaking citizens of Ukraine are also largely imperceptible: here, Ukrainian-Russian bilinguals feel least tense, with 17.2% of positive responses, this figure slightly increasing for Russian speakers (18.4%) and Ukrainian speakers (21.8%). More pronounced in all three groups is the perception of tensions between the residents of Ukraine's various regions and particularly between those living in the west and the southeast. The statistically significant difference here is found in the case of bilinguals and Russian-speaking respondents who are most sensitive to the "east-west divide" (37.9% and 38%, respectively). Taking into account the barely visible recognition of language-related success, as well as interethnic and interlinguistic collisions (around 20% in each case) in all three groups, we argue that language can hardly be viewed as a ground for serious social tension, nor should language be held accountable for any interregional clash in Ukraine. The absence of confrontation between the Ukrainian-speaking and Russian-speaking parts of Ukraine's population also found in previous studies (Masenko 2010: 112) testifies to the public acceptance of the sociolinguistic dynamics developing toward a greater embrace of the Ukrainian language, as well as to the public acceptance of bilingualism in general, i. e. the embrace of Ukrainian by Russian speakers, since Ukraine's independence in 1991.

A correlation between social inequalities and linguistic competence is detected in the case of foreign-language proficiency.

English-language proficiency, which prevails in the analyzed sample (45.1% of all respondents), correlates with the respondents' self-assessed social status and material welfare along with the sector of the economy where they are employed. The level of English proficiency is also significantly higher among those who have had an opportunity to travel abroad. Taking together the data on self-assessed social position (the seven-point imaginary ladder), material welfare (the five-point scale diagram) and external mobility (visits abroad within the past three years), we can suggest that the highest levels of English-language proficiency are found among respondents with self-assessed highest material and social positions. When the level of English-language proficiency is queried among the three studied groups (Ukrainian speakers, Russian speakers, Ukrainian-Russian bilinguals), it is the Ukrainian-Russian bilinguals who report on the highest proficiency. The bilingual respondents also tend to travel abroad more often. As a result of the study, a connection between the English language proficiency and the level of material status was recorded. But more research is needed to clarify whether English proficiency is a status-enhancing resource or an unattainable skill for low-status individuals.

The self-assessments that the monolingual and bilingual respondents provide for their social position and material welfare are similar: the average values on the seven-point ladder for social status and the five-point scale diagram for material welfare do not show statistically significant differences. Likewise, the figures on the employment of all the three groups in the various economic sectors do not differ. The only exception is the agrarian sector where the majority of Ukrainian-speaking respondents are employed (60.8%), followed by the bilinguals (32.9%) and Russian speakers (6.3%). This data suggests the absence of significant social inequalities among the three groups of Ukrainian-speaking and Russian-speaking monolingual respondents and Ukrainian-Russian bilinguals. This is in line with our previous finding on the absence of language-related social distinctions, whereby the majority of respondents in all of the identified groups do not report any tensions in interethnic and interlinguistic relations.

The results of the survey let us draw another set of conclusions. The data on regional distribution of monolingual and bilingual practices in Ukraine suggests that the traditional view of Ukraine's southeast as largely Russian-speaking is no longer valid. The figures on bilingual practices there highlight the importance of the Ukrainian language for the respective respondents and the growing shift from Russian monolingualism toward Ukrainian-Russian bilingual communication. Though these respondents still retain Russian in use, they also wish to rely on the utility of Ukrainian. Together with the abovementioned finding on the absence of significant material inequalities and social distinctions, this inference further suggests that language should not be viewed as a factor of social inequality in any part of Ukraine. The different ideologies underpinning the value of Ukrainian and Russian can coexist and be equally utilized by their speakers. In this respect, our data suggests that there may be, in fact, more linguistic capital related to Ukrainian-Russian bilingualism than to each of the monolingual practices, even in the absence of a legitimizing discourse.

This finding is of interest beyond the Ukrainian context as it implies a reconsideration of the view that a mode of speaking imbued with symbolic power is either established through the formal institutions (Bourdieu 1991) or legitimized as an accepted means of communication in the local economic domain (Woolard 1985). The finding that a bilingual practice, such as Ukrainian-Russian bilingualism, may relate to greatest material welfare invites a revision of the concept of the legitimate language as applied to only one language at once. This finding suggests that what is gaining "utility" (Sovik 2010) in Ukraine is no longer Russian on its own, but a Ukrainian-Russian bilingual practice, i. e. it is bilingualism that constitutes the "legitimate language" in this case. This finding is in line with findings from other similar contexts, such as the sociolinguistic situation in Catalonia, where the traditionally negative attitude to societal bilingualism has been reframed as plurilingualism, implying that "a bilingual repertoire is now more often a measure of acquisition of Catalan rather than displacement of it" (Woolard 2020: 276). Such a revision would entail a consistent departure from the view of the legitimate mode of expression as an ideal discrete language with clearly defined boundaries, which is the classic view of the legitimate language as understood by Bourdieu. These prospects would be fruitful avenues for future research in the current field of bi/multilingual studies.

The phenomenon of bilingualism and its symbolic power in Ukraine also requires further investigation, especially in view of the changes initiated by the 2019 Language Law as well as the dynamics of the language situation as influenced by the February 2022 full-scale Russian invasion. The inferences drawn from our data reveal the absence of discrimination on the basis of language as measured before the full-blown Russian war on Ukraine. This means that the allegations of tensions related to languages in Ukraine should be seen as unfounded.

Bibliography:

Bilaniuk, Laada. (2005). *Contested tongues: language politics and cultural correction in Ukraine*. Ithaca and London: Cornell University Press.

Bilaniuk, Laada. (2016). Ideologies of language in wartime. In *Revolution and war in contemporary Ukraine: The challenge of change*, Bertelsen, Olga (ed). Stuttgart: Ibidem Verlag, 139–160.

Bourdieu, Pierre. (1977). The economics of linguistic exchanges. *Social Science Information* 16(6): 645–668.

Bourdieu, Pierre. (1991). *Language and symbolic power*. Trans. by Gino Raymond and Matthew Adamson. Cambridge: Polity Press.

Csernicskó, István & Máté, Réka. (2017). Bilingualism in Ukraine: value or challenge? *Sustainable Multilingualism* 10: 14–35.

Friedman, Debra A. (2016). Our language: (re)imagining communities in Ukrainian language classrooms. *Journal of Language, Identity and Education* 15(3): 165–179.

Friedman, Debra A. (2021). Defending borders and crossing boundaries: ideologies of polylanguaging in interviews with bilingual Ukrainian youth. *International Journal of Multilingualism* DOI: 10.1080/14790718. 2021.1874386

Ganti, Tejaswini. (2016). 'Nobody thinks in Hindi here': language hierarchies in Bollywood. In *Precarious creativity: Global media, local labor*, Curtin, Michael & Sanson, Kevin (eds). Berkely: University of California Press, 118–131.

Geeraerts, Dirk. (2003). Cultural models of linguistic standardization. In *Cognitive models in language and thought. Ideology, metaphors and meanings*, Dirven, René, Frank, Roslyn & Pütz, Martin (eds). Berlin: Mouton de Gruyter, 25–68.

Heller, Monica. (1996). Legitimate language in a multilingual school. *Linguistics and Education* 8: 139–157.

Ivanova, Olga. (2013). Bilingualism in Ukraine: Defining attitudes to Ukrainian and Russian through geographical and generational variations in language practices. *Sociolinguistic Studies* 7(3): 249–272.

Irvine, Judith T. (1989). When talk isn't cheap: language and political economy. *American Ethnologist* 16(2): 248–267.

Kroskrity, Paul. (2004). Language ideologies. In *Companion to linguistic anthropology*, Duranti, Alessandro (ed). Malden, MA: Basil Blackwell, 496–517.

Kudriavtseva, Natalia. (2021). Standard Ukrainian in the multilingual context: language ideologies and current educational practices. *Journal of Multilingual and Multicultural Development* 42(2): 152–164.

Kudriavtseva, Natalia. (2023). Ukrainian language revitalization online: targeting Ukraine's Russian speakers. In *Teaching and learning resources for endangered languages*, Valijärvi, Riitta & Kahn, Lily (eds). Leiden: Brill, 203–223.

Kulyk, Volodymyr. (2009). Language policies and language attitudes in post-Orange Ukraine. In *Language policy and language situation in Ukraine: Analysis and recommendations*, Besters-Dilger, Juliane (ed). Frankfurt: Peter Lang, 15–55.

Kulyk, Volodymyr. (2015). The age factor in language practices and attitudes: continuity and change in Ukraine's bilingualism. *Nationalities Papers* 43(2): 283–301.

Kulyk, Volodymyr. (2017). Language attitudes in independent Ukraine: Differentiation and evolution. In *The battle for Ukrainian: A comparative perspective*, Flier, Michael S. & Graziosi, Andrea (eds). Cambridge, Mass.: Harvard University Press, 309–341.

Lakhtikova, Anastasia. (2017). Understanding passive bilingualism in Eastern Ukraine. *Critical Multilingualism Studies* 5(1): 144–173.

Masenko, Larysa. (2010). Movna sytuatsiia Ukrainy: sotsiolinhvistychnyi analiz [from Ukr.: Language situation in Ukraine: sociolinguistic analysis]. In *Movna polityka ta movna sytuatsiia v Ukraini: analiz i rekomendatsii* [from Ukr.: Language policy and language situation in Ukraine: analyses and recommendations], Besters-Dilger, Juliane (ed). Kyiv: "Kyiv-Mohyla Academy" Publishing House, 96–131.

Pavlenko, Aneta. (2011). Language rights versus speakers' rights: on the applicability of Western language rights approaches in Eastern European contexts. *Language Policy* 10: 37–58.

Riley, Kathleen C. (2011). Language socialization and language ideologies. In *The handbook of language socialization*, Duranti, Alessandro, Ochs, Elinor & Schieffelin, Bambi (eds). Malden: Blackwell Publishing, 493–514.

Seals, Corinne A. (2019). *Choosing a mother tongue: the politics of language and identity in Ukraine*. Bristol: Multilingual Matters.

Shevchuk-Kliuzheva, Olha. (2020). The sociolinguistic aspect of Ukrainian-Russian child bilingualism on the basis of a survey of Ukrainian families. *Cognitive Studies / Études cognitives* 20: Article 2323. DOI: 10.11649/cs.2323

Skokova, Liudmyla. (2018). Movni praktyky v ukrainskomu suspilstvi [from Ukr.: Language practices in Ukrainian society]. In *Kulturni praktyky v suchasnomu suspilstvi: teoretychni pidkhody ta empirychni vymiry* [from Ukr.: Cultural practices in modern society: theoretical approaches and empirical dimensions]. Kyiv: Instytut sotsiolohii NAN Ukrainy, 233–250.

Søvik, Margrethe B. (2010). Language practices and the language situation in Kharkiv: Examining the concept of legitimate language in relation to identification and utility. *International Journal of the Sociology of Language* 201: 5–28.

Stepanenko, Viktor. (2017). Movna polityka i movni praktyky v konteksti vijny [from Ukr.: Language policies and language practices in the context of war]. *Sotsiolohiia: Teoriia, Metody, Marketynh* [from Ukr.: Sociology: theory, methods, marketing] 2: 3–34.

Stroud, Christopher. (2002). Framing Bourdieu socioculturally: alternative forms of linguistic legitimacy in postcolonial Mozambique. *Multilingua* 21(2/3): 247–273.

Vaara, Eero, Tienari, Janne, Piekkari, Rebecca & Säntti, Risto. (2005). Language and the circuits of power in a merging multinational corporation. *Journal of Management Studies* 42(3): 595–623.

Vyshniak, Oleksandr. (2009). *Movna sytuatsiia ta status mov v Ukraini: dynamika, problemy, perspektyvy (sotsiolohichnyi analiz)* [from Ukr.: Linguistic situation and the status of languages in Ukraine: dynamics, problems, prospects (a sociological analysis)]. Kyiv: Instytut sotsiolohii NAN Ukrainy.

Woolard, Kathryn A. (1985). Language variation and cultural hegemony: toward an integration of sociolinguistic and social theory. *American Ethnologist* 12(4): 738–748.

Woolard, Kathryn A. (2008). Language and identity choice in Catalonia: the interplay of contrasting ideologies of linguistic authority. In *Lengua, nación e identidad. La regulación del plurilingüismo en España y América Latina*, Süselbeck, Kirsten, Mühlschlegel, Ulrike & Masson, Peter (eds). Frankfurt am Main: Vervuert/Madrid: Iberoamericana, 303–323.

LANGUAGE AND SOCIAL INEQUALITIES   135

Woolard, Kathryn A. (2016). *Singular and plural: ideologies of linguistic authority in 21st century Catalonia*. Oxford: Oxford University Press.

Woolard, Kathryn A. (2020). "You have to be against bilingualism!" Sociolinguistic theory and controversies over bilingualism in Catalonia. *WORD* 66(4): 255–281.

Woolard, Kathryn A. (2021). Language ideology. In *The international encyclopedia of linguistic anthropology*, Stanlaw, James (ed). Wiley Blackwell. https://onlinelibrary.wiley.com/doi/full/10.1002/9781118786093.iela0217 (accessed 20 July 2022)

Woolard, Kathryn A. & Schieffelin, Bambi B. (1994). Language ideology. *Annual Review of Anthropology* 23: 55–82.

Woolard, Kathryn A., Schieffelin, Bambi B. & Kroskrity, Paul. (1998). *Language ideologies: practice and theory*. Oxford: Oxford University Press.

Yavorska, Galina. (2010). The impact of ideologies on the standardization of modern Ukrainian. *International Journal of the Sociology of Language* 201: 163–197.

School Language Choice in Almaty, Kazakhstan, and Emerging Educational Inequality

Elise S. Ahn, Juldyz Smagulova

Abstract: *Since independence and particularly since the beginning of the 21ˢᵗ century, Kazakhstan has been undergoing rapid socio-demographic and geographic changes. This chapter explores how these socio-demographic and geographic changes have been contributing to emergent socio-economic stratification in urban contexts with a focus on the city of Almaty. Drawing on data from a survey conducted in 2014 among 29 public secondary schools involving 2,954 participants from grades nine to 11, the chapter examines the characteristics of the student bodies at these public schools according to medium of instruction (MOI) (primarily Russian or Kazakh). By looking at characteristics like ethnicity, reported language proficiency in Russian and/or Kazakh, factors like family migration, and various proxies for family socio-economic status (e.g., frequency of family vacations, family libraries, etc.), the study observed that there were patterns related to ethnic and socioeconomic stratification differentiating the Russian versus Kazakh MOI schools. While the dataset was a cross-sectional view into secondary school aged students during a single point in time (2014), the findings indicate that further research examining the ways recent education and other social policies may be reinforcing and/or reproducing historically structured inequalities, particularly in areas undergoing rapid urbanization like Almaty.*

Key words: *medium of instruction, language policy, education policy, school choice, Kazakh language, Russian language, socio-economic stratification, urbanization*

1. Introduction

Socio-spatial segregation between urban and rural areas has long contributed to the ways in which Kazakhstani society is structured. The nature of this segregation may be considered or characterized by the vestiges of social policies from the Soviet period. However, with the dissolution of the Soviet Union and the subsequent transition to a market economy, the physical segregation that previously existed has now become more diffuse due to increased mobility — internal emigration, regional immigration, return migration — suburbanization and urban expansion. Drawing on survey data collected among 2,954 students in Almaty comprehensive schools in 2014, this chapter aims to examine the differences between Kazakh and Russian medium of instruction (MOI) schools in terms of family migration, socio-economic status (SES), and academic aspirations to better understand the emergent nature of socio-economic stratification in contemporary Kazakhstan. We post that the urban-rural divide continues to be reproduced in contemporary Almaty due to or through the disparities in educational opportunities in rural areas, which may be connected also to the language of schooling, and proficiency in the Kazakh and Russian languages. In our study, we demonstrate that these disparities are persisting despite government attempts to elevate the status of Kazakh.

Urban areas like Almaty illustrate the complexity and uneven nature of how these different phenomena then coalesce in local settings. In urban areas, Russian language proficiency has historically been linked to both higher SES and income. This is in comparison to a lack of Russian proficiency, which was seen as a social detriment. Previous studies have demonstrated that speaking Kazakh continues to yield a negative wage premium even after it was made an official state language (Smagulova 2012; Aldashev & Danzer 2014). In contemporary Kazakhstan, Kazakhs and Kazakh language-speakers have gained more prestige and visibility; however, despite the government's language policy and planning efforts, the urban middle class (irrespective of ethnic background) has largely remained predominantly Russian-speaking in comparison to the rural areas, which have remained predominantly Kazakh-speaking.

Yet, despite the acknowledgement of different forms of social inequality, which have been further exacerbated by other processes like migration, there remains a dearth of empirical studies linking urbanization and city expansion (by incorporation of the neighboring rural villages) to school choice, family SES, and other attributes like student academic aspirations in the Kazakhstani context. This chapter is an attempt to contribute to this critical both scholarly and public discourse and is based on a study that was conducted during the spring of 2014 in Almaty, Kazakhstan. The study explored different facets of how education inequality and inequity were taking shape in the city due to rapid urbanization. The study utilized a survey instrument which was distributed in both Russian and Kazakh languages to secondary students attending public schools throughout the city. While the survey tool itself explored numerous variables that the research team posited might affect education access (as seen through students' stated education aspirations), this chapter focuses on how ethnic segregation is being reproduced through the schooling system reinforcing segregationist policies and structures that existed during the Soviet Union. Our analysis builds on the work of scholars like Tsui and Tollefson (2004) and Tollefson (2006) who have connected language and education to a range of important sociopolitical issues such as nation-building, migration, elite competition, the distribution of resources and power, as well as sociologists like Sassen (2006) who have looked at such issues with a focus on urbanization and globalization.

2. Background: Kazakhstan's Urban / Rural Divide

To understand the impact of internal migration on urban Kazakhstani contexts, it is critical to understand the structural segregation that existed during the Soviet period. Yessenova (2005), who studies urban migration in modern Kazakhstan, argued that

> The "city" was created in the Soviet past as a distinct cultural universe through a number of deliberate social and economic strategies, including residence permits, resource allocation, language, and education, which shaped a strong sense of entitlement among its citizens. (Yessenova 2005: 678)

In contrast to the material, economic, and political role that cities played within the Soviet political economy, rural areas with *kolkhozes* ("collective farms") and *sovkhozes* ("Soviet farms") were seen as critical mechanisms — not only to maintain the social contract through their agricultural contributions — but also to maintain social stability. As Wegren (2002) noted, this was evidenced by the amount of state capital investments that were made in and for rural areas. After the collapse of the Soviet Union, most of the *kolkhozes* and *sovkhozes* were disbanded, rural workers lost their jobs, and the massive amounts of state investments and subsidies drastically declined as the newly independent countries transitioned to become market economies (Wegren 2002).

According to the Census (1989), the difference between average monthly payment in agricultural and industrial construction sectors in Kazakh Soviet Socialist Republic (Kazakh SSR) was about 40%. In the well-paid urban construction sector, the average monthly salary was 275.6 rubles and in the agricultural sector, it was 199.3 rubles. Since then, rural incomes have plummeted. For example, in 2004, 75% of the rural population was categorized as being *self-employed* (which meant people were technically unemployed) and the average salary in the agricultural sector was 40% below the overall average salary. It is then unsurprising that the greatest area of socio-economic inequality due to the drastic decline in state economic investment has been reflected in the divergence of living conditions between urban and rural areas (World Bank 2004). In rural areas of Kazakhstan, housing conditions are poor, education is inadequate, unemployment is high, access to reliable municipal water lines, sewage system, and district heating are limited (World Bank 2004).

Geography inherently underpins discussions about the urban/rural divide and in elucidating the distribution of growing socio-economic stratification. In the Kazakhstani context, this divide also has an ethnolinguistic component as well. Until independence, ethnic Kazakhs were a minority population in Kazakhstan. For example, in the late 1950s, less than a third of the population of the Kazakh SSR were ethnic Kazakhs and in the late 1980s, this amounted to about 40.1% of the total population. Moreover, in 1970, only 20% of urban residents in the Kazakh SSR were Kazakhs. Thus, not only were ethnic Kazakhs a numerical minority, geographically, most were in rural areas. Consequently, many ethnic

Kazakhs were geographically excluded from the benefits of the modernization process which started during the later decades of the Soviet Union and then accelerated during following independence.

This system of segregation was then sustained and reproduced through the education system, namely, through limiting access to higher education because of a school's MOI. To rephrase, the stratification of the labor force by ethnicity was sustained and reproduced by restricting the educational attainment and social power for non-Russian language speakers. Higher education and professional training opportunities for children graduating from Kazakh MOI (and other linguistic minority schools) were limited to the humanities, arts, and agriculture in contrast to those graduating from Russian MOI schools, who would also have access to science and engineering opportunities.

On the other hand, for ethnic Kazakhs living in urban areas, the lack of access to Kazakh MOI schools, combined with being a numerical minority, also contributed to ethnolinguistic social stratification. Among urban Kazakhs, this was seen in a language shift to Russian as the language of home and school. For urban Kazakhs, the motivation to learn Russian was often to become *monopoly mediators*, i.e., people standing between Russian rule at the center and Kazakh society in the periphery (or region) (De Swaan 1993). Those who learned Russian and developed other forms of cultural capital were given chances of material and symbolic profit in power fields unavailable to those who were fluent only in the Kazakh language. Consequently, Russian became the trademark of educated urban Kazakhs (or *metropolitan elites* to use De Swaan's (1993) terminology) and the Kazakh language became associated with backwardness, uneducated, and/or being rural.

It is within this broader context that state-level language planning efforts since Kazakhstan's independence (1991) have been taking place. Given the rural/urban and population distribution aspect, it becomes evident why the government has robustly focused on population management, i.e., increasing share of ethnic Kazakhs in the country by repatriating ethnic Kazakhs from other countries and resettling Kazakhs from the southwest Kazakhstan to Russian-dominant east and north of the country. Then, given the role of language in nation-state building work and narratives, establishing the Kazakh language as the official state language and the pre-dominant language of education and society also is understandably a critical enterprise.

Unsurprisingly, language policy and planning discourses and efforts then in Kazakhstan have been (re)framed within a nation-building discourse. For example, official language policy discourses focus on issues of reviving Kazakh, restoring it as a national language, and the role of the national language in promoting national integration. Compulsory teaching of Kazakh as a second language in Russian MOI schools has been the chief language planning strategy directed toward spread of the Kazakh language to increase the number of users or the uses of a language or language variety in the context of adults' resistance to learn the new state language. At the same time, reestablishing Kazakh MOI schools, particularly in Russian-dominant urban areas, has been primarily viewed as a way of restoring linguistic rights of ethnic Kazakhs who were previously denied education in their native language. The aspiration of policymakers and other stakeholders is that learners will acquire high level of competence in Kazakh so that Kazakh can transform from the language symbolizing the Kazakh state to the dominant means of communication in the country.

Concurrently, as the government was navigating the transition from a command to a market economy and with the drastic decline in state support in rural areas, there has been a tremendous amount of migration taking place throughout the country into urban areas. How this has been translated in relation to school infrastructure is that new schools (which are often also Kazakh MOI) are primarily located in areas of new(er) urban growth and expansion. This is despite the continued interest and enrollment in Russian MOI schools. On the one hand, the increase in number of Kazakh MOI schools and growth in enrollment could be perceived as indicators of effective language planning. As previously mentioned, at the time of the study, many new Kazakh MOI schools were being established in the city outskirts or in new micro districts. Because these schools were in new(er) urban areas, the student population generally consisted of children from lower socio-economic backgrounds whose parents had recently migrated to Almaty from rural areas.

Thus, by situating processes of emigration, regional immigration, return migration, suburbanization and urban expansion to school expansion and language policy reform against a Soviet socio-linguistic backdrop, this chapter attempts to explore the geographic, structural, and socio-economic dimensions of emergent social stratification in Kazakhstan today.

3. Urban Context: Almaty

Almaty is Kazakhstan's largest city and was the country's capital until 1994, when the capital was moved to Astana. Despite rapid growth in the capital, Almaty has remained largely the main educational, cultural, and financial center of the country. A quarter of the annual state budget taxes are contributed by the city of Almaty. A third of Kazakhstani students are educated in Almaty universities (e.g., 30% of all universities in Kazakhstan are in Almaty oblast).

In 2014, the official registered population of Almaty was 1.5 million; however, with unregistered and short-term residents, officials estimated that the actual population was probably closer to two million (*Official website of Almaty city* n.d.). The ethnic composition of the city shifted from 1991 until the 2010s with Kazakhs and Russians constituting 53% and 33% of city's population respectively in 2009. The rest of the population consisted of Uighurs (five percent); Tatars and Koreans (two percent each); and other ethnic groups (five percent) (*Census* 2009). The share of Kazakhs in Almaty grew quite rapidly from 10% in the 1970s to 15% in 1979 and to 22.5% in 1989 before the collapse of the Soviet Union (*All-Union Census* 1970, 1979, 1989). Concurrently, the percentage of ethnic Russians declined from 45.2% in 1992 to 25% in 2021.

The changes in the number and enrollment of Kazakh MOI schools are just as — if not more — dramatic than recent socio-demographic changes. In the 1970s, there was a single Kazakh MOI school in Almaty for urban residents. This was in addition to the four Kazakh MOI boarding schools which were for rural pupils. During the Soviet times, in many rural places with small population only primary (grades one through three) or secondary schools (grades one through eight) were available. Rural children had to live and study in boarding schools to receive their high school diplomas (grades nine and 10) in nearby bigger towns. After the collapse of the Soviet Union, this system collapsed as well. Boarding schools and smaller schools were terminated and in many remote *auls* ("villages") schooling became inaccessible. This may be one of the many reasons of mass urbanization of ethnic Kazakhs, i.e., parents moved to cities where Kazakh MOI schools were available.

The number of Kazakh MOI schools eventually did begin to grow in the late 1980s and then exponentially in the 1990s. By the 2008-09 academic year (AY), there were 48 schools teaching in Kazakh, 79 schools teaching in Russian and 47 mixed schools, which is when Kazakh, Russian or other MOI classes share the same building. In 2023, out of 216 schools, 79 schools were Kazakh MOI and 76 schools were mixed (*Bilim Almaty* 2023). After a dramatic increase in enrollment in Kazakh MOI schools in the early 2000s, the trend has stabilized. The share of children studying in Kazakh and Russian has not changed much since 2008 (Table 1).

Table 1.   Almaty school enrollment by MOI (2008-2011)

Language of Education	2008	2008 (%)	2009	2009 (%)	2010	2010 (%)	2011	2011 (%)
Kazakh	64,999	41.0	68,157	42.6	64,144	43.7	70,954	44.5
Russian	91,112	57.6	89,532	55.9	86,709	54.8	85,827	53.9
Uighur	2,114	1.3	2,125	1.3	2,190	1.4	2,318	1.5
German	233	0.1	221	0.1	217	0.1	212	0.1
Total	**158, 458**		**160,035**		**158,260**		**159,311**	

Source: Almaty Municipality (2014)

Many ethnic Kazakh parents continued to choose Russian as the MOI for their children's schooling (Altynbekova 2010). Similarly, in a study conducted by Sadvakasova et al. (2011), ethnic Kazakh respondents whose highest level of education attained was university or higher were likely to enroll their children in Russian or English MOI schools (or schools that provide instruction through a combination of three languages: Russian, English, and Kazakh). This is in comparison to her ethnic Kazakh respondents with secondary school diplomas or vocational education and training diplomas, who appeared to favor schools that provided instruction exclusively in Kazakh for their children.

More generally, it was assumed that Russian MOI schools provide better quality education. Madiyeva (2010) found that parents often anecdotally commented on lack of teacher professionalism as the main reason for not sending their children to or withdrawing from Kazakh MOI schools. At one point, this was such a prevalent belief that the then Minister of Culture had to speak out to defend the quality of education in Kazakh schools. He spoke about his own experience as a parent. The minister claimed that all his four children had attended Kazakh MOI schools where they received an excellent education, allowing them to apply to the U.S. and U.K. universities (*Zakon.kz* 2010). Besides appealing to personal experiences, the other argument frequently used by government officials to defend Kazakh MOI schools was to show the differences in the number of Olympiad winners and *Altyn Belgi* recipients. Olympiads are discipline-specific academic competitions and the *Altyn Belgi* award is given to Kazakhstani students who show excellent academic performance during school years and then also get top scores in state secondary completion/university entrance exam (UNT). Yet, these statistics are by no means robust measures which demonstrate the qualitative differences of one MOI school over another.

Despite these debates and the Kazakhstani government's language policy and planning efforts, proficiency in the Russian language may continue to be a linguistic proxy for SES or social capital. In the Kazakhstani context, prior to the 2022 protests which were in part in response to the increasing socio-economic stratification being experienced throughout the country (Reed 2023), scholars like

Smagulova (2008) and Sadvakasova and Rakisheva (2011) have observed growing social inequality along the ethnic and language lines. The caveat to this is the changing reality that while Russian remains a valuable linguistic resource linked to upward social mobility, access to standard prestige-bearing varieties of Russian have also become increasingly restricted particularly in rural areas (where access was already quite restricted). Subsequently, in the Kazakhstani context, the Russian language is becoming what Blommaert (2003) called a *bourgeois resource* because the access to it is more restricted than during the Soviet period. More recently, the place of the Russian language has become further complicated by Russia's 2022 war in Ukraine, which has subsequently undermined Russia as a desirable destination for work and education; it should be noted that the longer-term impacts of the war on shifting geopolitics and the changing status on the status of the Russian language in Kazakhstan remain to be seen.

Parent's school MOI choices for their children were (and remain) particularly striking when set against the backdrop of the Kazakhstani government's proactive and comprehensive language planning campaign to elevate the prestige of the Kazakh language, along with the particularities of how urbanization is taking place in the country.

4. Method

Since Almaty is the largest and most densely populated city in Kazakhstan and has experienced rapid urbanization in a relatively short period of time, this study was conducted in 29 Almaty schools. The research team designed a survey instrument, which examined a number of attributes, e.g., the primary language of education, perception of the socio-economic conditions around the school, school ethno-linguistic composition, and future educational plans, and was broadly intended to better understand the student characteristics of Almaty public schools through a cross-sectional lens.

148   ELISE S. AHN, JULDYZ SMAGULOVA

The survey instrument was adopted from several sources. First, we looked at a survey that was conducted in 2005.[1] Several questions were also adopted from the PISA background information survey which has test participants answer questions regarding their homes, available and accessible resources, and their academic achievement. Since the PISA test is only taken by 15-year-olds (regardless of year in school), we thought it would be interesting to situate the data that we collected within the broader (theoretically representative) PISA data collected during the 2012 and 2009 cycles in Kazakhstan. Moreover, since students who are 15 years old are finishing secondary school, i.e., they are usually in 10th grade, we wanted to see what the education aspirations of ninth graders were. Ninth grade is the last compulsory form for students before they decide to go to college (vocational school) or look for other forms employment and is a major branching point in the Kazakhstani education system. Finally, questions from a survey conducted in six European cities by faculty members at Tilburg University were also adopted to compare the survey results in a more comparative way and over a broader age range. While the Multilingual Cities survey looked at students from grade four to 11, we initially decided to look at grades eight through 11.

The survey was conducted in nine schools in grades eight through 11. A total of 217 surveys were collected. The piloted survey was 58 questions and was distributed in both Russian and Kazakh to enable respondent choice. The pilot survey phase took place during late February and throughout March 2014. The collection period was extended by two weeks to make up for the fact that all schools were closed in late March due to various holidays and other vacation days. The finalized survey tool was a sample-based assessment, which produced data that was more flexible than what was available through the census-based statistical information provided by the Kazakhstani Institute of Statistics. It consisted of 52 questions which were divided into four sections (education, language and

---

1   The survey was conducted under the auspices of the international association for the promotion of cooperation with scientists from the independent states of the former Soviet Union (INTAS).

culture, household data, and personal) and were reorganized to have personal information placed in the later part of the survey.

The main criteria used to select potential participant schools were (1) schools that had larger overall student bodies; (2) schools that had a proportionate number of students continuing from ninth to eleventh grade; and (3) language of education (Russian or Kazakh), i.e., a balanced number of overall Russian and Kazakh medium schools needed to be surveyed to have a more representative aggregated sample at the district level. The finalized survey was conducted in April-May 2014 in 158 classes in 29 comprehensive schools in all seven Almaty districts. The total number of viable surveys was 2,749. Table 2 provides an overview of the survey respondents by the school's MOI.

Table 2.   Overview of the survey sample by MOI

	9th Grade		10th Grade		11th Grade	
	# of students	# of classes	# of students	# of classes	# of students	# of classes
Russian	673	31	300	17	244	17
Kazakh	484	27	333	19	241	18
Mixed	186	12	157	10	121	7
Total	1,343	70	790	46	606	42

5.   Findings

5.1. MOI and student profiles: ethnicity and migration

Table 1 provides an overview of official statistics on Kazakh and Russian MOI school enrollments from the Almaty City Department of Education. What gets lost in aggregated data is that the behavior or defining characteristics of smaller populations becomes subsumed. For this reason, we took a closer look at different populations within the schools to see what patterns emerged in our survey sample.

School ethnic composition

In our sample, there was a clear difference in the ethnic composition of the schools. As shown in Table 3, the Kazakh MOI schools we surveyed were primarily mono-ethnic enterprises, i.e., less than one percent of the pupils in these schools were from other ethnic backgrounds. On the other hand, Russian MOI schools were observably more multi-ethnic and diverse. These results were similar to the findings of the 2006–2007 INTAS survey (Smagulova 2008), which concluded that ethnic minorities consistently opted for Russian MOI schools. This similarity would suggest that this trend from 2006 was maintained or continued through 2014.

Table 3.   Ethnic composition of the schools surveyed by respondents

Nationality (self-Identified)	Kazakh MOI	Russian MOI	Mixed	Total
Kazakh	969	400	495	1,864
Russian	0	226	133	359
Uighur	1	72	114	187
Korean	0	32	13	45
Dungan	0	8	34	42
Tatar	1	23	14	38
Bi-cultural	3	25	9	37
German	0	10	7	17
Turk	2	10	4	16
Azeri	0	9	4	13
Others	3	48	29	80
Not available	84	85	85	254
Total	**1,063**	**948**	**941**	**2,952**

Birthplace and internal migration

Since Almaty has been undergoing rapid urbanization, it was also critical to understand how many of the respondents were also new(er) to the Almaty area. Our data indicates that most children in Russian MOI schools were at least second-generation urban dwellers. Also, when we cross-tabulated the choice of the MOI by students' birthplace, we found that slightly less than half of children in Kazakh MOI schools were born in Almaty (Table 4). Almost twenty percent of the Kazakh MOI student population in the survey sample had indicated that they were born outside of Almaty in the predominantly Kazakh-speaking rural Almaty oblast and southern regions of Kazakhstan. This contrasted with the observation that more than 60% of students in the sample that attended in Russian MOI schools were born in Almaty with only 8.3% originating from predominantly Kazakh-speaking areas.

Table 4.   **School MOI choice by students' birthplace (by frequency and proportion)**

School MOI	Almaty	Almaty Oblast	South. KZ	North, Central, East	West	Central Asia (Other)	Outside KZ (Other)	Not Avail	Total
Kazakh	525 (49.4%)	81 (7.6%)	125 (11.8%)	35 (3.3%)	18 (1.7%)	2 (0.2%)	9 (0.9%)	218 (20.5%)	**1,063 (100%)**
Russian	582 (61.4%)	35 (3.7%)	30 (3.2%)	38 (4.0%)	13 (1.4%)	17(1.8)	21 (2.2%)	163 (17.2%)	**948 (100%)**
Mixed	517 (54.9%)	67 (7.1%)	62 (6.6)	33 (3.5%)	4 (0.4%)	16 (1.7%)	11 (1.2%)	199 (21.1%)	**941 (100%)**
Total	**1,624**	**183**	**217**	**106**	**35**	**35**	**41**	**580**	**2,952**

SCHOOL LANGUAGE CHOICE AND EDUCATIONAL INEQUALITY 153

At the time the survey was conducted, we observed that the newly added city districts tended to have a higher share of Kazakh MOI schools in comparison to the older city districts. For example, in Almaly district, founded in 1957, there were 10 Kazakh MOI, 13 Russian MOI, and six mixed schools while in Alatau district, created in 2008 (and made of several former villages), there were 16 Kazakh MOI, 10 mixed schools, and three Russian MOI schools. Interestingly, among the participants, students born outside of Kazakhstan (48.6% vs. 5.7% of children from Central Asia and 51.2% vs. 22% of children were born in further abroad) tended to choose or were placed into Russian MOI schools or were in Russian MOI classes in mixed schools.

5.2. MOI and SES of participants' families

Since it was challenging to try to determine family socio-economic status from the survey instrument, we used various proxies. In term of parents' employment, we found that parents of children in Russian MOI schools were more likely to occupy white collar jobs (23% vs. 14.9%). The data on type of residence further supported the presumption that Kazakh MOI schools have largely catered to rural migrants or residents of former rural administrative units. Almost 71% of students from Kazakh MOI schools reported that they lived in their own houses and only 14.1% said they lived in apartments. The situation was the opposite for children in Russian MOI schools with less than third of Russian school students reporting they resided in private houses, but almost 60% lived in apartments (Table 5).

Historically, high rise apartment buildings were the preferred (or more frequent) choice for those living in the central, more urban parts of Almaty. Houses were more typical for peripheral parts of the older parts of Almaty as well as in newly established districts (because of city's expansion to and subsumption of previously rural places). Because the price of land was cheaper in newer districts, it was more affordable to build there than to buy a flat in the central part of Almaty.

Table 5. Housing types (by frequency and proportion)

School MOI	Own House	Rented House	Own Flat	Rented Flat	Relatives' Home	1 Room/ Dorm	Other	Not Avail	Total
Kazakh	753 (70.8%)	37 (3.5%)	150 (14.1%)	24 (2.3%)	25 (2.4%)	0	0	74 (7.0%)	**1,063**
Russian	291 (30.7%)	11 (1.2%)	547 (57.7%)	47 (5.0%)	11 (1.2%)	0	1 (0.1%)	40 (4.2%)	**948**
Mixed	558 (59.3%)	21 (2.2%)	243 (25.8%)	31 (3.3%)	15 (1.6%)	1 (0.1%)	2 (0.2%)	68 (7.2%)	**941**
Total	**1,602**	**69**	**940**	**102**	**51**	**3**	**3**	**182**	**2,952**

It is important to note that in these new districts, the infrastructure was less developed and there were fewer opportunities for students' educational and extracurricular activities.

Another difference between students attending Kazakh and Russian MOI schools was how they spent their vacations. Table 6 shows how students from Russian MOI schools reported travelling in and out of Kazakhstan (almost 60%) with less than third saying they spend vacations visiting relatives. This contrasted with students from Kazakh MOI schools (59%), who spent their breaks visiting relatives in *auls* or spending time with their grandparents or other extended family members. Less than third (29.1%) of Kazakh MOI school students reported traveling around Kazakhstan or abroad.

Table 6. Vacation location (by frequency and proportion)

School MOI	Visiting relatives	In Kazakhstan	In Central Asia	Outside of KZ and CA	Other (Unknown)	Not Available	Total
Kazakh	627 (59.0)	56 (5.3)	86 (8.1)	144 (13.5)	23 (2.2)	127 (11.9)	**1,063**
Russian	287 (30.3)	66 (7.0)	171 (18.0)	296 (31.2)	29 (3.1)	99 (10.4)	**948**
Mixed	514 (54.6)	74 (7.9)	126 (13.4)	109 (11.6)	22 (2.3)	96 (10.2)	**941**
Total	**1,428**	**196**	**383**	**549**	**74**	**322**	**2,952**

These differences between students at Kazakh versus Russian MOI schools may be interpreted in several ways. The most obvious explanation is economic, i.e., it seems that parents of students in Russian MOI schools had higher disposable incomes allowing them to go on vacations abroad. It may also have been that the relatives of most of the participants from Russian schools lived in Almaty (and

156 ELISE S. AHN, JULDYZ SMAGULOVA

most likely speak Russian). This contrasted with survey participants from Kazakh MOI schools, where the opposite seems to have been true, with their close relatives living in other regions of Kazakhstan.

Academic achievement

While these socio-demographic factors provide empirical insight into the student populations at different schools, they also have important implications for educational equity. Findings from PISA 2012 revealed a wide gap in academic achievement between students of Russian and Kazakh MOI schools (OECD 2014). Both language groups performed below the OECD average, but students from the Kazakh schools had significantly lower results in all subject areas, and the difference was highest for functional literacy results. The authors of the report noted that these results might be explained by differences in access to pre-school education as well as socio-economic and cultural differences between Russian and Kazakh speaking populations (OECD 2014).

With these results in mind, we also sought to compare college plans and supplementary educational opportunities of students of Kazakh and Russian MOI schools (Table 7). First, the respondents were asked whether they plan to take the Unified National Test (UNT) — a high-stakes, content-oriented exam used as both a high school exit and university entrance test. The results show that more students in Kazakh MOI schools indicated intent to take the test: 63.2% of students from the Kazakh MOI schools intend to take UNT in comparison to 55.6% of students from the Russian MOI schools.

SCHOOL LANGUAGE CHOICE IN ALMATY 157

Table 7. UNT plans (by frequency and proportion)

School MOI	Yes	No	IDK	Not Avail	Total
Kazakh	672 (63.2%)	157 (14.8%)	180 (16.9%)	54 (5.1%)	1,063
Russian	527 (55.6%)	185 (19.5%)	183 (19.3%)	53 (5.6%)	948
Mixed	544 (57.8%)	199 (21.1%)	139 (14.8%)	59 (6.3%)	941
Total	1,743	541	502	166	2,952

The survey results suggest that Russian MOI school students may have had more available choices in terms of higher education options and that they were less dependent on state grants to help fund their university schooling; that is, Russian MOI school students may perhaps opt out of taking the UNT because they have options to continue education which do not require the UNT results. For example, no UNT results are needed to study in Malaysia, and to study in the Russian Federation, one can take an oral exam at school instead of UNT.

This hypothesis was further supported by other survey results. For example, when students were asked about their college plans, it became apparent that more Kazakh MOI school students hoped to receive a state grant which would then allow them to study at university for free. Slightly more than half of the respondents indicated that they plan to apply for the state grant (Table 8).

158   ELISE S. AHN, JULDYZ SMAGULOVA

Table 8.   University choices (by frequency and proportion)

School MOI	Kazakh University (grant)	Kazakh University (pay)	International Branch Campus	Study Abroad	Don' t Know	Not Avail	Total
Kazakh	541 (50.9%)	26 (2.4%)	6 (0.6%)	138 (13.0%)	227 (21.4%)	125	**1,063**
Russian	168 (17.7%)	46 (4.9%)	8 (0.8%)	332 (35.0%)	246 (25.9%)	148	**948**
Mixed	380 (40.4%)	40 (4.3%)	5 (0.5%)	163 (17.3%)	244 (25.9%)	109	**941**
Total	**1,089**	**112**	**19**	**633**	**717**	**382**	**2,952**

In comparison to the respondents from Kazakh MOI schools, students from the Russian MOI schools indicated that they were less dependent on state support to continue education as over a third had plans to study abroad (35%) or intended to pay tuition (4.9%). Another inference we can make from these data is that children from Russian MOI schools had higher proficiency in Russian language that would then allow them to apply to universities in the Russian Federation (this was before the invasion of Ukraine in 2022).

Differences in college plans might also explain the difference in the levels of participation in extra-curricular activities. Twice as many students from the Russian MOI schools stated that they attended extracurricular tutoring (additional classes to help with school subjects). We also found that among the survey respondents, many Russian MOI school students started additional tutoring in secondary school and their parents spent more money on extra-curricular activities. Kazakh MOI students tended to start extra-curricular activities later in high school and, as seen in Table 9, nearly 20% of respondents reported attend UNT preparation courses, which focus on teaching to the test.

Table 9.   Extracurricular activity participation (by frequency and proportion)

School MOI	Tutoring	UNT Preparation	IELTS/ TOEFL	Other Languages	Other Courses	Sports	Not Avail	Total
Kazakh	193 (18.2%)	194 (18.3%)	73 (6.9%)	7 (0.7%)	80 (7.5%)	2 (0.2%)	514 (48.4%)	**1,063**
Russian	318 (33.5%)	96 (10.1%)	46 (4.9%)	23 (2.5%)	50 (5.3%)	2 (0.2%)	413 (43.6%)	**948**
Mixed	209 (22.2%)	161 (17%)	18 (1.9%)	56 (6%)	16 (1.7%)	5 (0.5%)	476 (50.6%)	**941**
Total	**720**	**451**	**137**	**186**	**46**	**9**	**1,403**	**2,952**

Differences in educational strategies between parents of Kazakh and Russian MOI school students were also noted in an OECD report (2014); it was observed that Kazakh-speaking families had more material wealth but invested less in symbolic wealth such as home libraries. During the Soviet period, many urban families had big home libraries, and to be considered literate one had to be well read. In this respect, the size of a home library and children's reading habits could further highlight differences between two populations. In Tables 10 and 11, students in Russian MOI schools reported that they had bigger home libraries and read more books for pleasure than students in Kazakh MOI schools.

Table 10.   Size of home library (by frequency and proportion)

School MOI	0–50	51–100	101–200	201–300	301–400	401–500	500+	Not avail	Total
Kazakh	358 (33.8%)	237 (22.3%)	153 (14.4%)	80 (7.5%)	46 (4.3%)	131 (12.3%)	4 (0.4%)	54 (5.0%)	**1,063**
Russian	207 (21.8%)	187 (21.8%)	140 (14.8%)	107 (11.3%)	79 (8.3%)	142 (15%)	55 (5.8%)	29 (3.0%)	**948**
Mixed	365 (18.8%)	203 (21.6%)	96 (10.2%)	67 (7.1%)	34 (0.4%)	114 (12.0%)	1 (0.1%)	61 (6.5%)	**941**
Total	**930**	**627**	**389**	**254**	**159**	**387**	**60**	**144**	**2,952**

SCHOOL LANGUAGE CHOICE AND EDUCATIONAL INEQUALITY   161

Table 11.   Reading for pleasure seen in books per year (by frequency and proportion)

MOI School	1–4	11–15	16+	Don't read	Not Avail	Total
Kazakh	370 (34.8%)	88 (8.3%)	94 (8.8%)	459 (43.0%)	52 (4.9%)	1,063
Russian	275 (29.0%)	111 (11.6%)	142 (15.0%)	395 (41.7%)	25 (2.6%)	948
Mixed	313 (33.3%)	78 (8.3%)	125 (13.3%)	374 (39.7%)	51 (5.4%)	941
Total	**958**	**277**	**361**	**1,228**	**128**	**2,952**

It is possible that many Russian-speaking families inherited their libraries and literacy practices. This snapshot may also mean that parents of students at Russian MOI schools bought more books—not because they valued books and/or had higher incomes—but because more titles were available in Russian than in Kazakh. Relatedly, the lack of books in Kazakh may also explain why Kazakh-speaking children reported reading less for pleasure. Wider accessibility of books in Russian also may suggest that Russian MOI schools had more choices of textbooks. Table 12 shows that more students in Russian MOI schools reported that their schools had not provided them with all textbooks.

Table 12.   Possession of required textbooks (by frequency and proportion)

School MOI	Yes	No	Not Avail	Total
Kazakh	784 (73.8%)	234 (22.0%)	45 (4.2%)	1,063
Russian	639 (67.4%)	283 (30.0%)	26 (2.7%)	948
Mixed	708 (75.2%)	184 (20.0%)	49 (5.2%)	941
Total	**2,131 (72.2%)**	**701 (23.7%)**	**120 (4.0%)**	**2,952**

Given the smaller population of students in Russian MOI schools overall and school budget allocations, it is unlikely that these students were being discriminated against. Anecdotally, parents of students at Russian MOI schools are frequently asked to buy additional or alternative textbooks to complement or replace the ones recommended by the Republic of Kazakhstan's Ministry of Education and Science (2018). Most of these textbooks are published in the Russian Federation.

Finally, the data seem to suggest that students' language proficiency could be one more potential source of inequality in education. The results on self-reported proficiency show that more students attending Russian MOI schools reported fluency in the MOI of the school they attended (speaking: 95.7%; reading: 92.8%; writing: 89.1%) versus students at Kazakh MOI schools (speaking: 86.4%; reading: 86.4%; writing: 84.6%). This suggests that many ethnic Kazakhs may have chosen to educate their children in their mother tongue because they are not able to transmit the language at home (Smagulova 2019). Kazakh MOI schools may then be a last resort for parents to raise Kazakh language users. Another category of students who may have low proficiency in academic Kazakh are *qandas*, i.e., Kazakhs who have been repatriated from other countries. They speak different varieties of Kazakh or sometimes other languages (e.g., Karakalpak or Chinese) and often have limited or no proficiency in Russian to compensate for a lack of proficiency in academic Kazakh. Socio-economically, many ethnic Kazakh returnees to Kazakhstan come from a socio-economically disadvantaged background as well (Sancak 2007; Kuşçu 2013). Comparing socio-demographic characteristics of students enrolled in Russian and Kazakh MOI schools in the sample that we collected revealed that populations of these schools are different in many ways. In addition to the observation that students in Kazakh MOI schools were almost exclusively ethnic Kazakhs, they were more likely to be from families who recently relocated (or were incorporated) to the city and who maintain close ties with their relatives back home; to come from less affluent families and live further from the school. This contrasted with students in Russian MOI schools were more likely to be fluent in the medium of instruction of their school, had more opportunities to study outside of school, read more and had more books, and were less dependent on state grants to continue education after graduating from upper secondary school.

This survey captured a cross-section of data at a specific point in time. However, it does seem that emergent socio-economic stratification as reflected in the changing nature of education (in)equality in urban Kazakhstan (with Almaty as an exemplar) is informed by the *ruralization* of urban areas. While this chapter does focus on providing a descriptive analysis of the socio-economic constitution of Almaty schools and is therefore limited in its analytic power, the intention of this study was to establish a baseline to better understand emerging SES in Kazakhstan to establish more robust causal roots by administering the survey over time.

6. Conclusion

This chapter draws on survey data collected among 2,954 students in Almaty comprehensive schools in 2014. By comparing Kazakh and Russian MOI schools in terms of family migration, SES, and academic aspirations, it aims to inform a better understanding of the emergent nature of socio-economic stratification in contemporary Kazakhstan.

Our results suggest that expanding Kazakh MOI school infrastructure in Almaty has provided ethnic Kazakhs of various backgrounds the opportunity to study in the Kazakh language; nevertheless, the macro-language planning goal remains still out of reach, because many students in Kazakh MOI schools seem to be new urban settlers who already speak Kazakh at home. Many Russian-speaking urban residents, especially those from other ethnic minority background, continue to resist Kazakh MOI education. Problematizing how education policy has been viewed, Asanova (2007) posited that in Kazakhstan "education policy makers tend to view the reasons of the achievement gaps as residing with schools, rather than occurring due to structural inequalities, including inequalities in learning opportunities for privileged and disadvantaged students" (Asanova 2007: 82). To move discussions beyond ongoing public debates regarding education access and language proficiency and identities, more empirical research focusing on issues of ethnic identity, socio-economic disparities, along with rural/urban divides related to the quality of education between Kazakh and Russian MOI schools is needed. Consequently, in this chapter, we tried to attend to multiple dimensions of MOI choice — socioeconomic and ethnic background of students, residential characteristics, and the adequacy of home and community resources — to better understand the nature of socio-economic stratification in Kazakhstan today. Our findings from 29 urban Almaty schools indicated that there are systemic socio-economic inequalities between students of Kazakh and Russian MOI schools.

This study was an initial attempt to critically evaluate the changing education market in the context of rapid urbanization. It is evident that more such interdisciplinary studies are needed. What is the impact of private education and shadow education on educational equity? What is the relationship between home language and literacy practices and academic achievement and social mobility? What is the impact of the current language-in-education policy on social cohesion? As the events of January 2022 demonstrated, understanding, and addressing the root causes of socio-economic stratification in the Kazakhstani context remains critical to understanding what may contribute to socio-political (in)stability and so, continues to warrant closer examination.

Bibliography:

Ahn, Elise & Smagulova, Juldyz. (2020). Examining education change in urban Kazakhstan. A short spatial story. In *Globalization on the margins: Education and post-socialist transformations in Central Asia* (2nd ed.), Silova, Iveta & Sarfaroz Niyazov (eds). Charlotte, NC: Information Age, 273–291.

Aldashev, Alisher & Danzer, Alexander M. (2014). Economic returns to speaking the right language(s)? Evidence from Kazakhstan's shift in state language and language of instruction. Discussion Paper Series No. 8624. London: University College London Centre for Research and Analysis of Migration, https://ideas.repec.org/p/crm/wpaper/1440.html

Almaty Municipality. (2014). Secondary education in Almaty. Database of the Almaty Education Department, http://www.almaty.kz.

SCHOOL LANGUAGE CHOICE IN ALMATY   165

All-Union Census. (1970). Itogi vsesoûznoj perepisi naseleniâ. Raspredelenie naseleniâ. Nacional'nyj sostav naseleniâ SSSR, soûznyh i avtonomnyh respublik, kraev, oblastej i nacional'nyh okrugov [from Rus.: The results of the All-union census of the year 1970. Distribution of the population. National structure of the USSR, Union, and autonomous republics, krai, oblasts and national districts]. Vol. IV, Books 1–3. Moscow, USSR: Statistika.

All-Union Census. (1979). Itogi vsesoûznoj perepisi naseleniâ. Raspredelenie naseleniâ. Nacional'nyj sostav naseleniâ SSSR, soûznyh i avtonomnyh respublik, kraev, oblastej i nacional'nyh okrugov [from Rus.: The results of the All-union census of the year 1979. Distribution of the population. National structure of the USSR, Union, and autonomous republics, krai, oblasts and national districts]. Vol. IV, Books 1–3. Moscow, USSR: Statistika.

All-Union Census. (1989). Itogi vsesoûznoj perepisi naseleniâ 1989 goda. Nacional'nyj sostav naseleniâ Kazahskoj SSR, oblastej i goroda Alma-Aty [from Rus.: Results of the All-union census of the year 1989. National structure of the Kazakh SSR, oblasts and Alma-Ata city]. Alma-Ata, USSR: State Committee of KazSSR on Statistics and Analysis.

Altynbekova, Olga. (2010). Âzykovye sdvigi v obrazovatel'nom prostranstve Kazahstana [from Rus.: Linguistic shifts in Kazakhstan's education space]. In *Dinamika âzykovoj situacii v Kazahstaneâ* [from Rus.: *Dynamics of the language situation in Kazakhstan*], Suleimenova, Elenora (ed.), Almaty, Kazakhstan: Lingua, 295–341.

Asanova, Jazira. (2007). Seeing near and far: Balancing stakeholder needs and rights in Kazakhstan's educational reform. *Canadian and International Education* 36(2): 71–90, http://ir.lib.uwo.ca/cie-eci/vol36/iss2/6

Bilim Almaty. (2023). https://bilimalmaty.kz/mektep.

Blommaert, Jan. (2003). Situating language rights: English and Swahili in Tanzania revisited. *Working Papers in Urban Language & Literacies*, Paper 23.

De Swann, Abram. (1993). The evolving European language system: A theory of communication potential and language competition. *International Political Science Review* 14(3): 241–255, https://www.jstor.org/s table/1601192

Kuşçu, Işık. (2013). Ethnic return migration and public debate: The case of Kazakhstan. *International Migration* 52(2): 178–197, https://doi.org/1 0.1111/imig.12055

Madieva, Gulmira. (2010). Simvoličeskie markery ètničeskoj identičnosti [from Rus.: Symbolic markers of ethnic identity]. In *Dinamika âzykovoj situacii v Kazahstaneâ* [from Rus.: *Dynamics of the language situation in Kazakhstan*], Suleimenova, Elenora (ed), Almaty, Kazakhstan: Lingua, 181–204.

Republic of Kazakhstan Ministry of Education and Science. (2018). Order No. 564. On the approval of the model rules for admission to studies in educational organizations, implementing general educational curricula of primary, basic secondary and general secondary education, October 12, https://adilet.zan.kz/eng/docs/V1800017553

Organization for Economic Cooperation and Development [OECD]. (2014). Obzor nacional'noj obrazovatel'noj politiki: Srednee obrazovanie v Kazahstane [from Rus.: Reviews of national policies for education: Secondary education in Kazakhstan], http://ncepa.kz/upload/ibloc k/f8f/reviews-of-national-policies-for-education_rus_iac2014.pdf

Reed, Cheryl L. (2023). Kazakhstan's bloody January: Day 6, Almaty. *The Diplomat*, January 7, https://thediplomat.com/2023/01/kazakhstan s-bloody-january-day-6-almaty/

Sadvakasova, Aigul, Rakisheva, Botagoz & Kalmykov, Sergei (2011). Âzykovaâ politika v Kazahstane (rezul'taty sociologičeskogo issledovaniâ) [from Rus.: Language policy in Kazakhstan (results of sociological research)]. Astana, Kazakhstan: Committee for Languages of the Ministry of Culture of the Republic of Kazakhstan.

Sancak, Meltem. (2007). Contested identity: Encounters with Kazakh diaspora returning to Kazakhstan. *Anthropology of East Europe Review* 25(1): 85–94.

Sassen, Saskia. (2006). *Territory, authority, rights: From medieval to global assemblages*. Princeton, NJ: Princeton University Press.

Smagulova, Juldyz. (2008). Language policies of Kazakhization and their influence on language attitudes and use. *The International Journal of Bilingual Education and Bilingualism* 11(3–4): 1–36.

Smagulova, Juldyz. (2012). *Language shift and revival: Multilevel analysis*. Unpublished PhD dissertation. London: King's College London.

Tollefson, James W. & Tsui, Amy B. M. (2018). Medium of instruction policy. In *The Oxford handbook of language policy and planning* (vol. 1), Tollefson, James W. & Pérez-Milans, Miguel (eds). New York City: Oxford University Press, 257–279.

Tollefson, James W., & Tsui, Amy B. M. (2004). *Medium of instruction policies: Which agenda? Whose agenda?* Mahwah, New Jersey: Lawrence Erlbaum Associates.

Wegren, Stephen. (2002). The rise, fall and post-Soviet transformation of the rural social contract. Washington, D.C.: The National Council for Eurasian and East European Research, https://www.ucis.pitt.edu/n ceeer/2002_816_14_Wegren.pdf

World Bank. (2004). Dimensions of poverty in Kazakhstan. Profile of living standards in Kazakhstan in 2002. Vol. 2, https://openknowledge.wo rldbank.org/handle/10986/15665/

Yessenova, Saulesh. (2005). 'Routes and roots' of Kazakh identity: Urban migration in postcolonial Kazakhstan. *The Russian Review* 64: 661–679.

Zakon.kz (2010). Ministr kul'tury RK nazval obrazovanie na kazahskom âzyke uspešnym [from Rus.: The minister of culture RK called education in Kazakh successful], *Vesti.kz*, https://online.zakon.kz/m/document/?doc_id=30845414

Pro-change or Safeguarding the Status-Quo
Language Ideological Debates Surrounding the 2019 Ukrainian Orthography[1]

Alla Nedashkivska

Abstract: *The aim of this chapter is to analyze discourses around the introduction of the new Ukrainian Orthography in 2019. Debates on the perceived or ideal standard of the Ukrainian language have been percolating for centuries in various social circles and contexts. Since May 2019, these debates have been receiving heightened attention, accompanied by politicization, conflicts, and strong responses on all sides. Societal reactions and emotional responses by the public towards these new orthographical norms are at the core of this investigation. The study relies on the sociocultural model of orthography (Sebba 2009, 2012), in which orthography is viewed as a social practice, going beyond its understanding as simply written representations of speech. The premise is that orthography is a set of symbols that are endowed with historical, cultural, and politicized meanings (Woolard & Schieffelin 1994), and these meanings are ideologically laden (Sebba 2009). Thus, this study focuses on the new orthographic policy, and analyzes various discourses on the new orthography and how these constitute language ideological debates. Texts from three social media platforms, Facebook, Instagram, and TikTok, are examined. These texts are viewed as "ideological sites" (Silverstein 1979) which allow us to explore people's beliefs, ideas, and sensitivities about particular language policies and practices, in other words, the underpinnings of societal positions about the new orthographic norms. The analysis of these language ideologies is also tied with the concepts of attribution, iconization, and branding (Sebba 2015), which are relevant in the context of the*

---

1   I am grateful to Dr. Debra Friedman for valuable and critical comments on drafts of this chapter. I appreciate Dr. Andrij Hornjatkevyč's insights into various features of different publications of the Ukrainian Orthography. Comments and suggestions made by anonymous reviewers enabled to crystalize several important aspects the manuscript. All oversights remain my own.

170 ALLA NEDASHKIVSKA

orthographic reforms and transformations taking place in Ukraine. The results allow us to discuss two major ideological positions: the position of pro-change and the position of safeguarding the status-quo, which display constructions and enactments of language ideologies in the society. The analysis reveals that these positions are distinct within and across generations.

Key words: *orthography, Ukrainian orthography, language ideologies, attribution, iconization, iconization, branding, orthography and generations.*

> "Orthographies are mirrors of their surrounding history"
> Michael Moser (n.d.: 2)

1. Introduction

This chapter provides an examination of the debates surrounding the 2019 reforms to Ukrainian Orthography (*Ukrains'kyi Pravopys* 2019), introduced as a result of lengthy and heated deliberations and disputes in the circles of Ukrainian language policy makers and the public, particularly since Ukraine's independence in 1991, with orthographic conflicts going as far back as the eighteenth century. As known from scholarship, introductions of new orthographies or implementations of orthographic reforms, particularly due to the prescriptive powers of these reforms, normally and most often lead to discomfort, fears, lack of acceptance, opposition, contestation, and protest (Schieffelin & Doucet 1994; Sebba 2009). These reactions and feelings in the context of language debates in general and orthography in particular are never about language alone (Woolard & Schieffelin 1994); they are always tied to social, political, and cultural processes and events in a particular community. Orthographies cannot be viewed as written representations of speech only: orthographic systems act as symbols loaded with historical, cultural, and often politicized meanings (Woolard & Schieffelin 1994: 65) with "all models of orthography as fundamentally ideological" (Sebba 2009: 14).

    Ukraine is yet another example among many in which, over centuries, a number of models of orthography have been politicized, conflicted, and accompanied by heated discussions. The 2019 Orthography, as is typical in these cases, elicited a strong emotional response from the public (for several other cases of often turbulent orthographic reform contexts, see Sebba 2009). The premise of this study is not to focus on the linguistic side of the new Orthography, but to view it as "complex social and cultural achievements, best viewed as sets of practices — some highly conventionalized and others relatively unconstrained... [which] are microcosms of language itself, where the issues of history, identity, ethnicity, culture and politics which pervade language are also prominent" (Sebba 2009: 167). Accepting Sebba's (2009, 2012) sociocultural model of orthography, which views orthography as social practice, this study draws on societal attitudes towards this social practice as reflected in social media discourses. These attitudes about orthography or "beliefs about what language is, should be, and should be used for" (Sebba 2009: 25) provide ideological stances for the debates, thereby allowing us to study discourses surrounding the implementation of the new orthography within the framework of language ideologies.

2. Background

2.1. Historical conflicts over the Ukrainian Orthography

Orthographic reforms contributing to language standardization processes in Ukraine as in many other cultures and societies have not been simple, but rather turbulent, debated, disputed, conflictual and importantly tied to historical and sociopolitical landscapes and contexts. Battles for a unified Ukrainian Orthography have been visible since the end of the eighteenth century, with crucial peaks of attention during the twentieth century, and most recently with the introduction and implementation of the newest 2019 Orthography (see Table 1). Without going too deeply into the historical past, it will suffice to note that the establishment of a Ukrainian state in 1919 facilitated the development and acceptance of unified Ukrainian language orthographic norms, published as the "More Important Rules of the Ukrainian Orthography" and later as the

"Most Important Rules of the Ukrainian Orthography." In 1925, a State Orthography Commission at the Council of People's Commissars of the Ukrainian Soviet Republic was formed, the task of which was to revise the earlier rules, developing a new all-Ukrainian orthographic canon. The work of this commission culminated in an orthography, unified and accepted by all areas of Ukraine, with Western Ukraine being part of Poland and Eastern Ukraine being a recent addition to the Soviet Union. This orthography came to be known as the 1928 Orthography, or *Skrypnykivka*, as endorsed by the People's Commissar for Education, Mykola Skrypnyk. The 1928 Ukrainian Orthography, primarily based on the language of Central Ukraine, was in use until 1933, when the Soviet authorities began to fear Ukrainian national sentiments, which they perceived as political threats. In the sphere of language practices of Ukrainians, the Soviet authorities were also afraid of the outcomes of the Ukrainianization movements of the 1920s and thus ruled the 1928 Orthography as "nationalistic." As Huzar notes about this time period, "Very often the Ukrainian identity in its essence (with the Ukrainian language and its Orthography being the major elements of this identity) was treated as potentially dangerous in the context of Russification, and therefore became an object of repressions" by the Soviet government (Huzar 2004: 506). In 1933, as a part of a general policy of Russification of the official languages of the Soviet republics, the Soviet authorities enforced a revised Ukrainian orthography, the goal of which was to bring the Ukrainian orthographic conventions closer to those of the Russian language, thereby promoting the similarity and "sisterhood" of the two languages and strengthening Russian imperial unity.[2] Among several tamperings with the Ukrainian language, the emblematic changes of the 1933 reform included abolishing the letter ґ from the

---

2 The policy of Russification affected not only the Slavic languages of the Soviet Union, such as Ukrainian and Belarusian, but also non-Slavic languages such as Kazakh, Tatar and other. The non-Slavic languages were required to switch to the Cyrillic alphabet and to include large numbers of Russian loanwords. These transformations were imposed allegedly to enhance languages' "proletarian" character (I am grateful to the anonymous reviewer for highlighting this point).

Ukrainian alphabet, with arguments being that Ukrainian cannot have two graphemes ґ/g and г/h while Russian has only one г/g (see Hornjatkevyč 1980), and replacing the genitive case ending of nouns of the third and fourth declensions of -и/-y with -і/-i, mirroring the Russian ending -і/-i (радости/radosty → радості/radosti 'joy').[3] These and several other changes in the 1933 Orthography constituted enactments of Russification policies in Ukraine, which Ukraine endured for many decades, leading to the reforms of 2019.

Table 1. **Ukrainian orthographies: A brief historical overview (based on *Ukrains'kyi Pravopys 2019*: 5-10; Moser n.d.)[4]**

Year	Event	Notes on importance/role/main features and/or changes
1798-1905	50 different orthographic systems were proposed and/or used	See Ukrains'kyi Pravopys (2019: 6)
1919	"The More Important Rules of the Ukrainian Orthography" & "The Most Important Rules of the Ukrainian Orthography" were published	The first official orthographic codex in the history of Ukraine

---

3   The change of -и/-y with -і/-i in the genitive case was imposed in most nouns of the third and fourth declensions, except those with the suffix -ат/-at most often used for baby animals. Therefore, the Ukrainian forms such as теляти/teliaty 'calf' remained unchanged. This exception was most likely because in Russian a similar noun group has a different suffix -ёнок/-ionok: телёнок /telionok 'calf'.

4   For a brief, but detailed historical overview of the codification of Ukrainian, with special attention paid to orthographic developments, see Belej (2020).

174 ALLA NEDASHKIVSKA

1928[5]	The "Kharkiv Orthography" (known also as the Skrypnykivka) adopted	The first orthography fully accepted by both Western Ukraine (Poland) and Eastern Ukraine (Soviet Union)
1929	Orthographic Dictionary published	Written by Hryhorii Holoskevych
1933	The new Ukrainian Orthography created	Enforced by Soviet authorities and changed to more closely resemble the Russian orthography, emphasizing the "similarity" of the Ukrainian and Russian languages *The 1933 Orthography was not accepted beyond the borders of the Soviet Union. The 1928 norms remained in use in Western Ukraine and in the Diaspora.
1930s/1946/1960	Additional changes to the Ukrainian Orthography are added	Continued Russification of the Ukrainian orthography
1989-1990	New Redaction of the Orthography published	*Return of the letter r/g
1999	Proposal for a revised Orthography were circulated and debated	Not made official
2019	The 2019 Ukrainian Orthography (Ukrains'kyi	Return to certain norms of 1928 (de-Russification);

---

5   Bold highlights indicate events that are particularly relevant for the focus of this study.

	Pravopys 2019) adopted and regulated	Allowance of variants (co-existence of "old" and "new" spelling and forms)
2021	In January, a 12-year-old from Kherson challenged the legality of the orthography at the District Administrative Court of Kyiv. The court found the acceptance of the new Orthography illegal, which led to protests. Later, the Appellate court ruled in favor of the Cabinet of Ministers' approval of the orthography.	Debates surrounding the new Orthography resurface

2.2. The key changes in the 2019 Ukrainian Orthography

The 2019 Orthography was developed by the Ukrainian National Committee on Issues of Orthography, which began its work in 2015 (*Ukrains'kyi Pravopys* 2019: 7–8). This committee consisted of linguists from the National Academy of Sciences of Ukraine and representatives from higher educational institutions from different regions of Ukraine. As noted in its introduction, the 2019 Orthography "returns to life some of the peculiarities of the 1928 Orthography, which constitute the Ukrainian orthographic tradition and renewal of which has a contemporary scientific basis" (ibid.: 8). This tradition also preserves the "inheritance in the language" strengthening "the connections between generations, which lived, live and will live in Ukraine" (ibid.: 10). Furthermore,

> At the same time, the orthographic committee was driven by the fact that language practices of Ukrainians of the second half of the twentieth — beginning of the twenty-first centuries has already become a part of the Ukrainian orthographic tradition. (*Ukrains'kyi Pravopys* 2019: 8)

The authors note that they view the abolition of the 1928 norms as a criminal act of repression of the Soviet totalitarian regime against

Ukrainians and their language (ibid.: 8). Nevertheless, considering Ukrainian as an "open and dynamic" language (ibid.: 8), they state that it is not possible "to ignore the fact that history creates people's languages: languages change and their orthographies need to reflect first and foremost their contemporary state" (ibid.: 8). This requires the language to reflect practices familiar to and currently used by the speakers of Ukrainian in Ukraine. The committee also underscores that the new Orthography, "reacting to challenges of language practices… widens boundaries for the use of orthographic variants" (ibid.: 9). The reasoning behind this is that "variance constitutes an organic part of any orthographic codex and is characteristic of every language at various point of its historical development" (ibid.: 9).[6]

In summary, the committee's main goals were to find a balance between the established and new developments in the contemporary language while also preserving, and in certain cases resurrecting, some traditional characteristics of Ukrainian (ibid.: 10). In other words, the new orthography represents a compromise between a re-establishment of historical authentication[7] (de-Russification practices within the Ukrainian language) and a reflection on the current trends in the Ukrainian language. Table 2 presents some main changes introduced in the 2019 Orthography, with the fifth column focusing on elements highly discussed in social media, corroborated by the analysis of the corpus under discussion.

---

6   The Ukrainian approach to allowing variance may also be viewed as a reaction to the imposed language standardization under the Soviet government. The Soviet Russian standard language ideology, imposed on other languages of the Soviet Union including Ukrainian, emphasized a prescriptive ideal of language not based on real practices and regarded any type of variance as highly undesirable (I am grateful to the anonymous reviewer for this observation).

7   For the discussion of the notion of "authentication" vs "authenticity" see Bucholtz (2003), who argues that "authenticity presupposes that identity is primordial" with authentication viewing identity "as the outcome of constantly negotiated social practices" (408).

PRO-CHANGE OR SAFEGUARDING THE STATUS-QUO   177

Table 2.1. New 2019 Orthography: Major changes[8]

Feature/Change	1928	1933→1990s→2000s	2019	Emblematic and highly discussed features of the 2019 Orthography
The use of the letter г/g vs. г/h [for the 'g' sound]	г (*in foreign words)	аґрус/ahrus 'gooseberries', ґава/hava 'crow'	аґрус/agrus, ґава/gava	г/g (*somewhat discussed)
Words with the Latin root -ject or suffix -e/-e vs. -є/-ie		проект/proekt 'project'	проект/proiekt	проект/proiekt 'project'
No hyphen in compound words		поп-музика/pop-muzyka 'pop music', веб-сторінка/veb-storinka 'web page'	попмузика, вебсторінка	(*not discussed)
Adjectival surnames from Russian -ой/-oi→-ий/-yi	Донской/Donskoi	Донской/Dons'koi	Донський/Donskyi	(*not discussed)
Changes based on corresponding norms: -н/-n→-нн/-nn		священик/sviashchenyk 'priest'	священник/sviashchennyk (similarly to письменник/pys'mennyk 'writer')	(*not discussed)
Renewed capital letters		бог/boh 'God', трійця/triitsia 'Holy Trinity'	Бог, Трійця	(*not discussed)
From capital letters to small letters		Президент/Presydent 'president'	президент (unless president of a country or state)	(*not discussed)

---

8   For detailed analyses of the orthographic norms implemented in 2019 and their comparisons to other versions of orthographies, including the 1928 Orthography, see Moser (n.d.) and Hornjatkevyč (2020, 1980).

Table 2.2. New 2019 Orthography: Major changes allowing variants

Feature	1928	1933→1990s→2000s	2019	**Emblematic and highly discussed features of the 2019 Orthography**
Expanding feminitives for professions	директор/dyrektor 'director', президент/prezydent 'president'		директорка/dyrektorka 'director Feminine form [Fem]', президентка/prezydentka 'president[Fem]'	**директорка, президентка** and also: **міністерка**/ministerka 'minister[Fem]' **філологиня** 'filolohist[Fem]'
The sound 'g' in surnames or place names: г/h vs. ґ/g	ґ (*discussed for foreign words only)	Гуллівер/Hulliver 'Gulliver'	Гуллівер/**Hulliver** and Ґуллівер/**Gulliver** 'Gulliver'	**Ґуллівер, Ґовартс**/Hovarts 'Hogvarts'
и-/y vs. і-/i word initially	Ірод/Irod 'Herod'	Ірод	Ірод/Irod and Ирод/Yrod	**индик**/yndynk 'turkey' (*this form is not present in 2019 Pravopys)
Words of Greek and Latin origin with -ау-/au vs. ав/av	**авдиторія**/avdytoriia 'auditorium', **павза**/pavza 'pause'	аудиторія/**audytoriia**, пауза/pauza	аудиторія and **авдиторія**, пауза and **павза**	**авдиторія**/avdytoriia **павза**/pavza
Words with Greek th: т vs. ф	катедра/katedra 'department', мітологія/mitolohiia 'mythology', етер/eter 'air'	кафедра/kafedra, міфологія/mifolohiia, ефір/efir	кафедра and **катедра**, міфологія and **мітологія**, ефір and **етер**	**катедра**/katedra, **мітологія**/mitolohiia, **етер**/eter
The genitive case of nouns of third and fourth declensions: -и vs. -і	радости/radosty 'joyGenitive[Gen]', смерти/smerty 'deathGenitive[Gen]'	радості/radosti, смерті/ smerti імени/imeny (1933) →імені/imeni (1945)	радості and **радости**, смерті and **смерти** імені/imeni and **ім'я**/imia	радости/radosty

3. Theory and Methodology

3.1. Theoretical framework

Because this study focuses on people's reactions, that is, their attitudes and beliefs towards a particular language reform, in this case an implementation of a new orthography, it is logical to rely on the concept of language ideologies, a concept very much favored by sociolinguists and linguistic anthropologists. The texts analyzed below, which I view as "ideological sites" (Silverstein 1979), represent social reactions to the new orthographic norms: acceptances or endorsements, protests or contestations. These reactions form language ideological debates (Blommaert 1999, cited in Ahmad 2012: 103), in which "the structure and use of language constitute the central axis of discussion and dispute" (Ahmad 2012: 103). Relying on Silverstein's understanding of language ideologies as "sets of beliefs about language articulated by users as a rationalization or justification of perceived language structures and use" (Silverstein 1979: 193), the goal of this project is to analyze people's sensitivities towards particular language issues. The analysis is carried out through the prism of language ideologies because language ideologies are beliefs and ideas that speakers have about their language, and these are interconnected with social processes in a particular sociopolitical environment (Kroskrity 2000, 2004). In addition, this study links the discussion of different language ideological positionings with concepts developed by Sebba (2009, 2015): attribution, iconization [iconisation], and branding. Sebba, who has studied many cases of orthographies, sees these three processes as relevant and recurring when orthographic reforms and transformations are in place.

Attribution, being a necessary precondition to iconization, "involves the perceived association of elements or practices with a group of people" (Sebba 2015: 209). In the present study, this concept is also extended to include the perceived association of language structures or practices with a particular language, language variety or language standard that people use, maintaining the view of orthography as social practice. According to Sebba, attribution is a process "whereby one group of people, A, make an association between a linguistic feature or language-related practice, X, and a group of people, B, who (supposedly) use that feature or engage in that practice. Use of the feature or practice in question can then be said to be attributed to the supposed user group B by the group A" (Sebba 2015: 209). In other words, attribution is "a process in which a particular linguistic [structure, sign, and] practice is constructed as characteristic of a (perceived) group" (Sebba 2015: 214) or a particular language, language variety or language standard.

Iconization, a concept originally introduced by Irvine and Gal (2000), follows an association of signs or language practices with a specific group of people, or a particular language, language variety or standard that people use. It involves "a transformation of the sign relationship between linguistic features (or varieties) and the social image with which they are linked" (Irvine & Gal 2000, cited in Sebba 2015: 212). After such a transformation takes place, "linguistic features that index social groups or activities appear to be iconic representations of them [not just a normal part of the linguistic practices of the group], as if a linguistic feature somehow depicted or displayed a social group's inherent nature or essence" (Sebba 2015: 212, citing Irvine & Gal 2000: 37).

Branding "highlights the strategic promotion of the branded product or concept, its distinctiveness or 'unique selling point' ...[and] may include visual images (in particular, logos) but refers more broadly to a process of identity creation by verbal and/or visual discursive means" (Sebba 2015: 213). I extend this definition of branding to encompass not only products or concepts, which, in this study, relate to language forms and practices, but also ideas and values around these forms and practices, which signal certain positioning geared towards making a particular impression on others.

With respect to orthographies, Sebba also notes that branding includes processes in which orthographic elements such as graphemes turn out to be emblematic of a particular community who use these elements in their language practices (Sebba 2015: 213). In addition, "[b]randing necessarily involves selection of a salient element from the relatively large repertoire of visual signs which are used in a script or orthography; this element then comes to be emblematic of the group who use it" (ibid.). Moreover, these salient elements, while being attributed to a particular group, prior to becoming emblematic may also be viewed as non-attributed to another group, thus differentiating the new brand from something else:

> The identity-marking potential of branding is increased when two alternative features, with similar functions, come to brand different groups. (Sebba 2015: 216)

These three concepts are pertinent to the orthographic debate in Ukraine and will be brought into the discussion below where relevant.

3.2. Data collection and procedures

Social media texts devoted to debates surrounding the implementation of the 2019 Ukrainian orthography constitute the core of this study's database. My initial observation revealed that discussions about the new Orthography were taking place on a variety of social media platforms, particularly on *Facebook, Instagram*, and *TikTok*, prompting my focus on these three platforms for the data collection. This selection allowed also for studying texts produced by different age groups or generations of users, with *Facebook* being favored by the oldest age-group participants while *TikTok* being represented by the youngest users.[9] In addition, a pilot search determined two peak time periods of the debates: i) May 2019 to early 2020, the time period surrounding the legislation of the 2019 Orthography; and ii) January 28, 2021, the proposed cancellation of

---

9   Statistics for January 2021 (midpoint of data collection for the present study) on social media use in Ukraine is available for *Facebook* and *Instagram*. With respect to age groups, the following is noted: (i) *Facebook*, with 21 920 000 users in total, displays: 13-24 age group→24.5%; 25-34 age group→26.5%; and 35-65 age group→49%; and (ii) *Instagram*, with 13 690 000 users in total, displays: 13-24 age group→34.7%; 25-34 age group→30.7%; and 35-65 age group→34.6% (https://napoleoncat.com/stats/social-media-users-in-ukraine/2021/01/).
The most comparable data for *TikTok* use in Ukraine could be found for August 2022 (1 654 148 users), with the following numbers: 18-24 age group→60.1%; 25-34 age group→25.9%; and 35-55+ age group→13.9% (https://www.start.io/audience/TikTok-users-in-ukraine).

the 2019 Orthography initiated by a 12-year old from Kherson, to March 2021, the toning down of the renewed discussions.

In *Facebook*, a key word search included the following: pravopys 'orthography;' Pravopys 2019 'orthography 2019'; Ukrains'kyi pravopys 'Ukrainian orthography;' and Novyi ukrains'kyi pravopys 'New Ukrainian orthography.' This search allowed me to delineate the following communities as devoted specifically to orthographic discussions: Pravopys 2018 'Orthography 2018' (created on November 7, 2017);[10] Kliasychnyi pravopys 'Classic Orthography' (created in 2012 and re-launched in 2019); Proty pravopysu 2019 'Against Orthography 2019' (created November 15, 2019[11]);[12] and Istoriia ukrains'koho pravopysu 'History of the Ukrainian orthography.' This last is not considered in the analysis because during the data collection period, this community did not have any posts about the 2019 Orthography. The first two groups were created prior to the legislation of the 2019 Orthography and display discussions since May 22, 2019. The data set from these two sites include the five-month time period of May 22, 2019 — October 30, 2019. The 'Against Orthography 2019' was created later; thus, in order to collect a comparable five-month set, an alternative timeline of November 2019 to April 2020 was determined. The second set of data from all three sites are from January 28, 2021 until March 28, 2021. For both *Instagram* and *TikTok*, data collection was limited to the same two primary time periods.

The data from *Instagram* were based on a key word search with the hashtags #pravopys 'orthography;' #Pravopys2019

---

10 The 'Orthography 2018' community was established before the 2019 Orthography was legislated. Discussions about the proposed orthographic changes began prior to its legislation.

11 On March 10, 2022, the administrator temporarily stopped posting on this site, most likely due to Russia's war against Ukraine, which had begun the previous month.

12 The 'Classic Orthography' site has another address: https://www.facebook.com/groups/pravopys. It appears that the sites were combined in a re-launched version in 2019. Administrators' note: "Created anew and re-launched, we return to our initial topics — problems of the Ukrainian orthography, including the new one." https://www.facebook.com/pravopys. Accessed July 28, 2022.

'orthography2019;' #Ukrains'kyipravopys 'Ukrainianorthography;' and #Novyiukrains'kyipravopys 'NewUkrainianorthography.'

Data from *TikTok* were most visible during the second timeline, the proposed cancellation of the 2019 Orthography, with young people reacting to and defending the new norms. Initial hashtags were #pravopys 'orthography,' #novyipravopys 'neworthography,' #pravopys2019 'orthography2019,' plus additional hashtags which emerged as relevant: #proiekt 'project' and #han'baOASK 'shameonRegionalAppealCourtofKyiv.' Please note that *TikTok* texts constitute short videos, on average 44 seconds long, which were studied based on the verbal content of the posts, including relevant comments.

These searches generated a corpus from all three social media communities, which was narrowed down using the following criteria: the topic of the post and comments relating primarily to orthographic discussion and/or debate; discussions that did not originate from a specific institution, establishment or political entity; posts that were not produced or managed by scholars or educators; and posts created within the specific time period. Posts and comments in both Ukrainian (predominant majority) and Russian (very few) languages were considered. Table 3 presents an overview of the entire corpus.

Table 3. Data set

Social media platform	Time period i) May 22, 2019-October 22, 2019 (*except FB:AO2019: November 15, 2019-April 15, 2020)	Time period ii) January 28, 2021-March 28, 2021	Posts and comments total
Facebook: Pravopys 2018 'Orthography 2018' [FB:O2018]	Posts: 19 Comments: 660	Posts: 30 Comments: 505	Posts: 49 Comments: 1,165
Facebook: Kliasychnyi pravopys 'Classic Orthography' [FB:CO]	Posts: 2 Comments: 22	Posts: 4 Comments: 113	Posts: 6 Comments: 135

Facebook: Proty pravopysu 2019 'Against Orthography 2019 [FB:AO2019]	Posts: 65 Comments: 925	Posts: 54 Comments: 401	Posts: 119 Comments: 1,326
Instagram [INS]	Posts: 22 Comments: 228	Posts: 7 Comments: 105	Posts: 29 Comments: 333
TikTok [TikTok]	Posts: 1 Comments: 106	Posts: 24 Comments: 1,075	Posts: 25 Comments: 1,181

The texts were studied and classified based on their most visible themes/positions, with respect to theme saliency, identifying key arguments of texts. This approach allowed establishing a number of themes (i.e. language and nation, language and Ukrainian identity, distancing of Ukrainian and Russian, cleansing of Ukrainian from Russian influences, uniqueness of Ukrainian, and timeliness of the new Orthography, as well as indifference towards the Orthography and criticism towards the proposed changes, among other themes). These specific themes were then grouped into two broader categories of pro and against the new Orthography, representing language ideological positions with respect to orthography and the Ukrainian language in general (see analysis below).

The goal of this project is not to present statistical significance of certain positions and attitudes towards the 2019 Ukrainian Orthography. Rather, the analysis seeks to provide a close reading of the texts under discussion, pointing out the evident positions, attitudes, and interests of particular communities as representing these communities' language ideological stances, which are visible in the context of orthographic debates.

4. Results

The analysis of main arguments and themes allows us to establish two distinct positions underpinned by multiple language ideologies surrounding the debates about the 2019 Ukrainian Orthography: the position of pro-change, liberation and progress and the position of safeguarding the status quo. These two main ideological positions, pro and contra arguments regarding the implementation of the new Orthography, are in no way surprising and are common in most cases of orthographic reforms. With respect to the Ukrainian orthography studied here, each of these positions is built on a number of language ideologies, some of which are peculiar to the Ukrainian context.

4.1. The position of pro-change, liberation and progress

The analysis reveals that texts classified under the position of pro-change, liberation and progress demonstrate a number of key language ideologies. First and foremost, in the orthographic debates, the language ideology of an inherent role of the Ukrainian language in nation- and state-building of independent Ukraine is present. This ideology, also encompassing an idea of the importance of language to the stability and vitality of the Ukrainian national identity, is visible. The following representative examples are cases in point:[13]

1. [*in response to the contra Orthography arguments*] Why are you against the orthographic changes? Are you against interests of the Ukrainian nation? Why are you against the evolution of Ukrainian?
   I'd like to repeat for those who are conservatives: conservatism is bad for building of our Ukrainian national state! [FB:AP2019]
2. … To the new Ukrainian spirit, the ORTHOGRAPHY,[14] we need to say 'YES', because if we say to the ORTHOGRAPHY 'NO', we will destroy our true essence and will once again resemble others. [FB:AP2019]
3. The language is not a toy for you to like or dislike. It is our history, history of language creation, our genetic and mental code. We will not be a deserving nation until we defend and love our own. [INS]

All three posts demonstrate the connection between language and nation, language and state, language and the Ukrainian "self," and

---

13 Examples are translated to resemble the original text as much as possible.
14 Capitalization is preserved as in original texts.

186   ALLA NEDASHKIVSKA

language and the Ukrainian identity. The messages also caution Ukrainians not to retreat into resembling others and not to return to the dominance of the Soviet past with influences of the Russian language (2). Instead, Ukrainians should defend and love their own identity, their Ukrainianness (3).

The ideology of Ukrainian as a national and state language of Ukraine is strengthened by the thesis that the new Orthography, by reinstating some elements from the 1928 Orthography, is a marker of pre-Russified Ukrainian. Therefore, in view of those who support the 2019 Orthography, the new norms promote de-Russification of Ukrainian, liberate the language from Russian influences, thereby distancing Ukrainian from Russian and detaching Ukrainian from the Soviet past:

4. We need to cleanse the Ukrainian language from the russianism![15] All the words that have Russian provenance are to be expelled. We need to return our [Ukrainian] words that have been repressed. [FB:O2018]
5. We need to erase the russianisms such as ефір/efir 'air', проект/proekt 'project,' аудиторія/**auditoriia** 'auditorium' ... from our orthography. Everything that brings us closer to Russian needs to be erased! To cleanse our language! We need a correct orthography... [FB:AO2019]
6. We ought to save our language from russianisms. We need to renew words that begin with the letter **И**/Y. [FB:CO]

In posts (4)-(6), the distancing of Ukrainian from Russian is transmitted via the idea of cleansing the Ukrainian language from Russian influences and erasing any traces of Russianisms, thereby liberating and saving the language. The return of repressed but symbolic elements, such as words that begin with **и**/у (6), as in **И**род/**Y**rod 'Herod' (previously with **i**/i: Ірод/Irod), and words such as етер/eter 'air,' проект/proiekt 'project,' or **ав**диторія/**av**dytoriia 'auditorium,' instead of those with the Russian spelling mentioned in (5), signals the process of attributing these elements to the 'true,' pre-Russified Ukrainian self. By non-attributing these

---

15   Lowercase is preserved as in original texts.

features to the Russian language, participants present them as iconic cases of the de-Russification of Ukrainian.

Several posts discuss the authenticity of the newly introduced orthographic rules. Many posts stress the distance and differences between the Ukrainian and Russian languages:

7. The 2019 Orthography is authentic and Ukrainian. I love it for its павзи/pavzy, лицарі чести/lytsari chesty and філологині/filolohyni_Fem. [INS]
8. Ukrainian and Russian have very little in common…Indeed, great forms all of these Етери/Etery, Индики/Yndyky and Міти/Mity. Now the Russians will not understand us for sure ☺ [INS]

Both (7) and (8) underscore the uniqueness of the re-introduced forms, which participants view as truly Ukrainian because they are absent in the Russian language. These examples reinforce the processes of differentiation of Ukrainian from Russian and of iconization of these "true" emblematic Ukrainian elements that augment the distance between the two languages.

The new orthographic changes are discussed as contributing to the preservation of the long history and rich traditions of the Ukrainian language, "which should not be abandoned, but nourished and advocated for" [FB:O2018]. This is seen in the following two posts:

9. Our new Orthography returns us to our everlasting Ukrainian language. [FB:AO2019]
10. Skrypnykivka [the 1928 Orthography] is really special, feels dear and magical because it is ours, it carries and cherishes our history. [INS]

In these posts, advocacy for the 1928 orthographic forms to be returned and accepted as 'special,' 'dear,' and 'magical' because these are seen as truly Ukrainian and not at all archaic, is visible. These forms, which Hornjatkevyč (2020) calls 'old—new again,' are accepted and promoted by some participants in the studied communities. Such forms, being associated with the "everlasting Ukrainian language" (attribution), contribute also to the process of iconization of the truly Ukrainian elements of the language that have a long history and established traditions. However, it should be noted that many on *Facebook* and a handful of participants on *Instagram* are against these forms, which is discussed below.

Texts that argue for Ukrainian as lively, vibrant, dynamic and progressive are of especial interest. Indeed, a language ideology of vitality and progress of Ukrainian is present in all three social media spaces, but particularly prominently on *Instagram* and *TikTok*. The most noticeable stance found on *Instagram* could be summarized by the following quotation of one of the participants:

> The New Orthography is not as monstrous as depicted by some.

In fact, this space demonstrates that the new Orthography signals language advancement, is a "recipe for youth and vitality" [INS], and is a fact of life, because the Ukrainian language is dynamic and needs to move forward, thereby demonstrating the language ideology of vitality and progress. *TikTok* posters also advocate for a new Ukrainian as lively and progressive. For them, "knowing Ukrainian, and knowing the correct Ukrainian (that is, following the new orthographic norms) is cool and fashionable!". This language ideology is reinforced by slogans such as "Let's make our language more elegant" [TikTok].

Both *Instagram* and *TikTok* figure as consultation spaces, in which users share their knowledge on how best to use the new forms, what is correct, and which practices reflect the new orthographic norms. These educational practices reflect participants' promotion of, advocacy for, and ultimately acceptance of the new norms.

Continuing with the language ideology of language vitality and progress, in all three social media spaces, feminitives stand out. These highly debated forms, which deserve a separate investigation, are feminine forms of words used for traditionally male professions or names of professions for which only masculine forms existed until recently (e.g., *chairman* and *chairwoman*). The new Orthography includes these lexical forms, accompanied by morphological rules on how to form them (please note that feminitives are not commonly included in Orthographies nor discussed in studies of orthographies).

On *Facebook*, feminitives are not accepted by all. Those very few who do accept these forms see Ukrainian as lively and not static, and as a language that needs to reflect new social processes and transformations:

11. A living language, such as ours, needs to move forward... feminitives definitely need to be a part of the new orthography. [FB:O2018]

Some *Facebook* participants see feminitives as necessary (11), but those who are still hesitant see them as "acceptable-to-be" because social realities change, "whether we like it or not" [FB:O2018]. Therefore, on *Facebook*, some examples point to a process of attribution of the new orthographic norms to users of the new Ukrainian that accept the new social reality into their language.

On *Instagram* and *TikTok*, feminitives are much more widely accepted and advocated for, notwithstanding some resistance (see below):

12. Feminitives are markers of the Ukrainian language! This allows us to establish borders with Russian, in which feminitives are practically absent. [INS]
13. [*female participant*[16]] Women more and more become a part of the public space, that is the society; therefore, feminitives constitute the norm. Why would I be called an artist$_{Masculine}$ and not an artist$_{Feminine}$? [INS]
14. We should be proud that Ukrainian changes according to its history and embraced changes in the society. [TikTok]
15. I am for the introduction of feminitives. Such changes are cool. [These forms] sound in a new way, contemporary. [TikTok]

In these posts we see an endorsement of new feminine forms as characteristic of the Ukrainian language, including its distinctness

---

16 In this study, the gender of participants was not taken as a variable; this may prove deserving of further investigation.

190 ALLA NEDASHKIVSKA

from Russian, as discussed above (12), as reflecting changes to professional gender roles (13) and (14) and the newness, coolness, and timeliness of these changes (15). Such reactions on *Instagram* and *TikTok* to many feminitives, and their enthusiastic acceptance and promotion of these forms on their respective platforms, may be viewed as a process of attribution of these features to speakers of the Ukrainian language who are progressive and cool, and of their non-attribution to speakers of Russian. Additionally, processes displayed in posts (12)-(15) may be viewed as branding, in Sebba's terms (2015). In other words, youth has picked up on feminitives as elements that distinguish and differentiate Ukrainian and make it modern and cool. Thus, young people brand their language and advocate for a progressive Ukrainian.

4.2. The position of safeguarding the status quo

Two major stances emerge contributing to the position of safeguarding the status quo: indifference or criticism towards language change in general and opposition to the new orthographic norms in particular on the grounds that they are "foreign," "artificial," or "archaic." Crucially, these two stances are found predominantly on *Facebook*, with *Instagram* and *TikTok* featuring only minor contributions.

On *Facebook*, in all three communities studied, the common themes with respect to indifference and criticism are based on the ideology that languages should not change; for example, "Why do we need changes?"; "We are fine without the new rules;" and "There are many other issues that matter more than language." Commonly, the government is criticized for "allocating resources for unnecessary matters" rather than focusing on "people's wellbeing."

The stance of opposition to the new orthographic norms surfaces in the expressions on awkwardness, absurdity and unacceptance of the "new-old" forms. These arguments are particularly made against many older Ukrainian forms that go back to the 1928 Orthography, as in the following meme:

16.

индик/yndyk 'turkey'...
етер/eter 'air'...
авдиторія/avdytoriia 'auditorium'
[from *Typove Rivne*, share on FB:AO2019]

The image in (16) lists the "new-old" forms, most of which are presented in Tables 2.1. and 2.2. (see the fifth column). These forms are disliked, as Robert DeNiro's facial expression in the image indicates, and are heavily criticized by those who believe that contemporary Ukrainian should not bounce back in time. These emblematic and widely-debated forms are clear examples of attribution to the "old" Ukrainian. This process is particularly present in the community of *Facebook* in the posts of those who are against the new Orthography. Language elements which they use as symbols for their arguments, such as индик/yndyk 'turkey,' етер/eter 'air,' and авдиторія/avdytoriia 'auditorium,' are associated with not-own, foreign, and often the Ukrainian diaspora group, which is "frozen in time" [FB:AO2019]. Moreover, the debate around these forms exemplifies the process of iconization with these language elements as marking old and archaic Ukrainian or diaspora Ukrainian.

The opposition views also stress that the new 2019 Orthography, "by returning to the past, cripples the language of contemporary Ukrainians" [FB:AO2019], destroys the contemporary language, and halts the development of Ukrainian. In these arguments, the new Orthography prompts the Ukrainian language to depart from the "self" and abandon its true nature, even becoming a "foreign tongue" for many Ukrainians:

17. Soon we will learn Ukrainian as a foreign language, with a dictionary, because hearing "Ateny" 'Athens' one would not get it right the way that it is Afiny 'Athens.' These, of course, are my emotions and I am not sure how can I influence the situation. But, I, my children, and my grandchildren will speak the LANGUAGE, and not the artificially created codes. [FB:AO2019]

Example 17 demonstrates the opposition to the new norms and even a protest again using the "old-new" forms, albeit in their status as variants (see Table 2.2.). These reintroduced elements are viewed as artificial and foreign to the Ukrainian language, reinforced by the capitalization of "language" (17).

A protest is also seen in texts that relate to language practices of formerly Russian-speaking Ukrainians. Following the series of political events that have transpired since the early 2000s, those who switched from speaking Russian to speaking Ukrainian declare that because of the new Ukrainian Orthography, they will go back to their previous language practices:

18. Out of all of my friends I am the only one who reads the new Orthography. Everyone else said that they will not learn the new rules and will go back to speaking Russian or Surzhyk (=mixture of Ukrainian and Russian)… Our language is being turned into something incomprehensible and foreign. [FB:AO2019]
19. (*in Russian*) And do not criticize me that I write this post in Russian. Now, I do not know how to write in the new Ukrainian. I will not destroy my ability and knowledge of my beautiful and melodic Ukrainian while discussing the new strange words. [FB:AO2019]

In post (18) and similar examples of oppositional discourse, participants attribute the new norms to unnatural and foreign processes, and these may be seen as signs of language protest. Example (19) is a clear example of a participant switching to using the Russian language because, due to the new Orthography, "they do not know how to write in Ukrainian" and they do not want to damage their "beautiful and melodic Ukrainian" language.

In the opposition discourses, feminitives also play an interesting part in the debate. In the *Facebook* communities studied here, these forms are often ridiculed and presented as "absurd," "nonsense," "insane," "painful," and a "joke" by those who oppose the new orthography. The opponents, noting that feminitives "destroy the language," attribute these "unnatural for the Ukrainian language" elements to some strange external and imposing powers and "uneducated language specialists:"

20. Those who introduced the new feminitives should be ashamed of themselves. They do not have any sense for the native language, or this [Ukrainian] language is not their native. [FB:AO2019]
21. 21. The majority of these "language specialists" [that introduced feminitives] most likely, crawled out of the forest and have never heard about education in schools… they are language idiots that imitate their wild activities with their crazy new forms. [FB:AO2019]

In posts (20) and (21), participants project negativity towards the Orthographic committee, criticizing their knowledge of the "true" and "native" Ukrainian and their educational training. In some posts about feminitives, one can even trace a thread of conspiracy-theory thinking, with accusations that Western organizations paid activists and professional linguists to include feminitives in the new Orthography, and that this constituted an experiment on the Ukrainian society, mirroring changes taking place in Western societies [FB:AO2019]. These examples could be viewed as examples of attributing the proposed orthographic innovations to non-Ukrainians and foreigners or uneducated Ukrainian "language specialists."

On *Instagram* and *TikTok*, there are very few posts that criticize feminitives. In those that do, feminitives are presented as disrespectful and unnecessary. However, in these spaces, the participants, acknowledging their initial opposition to feminitives, now see them as necessary, and this theme stands out:

22. I do not understand why people dislike feminitives? At first, I also did not like them, but in the language, they sound beautiful. [TikTok]
23. Well, if you do not like the feminitives now, later you will adapt. [TikTok]

This transformative position of young people is seen particularly on *TikTok*, where, in the course of discussions about the new Orthography, some youth who initially opposed the new rules have learned to embrace these innovations and declare, "The new Orthography is to be!" and "The old Orthography is to be forgotten!" [TikTok]:

24. Initially I really hated the N.O. (new Orthography). Then, I decided to look at it a bit closer, I read explanations to each of the new rules. And, now I consider the new Orthography the most logical. [TikTok]
25. …At first I did not accept the new O., but later I got used to it, and also understood that it is necessary. [TikTok]
26. When I was still a Russian-speaker, I criticized the new Orthography then, but now I am in awe. My favourites are: проєкт (/proiekt 'project), етер (/eter 'air'), мітологія (/mitolohiia 'mythology'), Гоґвартс (/Hogvarts 'Hogwarts'). [TikTok]

In the above three posts, the openness of youth to change and their acceptance of the new Orthography are pronounced. In fact, young people demonstrate the compromise with and adoption of forms that they did not perceive earlier as suitable for the language in their practices, now viewing these new forms as logical (24). Even for those who switched from being Russian-speakers to Ukrainian-speakers, the emblematic new forms became their favorites in their Ukrainian language (26). All of these examples from *TikTok* show how youth select salient elements from the language and use these elements as emblematic of their Ukrainianness, signalling a branding of the language that is carried out by young people.[17]

4.3. Summary of the analysis

All three social media spaces studied here present evidence of pro and contra arguments regarding the implementation of the new Orthography, allowing us to group these into the language ideological position of pro-change, liberation and progress and the language ideological position of safeguarding the status quo. As the analysis above shows, the three different social media spaces offer distinct results. Notably, these differences align with generational or age-group differences, with *Facebook* being preferred by older generations, and younger age-groups favouring *Instagram* and *TikTok*. The age factor was not a focus when the study was initially devised but has proved significant over the course of the analysis.

The *Facebook* communities present the most conflicting discourses with respect to the new 2019 Orthography, with opinions very heated, at times aggressive, and very much split between the two established ideological orientations. Texts here exemplify various attributions of the new norms and orthographic practices with either selves (pro arguments) or other communities (contra arguments). The distinct discourses attribute, or even iconize, certain elements of the Ukrainian language with certain communities. The most visible are the symbolic elements, as in индик/yndyk 'turkey,' етер/eter 'air,' and авдиторія/avdytoriia 'auditorium,' which are being attributed to or iconized as characteristic elements of archaic, distant Ukrainian or the language of the Ukrainian diaspora by those who oppose the 2019 Orthography. Those who support the 2019 Orthography are tolerant towards the new emblematic forms introduced, but mostly via non-attribution arguments foregrounding the differentiation of Ukrainian from Russian.

---

17 Similar tendencies among language practices and attitudes of Belarusian youth have been noted by Woolhiser (2013). Namely, active young users of Belarusian, including formerly Russophone "new speakers" of Belarusian, in the beginning of the 21st century, turn to older pre-1933 Belarusian standard forms. They view these forms as less Russified, thus more authentic, indexing their Belarusian identity.#

The process of iconization is somewhat visible on *Instagram* as well. However, importantly, the study of the younger generations on *Instagram*, but even more so on *TikTok*, reveals the prominence of what Sebba (2015) calls branding. Demonstrating acceptance of the 2019 Orthography, youth, through quick attribution of emblematic elements to the "Ukrainian of today," that is, to the language of young, educated, and cool Ukrainians, strategically promotes and popularizes the new Ukrainian norms, their distinctiveness and uniqueness, thus creating its new brand.

This new brand of the Ukrainian language continues to create discomfort, particularly for the older generations and groups such as those on *Facebook*, which continue their discussions within the processes of attribution and iconization. Moreover, the process that is being created by youth may be viewed as a re-branding of Ukrainian. Earlier or before the 2019 Orthography, the forms such as индик/уndyk 'turkey,' етер/eter 'air,' or авдиторія/avdytoriia 'auditorium' were attributed to and iconized as the language of old Ukraine or the language of the distant Ukrainian diaspora. As the data in this study show, some youth initially opposed these forms, but many of them now recognize that change is taking place and "The new Orthography is to be!" The previously symbolic, but now real, language elements and practices contribute to creating a new brand of Ukrainian, which is lively, fashionable, timely, and progressive.

5. Conclusions

This chapter presented a number of competing and conflicting debates on social media surrounding the legislation and implementation of the new 2019 Ukrainian Orthography. The texts were approached as sites of ideological debates that are constructed within a specific sociopolitical context, representing a multiplicity of stances towards the new orthographic rules. The analysis presented yet another proof that language debates are not only debates about language (Woolard and Schieffelin 1994; Nedashkivska 2020, 2021). On the basic level, discourses of orthographies are about correctness of certain forms or appropriateness of language practices in a particular environment or setting. However, at a more profound level, these discourses are about people's positionings in a specific sociocultural or sociopolitical context. This also includes positionings of representatives of different generations, which yielded the most important findings in this study. Indeed, the analysis displayed very vivid generational differences between how the new language legislation, new orthographic norms, and practices are being perceived, contested, accepted, or advocated for. The *Facebook* communities continue to argue and oppose. Those who argue for the new Orthography try to defend and liberate Ukrainian, stressing its differentiation from Russian and therefore showing tolerance towards the new norms. For those opposing the reforms, changes are constructed as ruining the "good" current norms of the language and going back to unknown and distant past forms. By contrast, the younger generations, with more progressive views, are responsive to change. They are ready to leave the past behind, and they are enthusiastic to move forward.

I would like to conclude this chapter by underscoring remarkable persistence and dedication of Ukrainian policy makers and those who invested their time, efforts and expertise in the new Orthography, despite the possibility that these orthographic reforms might not be readily acceptable by a sizable number of Ukrainians. Indeed,

> Any linguistic policy that would be exclusively based on 'purely linguistic facts' takes the risk of going the wrong way, because language is not only an instrument of communication but also carries symbolic values that condition social, political, and economic spheres. (Schieffelin & Doucet 1994: 193)

Sebba also noted that "successful reforms of orthographies, whether marginal modifications or total replacements, are rare. Conservatism is almost always the most attractive option for the majority of language users" (Sebba 2009: 155). In the Ukrainian case, the proposed 2019 orthographic changes are, in general, viewed by the younger generation as progressive and timely, and thus are accepted, popularized, promoted, and advocated for, pointing to the new Orthography's potential success. As for the *Facebook* generation, one participant wrote:

198   ALLA NEDASHKIVSKA

> Of course, old folks, like me, will need to move around a few rules in our
> heads...But! (we will learn to live with the new Orthography).

Bibliography:

Ahmad, Rizwan. (2012). Hindi is perfect, Urdu is messy: The discourse of delegitimation of Urdu in India. In *Orthography as social action*, Jaffe, Alexandra, Androutsopoulos, Jannis, Sebba, Mark & Johnson, Sally (eds). Boston & Berlin: De Gruyter Mouton, 103–133.

Belej, Les'. (2020). Vektory ukrains'koii orfohrafii [from Ukr.: Vectors of the Ukrainian orthography]. *Ukraisns'kyi tyzhden'*, 13 September, https://tyzhden.ua/History/247336?fbclid=IwAR3PCq_Xhd6hMWQw_N_WaIZL6P4cM-Ao4Z0_6XBmpw0VwdfhaNdgNiJlr0o (accessed 18 May 2021).

Blommaert, Jan. (1999). *Language ideological debates*. Berlin & New York: De Gruyter Mouton.

Bucholtz, Mary. (2003). Sociolinguistic nostalgia and the authentication of identity. *Journal of Sociolinguistics* 7(3): 398–416.

Hornjatkevyč, Andrij. (1980). Ukrains'kyi pravopys 1928 vs. 1960 [from Ukr.: Ukrainian Orthography 1928 vs. 1960]. *Journal of Ukrainian Studies* 5(1): 15–32.

Hornjatkevyč, Andrij. (2020). Ukrains'kyi pravopys 2019 r.: Stare znov nove [from Ukr.: Ukrainian Othography 2019: Old is new again]. In *Zakhidniokanads'kyi zbirnyk* [from Ukr.: Western Canada collection of essays], special volume *Language, Culture, and Society in Ukraine and its Diaspora*. Tsymbala, Lada & Nedashkivska, Alla (eds). Edmonton: Shevchenko Scientific Society of Canada publications 9, 142–149.

Huzar, Olena. (2004). Pravopysnyi standart ukrains'koi movy: istoriia ta realii [from Ukr.: Orthographic standard of the Ukrainian language: History and reality]. *Visnyk l'vivs'koho universytetu* (Ser. Philolohia) 34(II): 501–506.

Kroskrity, Paul V. (2000). Language ideologies—evolving perspectives. In *Society and language use*, Jaspers, Jürgen, Östman, Jan-Ola & Verschueren, Jef (eds). Amsterdam & Philadelphia: John Benjamins Publishing Company, 192–205.

Kroskrity, Paul V. (2004). Language ideology. In *Companion to linguistic anthropology*, Duranti, Alessandro (ed). Oxford: Blackwell, 496–517.

Moser, Michael. (n.d.). Vid "Kharkivs'koho pravopysu" 1928 r. do "Ukrains'koho pravopysu" 2019 r. [from Ukr.: From the 1928 Kharkiv orthography to the 2019 Ukrainian orthography]. *Zbirnyk Movoznavchoi komisii NTSh: Zolota knyha* [38mpp; forthcoming].

Nedashkivska, Alla. (2020). Language ideologies in Ukraine following the Maidan revolution. In *Language of conflict: Discourses of the Ukrainian crisis*, Knoblock, Natalia (ed). London: Bloomsbury Academic Press, 157–177.

Nedashkivska, Alla. (2021). Native language activism: Exploring language ideologies in Ukraine. *Journal of Belonging, Identity, Language, and Diversity*, Special Issue *Boundaries and Belonging: Language, Diaspora, and Motherland* 5(1): 107–139.

Ukrains'kyi Pravopys [Ukrainian Orthography]. (2019). Kyiv: Naukova dumka.

Schieffelin, Bambi B., & Doucet, Rachelle Charlier. (1994). The "real" Haitian Creole: Ideology, metalinguistics, and orthographic choice. *American Ethnologist* 21(1): 176–200.

Sebba, Mark. (2009). *Spelling and society: The culture and politics of orthography around the world*. Cambridge: Cambridge University Press (online).

Sebba, Mark. (2012). Orthography as social action: Scripts, spelling, identity and power. In *Orthography as social action*, Jaffe, Alexandra, Androutsopoulos, Jannis, Sebba, Mark & Johnson, Sally (eds). Boston & Berlin: De Gruyter Mouton, 1–21.

Sebba, Mark. (2015). Iconisation, attribution and branding in orthography. *Written Language and Literacy* 18(2): 208–227.

Silverstein, Michael. (1979). Language structure and linguistic ideology. In *The elements: A parasession on linguistic units and levels*, Clyne, Paul R., Hanks, William F., & Hofbauer, Carole L. (eds). Chicago: University of Chicago Press, 193–247.

Woolard, Kathryn A., & Schieffelin, Bambi B. (1994). Language ideology. *Annual Review of Anthropology* 23: 55–82.

Woolhiser, Curt. (2013). New speakers of Belarusian: Metalinguistic discourse, social identity and language use. In *American Contributions to the 15th International Congress of Slavists*, Bethea, David M. & Bethin, Christina Y. (eds). Bloomington, IN: Slavica.

Deconstruction of Russia's *Newspeak* in Ukrainian Humorous Translation and Digital Folklore[1]

Lada Kolomiyets

Abstract. *The paper analyses digital folklore and humor as a weapon in Ukraine's defensive war with Russia. The discussion is focused on the specifics, forms, genres, and scope of the Ukrainian people's cyber war against Russia's propaganda from the perspective of ordinary people's ability to influence an ongoing conflict in real time via virtual conversations. Ukrainian digital folklore is viewed as a new phenomenon in the history of war culture and a new age of cyber-war culture. The paper relies on works exploring identity issues and change in communities affected by war through the prism of popular culture and Ukrainian contemporary art (Iryna Shuvalova, Nataliya Yarmolenko, Viktoriya Sukovata, and others). After a brief historical review of Russian imperial narratives towards Ukraine that led from a hybrid to total war, the chapter concentrates on the avenues of parodistic translation-deconstruction of Russia's Newspeak by means of puns, meta-derivatives, and neologisms. The perspective broadens still further with the study of new proverbs, jokes, aphorisms, and quotes analyzed as the public voice of Ukrainians debunking Russian propagandistic discourses on social platforms. At that, funny pictures, memes, and cartoons are analyzed separately, through the prism of historical reminiscences which they awaken. The strategies of explicating the Kremlin's geopolitical, historical, and cultural ambitions are highlighted. Contextualization of favorite poetic quotations and a new angle of poetic mystification are also considered separately, from the vantage point of deconstruction of Putin's neo-imperial myths. The chapter concludes that various deconstructive strategies were spontaneously developed in numerous works of verbal and syncretic humor art and poetry posted and*

---

1   I gratefully acknowledge the Wenner-Gren Foundations (Sweden) for their generous support (under contract number GFU2022-0029) of this research at its final stage.

202   LADA KOLOMIYETS

disseminated on public platforms in connection with the Russian war against Ukraine.

Key words: *deconstruction, digital folklore, humor, parody, poetic mystification, translation, wartime Newspeak*

> Our values matter most not when it's easy to embody them, but when it's really hard. We must not become a mirror of the aggressor state.
> Oleksandra Matviichuk,
> From the Nobel Lecture given by Nobel Peace Prize Laureate
> Oslo, December 10, 2022

1. Introduction[2]

In this chapter, I will examine public posts and tweets on various social platforms, created in the Ukrainian and Russian languages in the Ukrainian sector of social platforms since February 2014 and mostly after February 24, 2022, when Russia's full-scale invasion into Ukraine started. In my analysis, I will hone in on the strategies of deconstructing Russia's *Newspeak* in Ukrainian humorous translation and digital folklore and ascertain the theory of deconstruction as the common theoretical framework for these spontaneous strategies as people's creativity in dismantling Russian (neo)imperial narratives and myths in cyberspace.

To this end, I will look specifically for the (new) forms and genres of digital folklore and humor as the propeller of a massive and ramified phenomenon of Ukrainian digital folklore under the umbrella of deconstruction theory applied to popular culture and adjusted to the circumstances of the newest cyber war culture, which continues to rapidly develop in the ongoing Russo-Ukrainian war conflict. I will employ the methods of critical and deconstructive discourse analysis (Wodak & Meyer 2012; Derrida 1976; 1978; 1979; 1981; 1982; McDonald 1995) for the analysis of Russian *Newspeak* and its humorous debunking on social platforms, which are effective in revealing the ways in which propagandistic

---

2   The study is based on the author's paper presentations at the 2021 and 2022 ASN World Conventions, Columbia University, 6 May 2021 and 4 May 2022.

language is constructed, as well as structural-semantic analysis and translation analysis; the latter two will both acquire a critical shade in the light of deconstructive method in my research. The analysis will result in some observations on the kinds and workings of spontaneous deconstructive approaches in the humorous genres of Ukrainian digital folklore aiming at dismantling Russian *Newspeak* and identify the most effective deconstructive strategies that can be singled out for different genres of cyber folklore, including parodistic translation.

2. Features of Digital Folklore

Average Ukrainians did not remain passive witnesses to the Russo-Ukrainian war. Social platforms offer people the agency to reflect on how they managed life during war. Ukrainians act on media platforms as the diarists and chroniclers of their experience and events of the war unleashed by the Kremlin.

As the study of popular and folk art, the paper relies on works exploring identity issues and change in the communities affected by war through the prism of popular culture. First, these are the recent publications on popular art coming from the occupied Ukrainian territories of the self-proclaimed Donetsk People's Republic (DPR) and Luhansk People's Republic (LPR) and the war in Donbas since 2014, such as the PhD thesis and articles by Iryna Shuvalova (2020; 2022), Viktoriya Sukovata (2017), and others. Among important works I draw on are the public lectures by Nataliya Yarmolenko, which derive from research on a similar project—the study of digital folklore in the case of Ukraine in wartime. In her public lectures about the internet folklore of the Russo-Ukrainian war, given on May 12, 2022 and June 21, 2022, Yarmolenko highlights the traditional and innovative features of Ukrainian digital folklore (Yarmolenko 2022a, 2022b). Specifically, Yarmolenko suggests an exhaustive list of the genre composition of digital folklore about the ongoing war, namely, ritual folklore (incantations, curses, prayers, lamentations), folk epic (author's tales, legends, folk tales, narratives, anecdotes), small folklore genres (praises, greetings, wishes, sayings, proverbs, etc.), children's folklore (tongue twisters, rhymes), song folklore, post-folklore (church parish folklore, holy messages, "letters of happiness"). At that, she highlights several new genres featuring the generic novelty of Ukrainian digital folklore. They are greetings, roll calls, news from the frontline, thank you notes to God, the Armed Forces, medics, firefighters, countries, cities, volunteers, etc., appeals, warnings, mutual aid announcements, bans, words of advice, warnings, quotations, remakes of songs (Yarmolenko 2022b).

The study presented here concentrates on humorous pieces of verbal and syncretic art (re)posted in social networks by private Ukrainian users and on webpages of private Ukrainian companies as well as in Ukrainian electronic media. These humorous works began to appear in the cyberspace in great measure from the first days of Russian full-scale invasion, which happened on February 24, 2022. To a large extent, they have been aimed at criticism of Russia's neo-imperialistic rhetoric and actions. The world press almost immediately drew attention to the successful use of humor as a powerful "latest weapon" (Matloff 2022) in the Ukrainians' virtual struggle against Russian aggression.

Thus, the largest number of works on Ukrainian digital art and social platforms which I studied as thematically related to my paper are the popular articles in the Internet media devoted to Ukrainian humor as a weapon in the Russo-Ukrainian war (Matloff 2022; Maksymiv 2022; Novak 2022; Shaw 2022; Charles 2022; Bishara 2022; Opanasyk 2022, etc.). Such publications highlight the importance of "a comic lens" for survival in drastic situations, but they are not looking for an answer to the fundamental question of why Ukrainian humor has become such an effective brand weapon. Of course, an obvious answer to this question may be the creativity of the population, i.e., ordinary Ukrainians have the time and ability to invent and repost funny texts that quickly spread on the networks. The absolute majority of these are anonymous texts. Syncretic works, such as posters, comics, funny pictures, are about the same, although most of them had a separate author and/or source of origin in the first publications. Numerous reposts, however, quickly anonymize even these artistic genres, if they accurately reflect the "need of the day."

The data for this study come from the following social networks: *Facebook, Twitter, Instagram, LiveJournal, Reddit, Idaprikol, VKontakte, YouTube Channel, Telegram Channel*; on webpages: *Ukrainian Memes Forces, Занавес, Zbirnyk ukraïns'kykh anekdotiv* [Collection of Ukrainian Jokes], *Persha pryvatna memarnya on Twitter* [The First Private Museum of Memes on Twitter], *Mala Storinka,* etc.; and in Ukrainian digital media: *Komsomol's'ka Pravda v Ukraïni* (KP in Ukraine), *Holos Ukraïny: Hazeta Verkhovnoï Rady Ukraïny* [Voice of Ukraine: Newspaper of the Verkhovna Rada of Ukraine], *Obozrevatel, Typovyĭ Kyiv / Tipichnyĭ Kiev* [Typical Kyiv], *News of Zakarpattia, UkraineWorld, Hlyboka.Info, YHIAH* [UNIAN], *TCH* [TSN], *Liha.Novyny, Liga.net, Radio Track: Novyny* [News], and some others.

Broadly understanding digital folklore as multimedia folk art that spreads in cyberspace on various social media platforms, one can come across different types of digital folklore, such as verbal type (jokes, proverbial saying, etc.), mixed type (memes, photo frogs), video and animated texts type (gifs). The discussion in this chapter will focus primarily on the verbal type and extend to the mixed type of digital folklore.

Although in most of its features, digital folklore functions like traditional folklore (it is a syncretic art, with relative constancy and at the same time certain variability of the folk text, its anonymity and collectivity), it nevertheless steps forward as an innovative form of folklore. Stylistic innovation of digital folklore consists in its parodistic and humorous varieties: jokes, anecdotes, satirical rhymes, etc., in addition to such new features as mediality, absence of direct contact between the performer and the listener, absence of oral form of communication (with the exception of songs), as well as its synchronization with current events and focus on the present moment. I also consider a deconstructive translation of Russian propaganda *Newspeak* as a separate branch of parodistic folklore, which, by the way, travels mainly in oral form in news media and on video platforms. It will be discussed in detail in the third section of this paper. From three hundred units of samples of digital folklore that I have collected and researched, I selected three dozen units of the most vivid samples of digital folklore and two dozen

206 LADA KOLOMIYETS

samples of parodistic translation for the demonstration and analysis in this chapter.

English-speaking audience remains broadly unfamiliar with Ukrainian digital folklore (not to mention other audiences), although small humorous genres and syncretic art, such as funny pictures and memes, can be found more and more often in the English-language digital media, in particular, in such well-known ones as *Al Jazeera, Radio Liberty, The Washington Post, The New Yorker, The New York Times,* etc., and also in smaller press, such as *Geneva Solutions, Hyperallergic, VOA Learning English,* and so on. Therefore, my English translations of the Internet samples of Ukrainian folk art, given in the chapter, can be considered an important practical and popularizing task, in addition to the main research tasks of this chapter.

The primary objectives of this paper are to analyze 1) the present-day ability of ordinary people to influence an ongoing conflict in real time via virtual conversations aimed at debunking Russian imperial myths and narratives; 2) humor as Ukraine's digital weapon and a tool of deconstructing the Kremlin's *Newspeak* on social platforms; 3) the forms and genres of Ukrainian people's digital folklore in the war with Russian propagandistic discourses; and 4) the strategies of dismantling Russia's *Newspeak*, peculiar to particular genres of digital folklore.

The chapter brings into focus a new paradigm in the Ukrainian civilians' perception of the Kremlin's neo-imperial rhetoric and conquering policy. The paradigm shift became particularly broad and conspicuous since the beginning of the full-scale invasion of Ukraine. In their defensive war, Ukrainians seem to have overcome their ages-old victim complex of Russian colonialism and are attacking the enemy with flurries of their natural sparkling humor. Ukrainian digital folklore is ridiculing the Kremlin's imperial *Newspeak* and its aggressive actions and intentions by means of parodistic translation, anecdotes, snarky sayings, witty wellerisms, and other varieties of humor genres, which spread in social media networks. Digital folklore unites disparate Ukrainian voices in cyber space and forms a single national narrative aimed at resistance to Russian invasion and defeating its aggressive policy. Digital platforms reveal the peculiar features of Ukrainians' inborn humor as being uniquely striking, bitingly sharp, but also life-affirming, full of positive energy and invincible laughter.

The focal research question, thus, is to trace the linguo-semiotic resources and strategic ways of combating Russian war discourses on virtual fronts so that to win in the Russo-Ukraine information cyberwar of civilians. With this purpose in mind, first of all, it is crucial to outline and describe the phenomenon of mass Internet activity of Ukrainian civilians, refugees, and diasporas all over the globe, synchronized with real events, as a people's war, and consider this phenomenon in the broader conceptual framework of war cultures as a new stage in the development of the concept of war culture, namely, as a people's cyber war.

In what follows, I will analyze the structure of Russian neo-imperial *Newspeak* as an object of deconstruction and reveal the ways in which propagandistic language is constructed. Then, I will consider the strategies of deconstructing the *Newspeak* in parodistic translation, with the focus on puns, meta-derivatives, and neologisms. I will also examine the most popular units of verbal digital folklore belonging to small humorous genres: (reinterpreted) proverbs, (new) jokes, funny aphorisms, and facetious quotes, from the vantage point of public dismantling of the myth of Russian greatness. In the same section, I will analyze the most popular samples of syncretic genres of digital art — comical pictures, memes, and cartoons, which may still partially retain their authorial origin, but are rapidly losing it due to mass distribution in social networks — in terms of explicating contradictions and reinterpreting Russian historical narratives and reminiscences. I will also probe into the phenomenon of poetic mystification in cyberspace and recontextualization of popular verses during the ongoing warfare.

3. Deconstruction in Translation and Digital Folklore

The theoretical research framework of this research is the theory of deconstruction worked out by Jacques Derrida (1976; 1978; 1979; 1981; 1982; McDonald 1995). Deconstruction is important for the concept and procedures of parodistic translation as well as for the understanding of how the humorous genres of digital folklore are created. The theory of deconstruction is based on a rethinking of the traditional hierarchy of speech over writing as a practice of signification (in Derrida's early work *Of Grammatology*, [1967] 1976). Deconstructing closure and grounding, Derrida asserts the importance of "absence" in which meaning, closure, and grounding is always and forever moving away. For Derrida, the connection between thing and language, or concept and sign, is not based on the metaphysical connection between word and object and the adequacy of language in providing knowledge about the "thing in itself," but rather on the principles of difference—the insurmountable gap between the word and the thing, the signifier and the signified—and the permanent deferral of a stable and unambiguous meaning. Therefore, according to Derrida, writing is a field for an unlimited game of meanings, which is characterized by the movement of distinction. As a result of this movement, meaning no longer acts as isolated and determined—for Derrida, these qualities are always illusory; meaning becomes a series of deferrals, supplements, and substitutions rather than remaining stable and fixed.

Comparing translation with historiography, Derrida (1979: 76) notes that each translation necessarily "infects" the original with new meanings and re-creates it anew. Thus, if even a neutral translation in terms of the translator's modality re-creates the original, then a parodistic translation is disproportionately more a product of the target culture than of the source text.

Deconstruction is applied in the works of Ukrainian digital humor at various structural levels of language: at the word and phrase level (parodistic translation), at the text level (mini genres of digital folklore), and at the level of Russian historical, geopolitical, and cultural narratives, wittily transformed in Ukrainian artistic interpretation into the pieces of humorous syncretic art. Deconstruction breaks the (original) meaning into parts. It is always a sarcastic, critical look at the (original) decontextualized text or utterance as having a single/unified/cohesive/non-contradictory meaning. This is why deconstruction works so well for Ukrainians in dismantling Russian propaganda, which is already constructed as very shaky and unsubstantiated statements — perfect material for a deconstructor, even for a non-linguist one.

When the meaning disintegrates, Russian political concepts and slogans, on the one hand, lose their meaning, and on the other hand, acquire an endless interpretive potential, which Ukrainians jokingly exploit. In theory, deconstructive criticism doesn't take even itself very seriously, and in practice, Ukrainians always remain self-ironic, ready to make a funny joke about themselves and have a good laugh at it. Self-irony is very helpful in making quality jokes about others. Ukrainian citizens create dozens of jokes every day, and hundreds of jokes every week. In particular, the online Collection of Ukrainian Jokes already includes almost thirteen thousand samples of the best Ukrainian jokes. Russian-language jokes also circulate in cyberspace, contrasting even more with Russian *Newspeak*. The whole of Ukraine, all its ethnic representatives, is joking.

The deconstructive procedures of picking apart and breaking down the meaning in Russian *Newspeak*, this ambiguous euphemistic language used chiefly in political propaganda, reveal its absurdity. The process of breaking the meaning apart matters itself — to demonstrate how the concept or statement is controlled and reduced by the values and prejudices of certain individuals. This is how and why Ukrainian parodies and jokes are created.

4. Russian Neo-imperial *Newspeak* as an Object of Deconstruction

The specific reasons for a manipulative linguistic strategy in Russia's media, aimed at distortion of political reality, appear to be grounded in the justification of expansionist policy. Linguistic manipulations have proved to be a highly effective tool of hybrid warfare on the part of the Kremlin officials and Russian media. The basic functional mechanism of Russian political propaganda consists in constructing an alternative reality by linguistic means, blatantly pretending on the eve of February 24, 2022, that it was not Russia but Ukraine who was preparing an invasion against Russia. Deliberate semantic shifts of the words and phrases to the opposite meaning comprise a linguistic phenomenon known as the "Newspeak" from George Orwell's dystopian novel *Nineteen Eighty-Four* (1949). The *Newspeak* is a controlled language designed to limit the individual's ability to think and articulate the concepts of personal identity, self-expression and free will, which are criminalized in a totalitarian superstate.

The study of the linguistic component of Russian hybrid warfare against Ukraine reveals its features as *a new* totalitarian *Newspeak*. It is a "development" of the performative ideological ritual language, well known to the former Soviet Union citizens as a legacy of the late Stalin — Brezhnev era, masterfully described in Alexei Yurchak's study *Everything Was Forever, Until It Was No More: The Last Soviet Generation*, which was originally published in English and later reprinted in Russian translation (Yurchak 2005; 2014). It was the system of "late socialism" (mid-1950s — mid-1980s) when the consciousness of so-called "homines sovietici," the "split personalities," and the "masked hypocrites" prevailed in the masses over any other consciousness. The consciousness of "masked hypocrites" seems to have deeply stuck in the minds of citizens of the Russian Federation until today. The task of constructing an opposite, alternative reality by means of the *Newspeak,* limiting a person's ability to think and express free will, which was analyzed by Orwell in his 1949 novel, has been unfolding in Russian media with a dizzying speed recently.

Throughout the year 2021, the Russian *Newspeak* was aimed at creating *a myth* that an invasion was being prepared against Russia by Ukraine (herewith, Russian troops on the border with Ukraine were allegedly located in a defensive position). Russian TV "journalists" were successfully convincing their listeners of this opinion with statements about "the peacemaking of Russia" (миротворчество России), Russia as "the only real peacemaker" (Россия единственный настоящий миротворец), etc., which sounded directly opposite to the real situation. Simultaneously, the rhetoric of peacemaking was used on par with the militaristic rhetoric, which included, for example, aggressive calls to resort to "coercion into peace" (принуждение к миру), "coercion into fraternity" (принуждение к братству), "forced denazification of

Ukraine" (насильственная денацификация Украины), as well as other older and newly coined phrases and slogans produced on Russian TV channels and political shows, such as "Russia 1," "Russia Today," "News of the Week with Dmitry Kiselyov," "60 Minutes" show, etc.

Russian propagandists count on the assumption that people do not want the truth as much as they want reassurance that what they believe *is* the truth. It is enough for the Kremlin mouthpieces to spread lies more and more intensely because this is what the TV viewers in Russian want to hear, and the pressure, fear, and manipulation act most effectively on totally disoriented people.

The Kremlin's *Newspeak* as a linguistic component—with its simplified grammar and limited vocabulary interspersed with prison jargon—of hybrid warfare with the aim of constructing the myth of alleged Ukrainian military aggression. Perceived threats to Russia from Ukraine have deep historical roots in the rhetoric of the Communist Party of the Soviet Union (CPSU), with its tradition of substituting objective facts with an alternative reality by means of linguistic manipulation. The rhetoric of generalized Party totalitarianism with its devastating impact on society was analyzed by Orwell in the already mentioned *Nineteen Eighty-Four*. To establish in the minds of citizens the idea that "[n]othing exists except an endless present in which the Party is always right" (Orwell 2003: 249) turned out to be the most important purpose of the Party's *Newspeak,* a language created to meet the ideological requirements of the ruling political regime. As in Orwell's novel, the Russian *Newspeak,* which is largely based on the rhetorical experience of the CPSU, affirms the infinite present for the Kremlin leader: Putin's Russia must "defend" itself forever while conducting at that very time its covert or overt offensive operations, that is, a real war of aggression against Ukraine and the rest of the democratic world. The catastrophic consequences of the influence of lies on the consciousness and emotional state of the deceived Russians are becoming more and more obvious with each new day.

The Soviet totalitarian state was built on historical myths inherited by its successor, the Russian Federation. Exploitation of the performative function of *Newspeak*, that is, using the language as a

212   LADA KOLOMIYETS

means of constructing a "correct" reality in the minds of millions rather than as a means of comprehending the objective facts, has been practiced for decades in the rhetoric of the CPSU, and in the early 2020s the neo-imperial Russian *Newspeak* dominates in the rhetoric of Russian government and media.

The *Newspeak*-ish rhetoric is being actively deconstructed in numerous ridiculing neologisms built on a range of clichés from the Russian *Newspeak,* which have been coined by Ukrainians recently. Moreover, a dynamic process of deconstructing the narratives of Russian *Newspeak* is observable not only in public but also in academic Ukrainian discourse, both at the levels of verbal form and semantic content. While Ukrainian academics efficiently decompose the mythmaking of modern Russia, revealing the linguistic mechanisms of geopolitical expansion of the Russian Federation and accurately defining its policy towards Ukraine, in particular in 2021, as "progressive hybression," from *hybrid + aggression* (Martyniuk 2018), Putin's geopolitical values are being industriously dismantled and reconsidered by Ukrainians on social media platforms. For instance, a witty philological riddle, posted by Юлія Бондаренко (Iūliiā Bondarenko) on her official Facebook page as early as 19 April 2021 (reposted on 19 April 2022), humorously points at the grammatical lacune in the future tense, first person singular of the Russian verb *победить* (to win) as a philological curse of the "russian world" (the author's spelling is kept):

> Філологічне прокляття "русского мира:" це коли бажання є, амбіції тиснуть, а велікій і могучій цього не передбачає. Бо яке б войовниче не було чиєсь Я, слова "переможу" в російській мові не існує. (See *Bol'shoĭ akademicheskiĭ slovar' russkogo iāzyka.* Vol.17, 2011, note by the author)
> A philological curse of the "russian world:" this is what happens when the desire is there and the ambitions are pressing, but "the great and mighty" [an imperialistic cliché for the Russian language, L.K.][3] does not provide for their implementation. Because no matter how militant someone's Self is, the

---

3   Quote from a poem in prose by Ivan Turgenev "Russian language" (1882): "In the days of doubt, in the days of painful reflections about the fate of my homeland, you are my only support and pillar, O great, powerful, truthful and free Russian language!" (Serov, Vadim, ed. (2003). Encyclopedic Dictionary of catchy words and expressions. Moscow: "Lokid-Press"). Unless otherwise noted, all translations from the Ukrainian and Russian languages are by the author.#

word "I-will-win" [Ukr. *peremozhu*] does not exist in the Russian language. (See *The Great Academic Dictionary of the Russian Language*. Vol.17, 2011, note by the author)

Only descriptive constructions *смогу победить* (I will be able to win), *буду победителем* (I will be a winner), etc. are possible and considered to be normative in the literary Russian language (Kak pravil'no n.d.).

The process of deconstruction of Russian *Newspeak* has become a mass entertainment, an element of Ukrainian pop culture in social networks. Deconstruction appertains to a play and amusement of pointing out flaws and gaps in the "serious" texts and statements of the "other." The process of deconstruction is related, first, to the search for meaning and pointing out the failure / error in meaning by revealing the tension/contradictions in the text; second, to the discovery of a new unity that resolves the tension, demonstrating that oppositions can be reversed and restructured in many different ways, and meaning can be re-created by many different contexts; and thirdly, deconstruction indicates that the tension is not really an opposite. In the case of Russian propaganda *Newspeak*, one can conclude that it has no meaning, since the euphemistic language within it fails, it does not work as a (true/false) statement, neither has an authentic/credible context for itself as a text.

5. Deconstruction of Russia's *Newspeak* in Parodistic Translation and Digital Folklore

For Ukrainian civilians the Russian war on their country began in 2014. Since then, Ukrainians have been at the center of Ukraine's virtual mobilization. Many of them took up real arms in the first days of Russian invasion, and many more engaged in virtual battles. With the expansion of Russia's war on February 24, 2022, ordinary people in Ukraine not only volunteered and sacrificed for their country's war effort, but quickly began describing their experiences to one another while engaging broader audiences—in Western and Central Europe, the United States, as well as Russian audiences—alongside Ukrainian bloggers with a social media presence.

5.1. Puns, meta-derivatives and neologisms produced in parodistic translation

Humorous deconstructive translation has been employed as a popular method of debunking those imperial mythologies which underlie the ideology of the "Russian world," better translated as "Russian (way of) life." With the help of semantic shifts, deconstructive translation explicates the language of Russia's war against Ukraine. Due to the deconstruction of Russian narratives, dozens of ironic neologisms appeared in the Ukrainian language prior to February 24, 2022, such as the concept of *viĭnomyr*, meaning "neither war nor peace," which characterized the (non)observance by Russian mercenaries of ceasefire on the demarcation line.

Among diverse examples of deliberately shifting translation of the concepts generated in the Russian *Newspeak* since 2014 are the following neologisms:

1. mocking neological compound noun *krymnashyst* (suffix -yst/ist indicates belonging to a certain party, ideology, or faith), which derives from the Russian imperialistic slogan *Крым наш*, "The Crimea is ours [Russia's]," and is used to designate a person who supports the annexation of Crimea by the Russian Federation; literal translation into English: *the-Crimea-is-ours-believer*;

2. mocking neological compound noun *ikhtamnet* (pl "ikhtamnety"), which derives from Putin's phrase *их там нет*, "they are not there," said about the supposed absence of the Russian military in Ukraine during the capture of Crimea in 2014; the word is used to designate Russian military men without insignia, who secretly fought in Ukraine on Russia's side; literal translation into English: *one-of-those-who-are-not-there*;

3. mocking neological compound noun *adinnarot*, which derives from Russia's imperialistic ideologeme *один народ*, "one/unified nation," formulated by Putin about the unity of Russians and Ukrainians, asserting that Ukrainians are Russians, and have always been; the word is used to make senseless the ideologeme that Russians and Ukrainians are the one nation through a grotesque imitation of the sound

form of this phrase in Russian (*адин на рот*, where *рот* means "mouth") while completely distorting/shifting its meaning; literal translation into English: *one-for-the-mouth*;

4. mocking neological compound noun *myshebrat'ia*, which derives from the manipulative phrase of Russian propagandists *Мы же братья*, "Brothers we are," addressed to Ukrainians; the word in Ukrainian is a mockery of the meaning of this Russian phrase through a grotesque imitation of its sound form in Russian (*мышебратья*, where *мыши* means "mice") depriving it of its initial sense altogether; literal translation into English: *mice-brothers*;

5. mocking noun *povtorun*, which alludes to the phrase "we can repeat" and designates a person, who is repeating or ready to "repeat" ("povtor" means "repetition" in both Russian and Ukrainian, and suffix -un indicates an actor); literal translation into English: *a repeater*; the phrase "we can repeat" per se is a part of a broader Russian militaristic and political slogan: *деды воевали, можем повторить*, "dedy voyevali, mozhem povtorit'" (*grandfathers fought, we can repeat*), which alludes to the "Great patriotic War" (a part of WWII) and signals the willingness of contemporary Russians to fight/conquer Europe, reach and invade Berlin, as their "grandfathers" did in 1945; the oppositional activists in Russia and elsewhere call this aggressive sentiment *pobedobesiye*, "victory madness;"

6. mocking phrase *uzkiy mir*, which derives from the key Russian ideological and cultural cliché *русский мир*, "Russian world;"[4] the phrase is used to shift the sense of this Russians ideologeme through a grotesque imitation of the sound form of the adjective *русский* (Russian) as "uzkiy" (narrow); thus, literal translation of "uzkiy mir" is *a narrow world* ("uzkiy" rhymes with "русский");

7. neological compound adjective *analogovnetnaya*, used ironically, which derives from the laudatory phrase "there are

---

4   In response to Putin's recent strategy directed at knocking out power substations in Ukraine and thus at breaking the spirits of everyday Ukrainians in the cold of winter, Ukrainians came up with jokes that they are ready to be without electricity, but not a part of the *Russian world* (Eggers 2023).

no analogues" spread by Russian propaganda media about the Russian army; before February 24, 2022, there was a common belief that the might of Russian army had no analogues in the entire world; literal translation into English: *no-analogues* (army);

8. mocking neological noun *mobik* (pl *mobiky*), which derives from the adjective "mobilized" and refers to those Russians who were mobilized (often by force) to the front half a year after the start of Russia's full-scale invasion of Ukraine, where Russia suffered numerous setbacks; this disparaging abbreviation "mobik" reflects a low motivation, poor training and insufficient equipment of the mobilized; semantic translation into English: *a mobilized loser*;

9. mocking neological apposition *mobik-chmobik* (pl *mobiky-chmobiky*): the added neological noun "chmobik" to the newly coined "mobik" exacerbates a scornfully negative, although not without a touch of compassion, attitude towards the hastily mobilized Russian citizens, contemptuously called the *mobiks* and destined to mass demise in Ukraine; the newly coined noun "chmobik"[5] derives from the abbreviation *чмо* in the Russian criminal jargon that stands for the phrase *человек, морально опущенный* (a man, morally degraded), which can be translated as "schmuck;" therefore, the neological noun "chmobik" is a blending, which consists of two parts: "chmo" and "mobik" and points to a double derision: *a morally degraded mobilized Russian, who is a loser*; as well as others.

Concurrently, Russian propagandistic media in Ukrainian public discourse is ironically referred to as the "automatic machines of throwing fakes" (*feĭkomety*) and the "staples of the Russian world" (*skriēpy russkoho* mira), ironically alluding to the key Russian ideological and cultural cliché *духовные скрепы* (*dukhovnye skrepy*), "spiritual bonds" (literally: spiritual staples), which supposedly denotes for Russians the "traditional values" of their country, its "spiritual bonds" with Kyiv (Russian: Kiev) and Kyivan Rus; the phrase

---

5 Originates from the abbreviated phrase in Russian «частично мобилизированный» (partially mobilized), *чмо*.

духовные скрепы first came into use on December 12, 2012, in the Address of the RF President Vladimir Putin to the Federal Assembly.

Since February 24, 2022, the RF citizens influenced by anti-Ukrainian propaganda with its calls to fight Ukraine have broadly acquired the name *rashyst* [ruscist] (pl *rashysty* [ruscists]) in Ukrainian media. The meaning of this new terminological designation is "a supporter of the Kremlin's aggressive policy against Ukraine." The neological terms *ruscist [rashist]* (рашист, рашистський), *ruscistka [rashistka]* (рашистка) originate from the term Ruscism/Rashism, an umbrella term for a popular ideology in Russia. The etymology of the concept of Ruscism points to a blend of English pronunciation of the country name *Rasha* [Russia] and the term "fascism."[6] *Ruscism* is considered as a form of Nazism, or fascism, or both, and it is most frequently defined as synonymous with the term "Russian Nazism," analyzed by Timothy Snyder (2022a).

On April 14, 2022, the Verkhovna Rada of Ukraine recognized the Russian Federation as a terrorist state with a totalitarian neo-Nazi regime and banned its propaganda on the territory of Ukraine (Rebryna 2022). At the same time, *ruscism*, or Russian fascism, is recognized in Ukraine as a political ideology and social practice of the ruling regime of Russian Federation in the late 20th — early 21st century, based on the ideas of the "special civilizational mission" of Russians and intolerance of cultural elements of other nations (TSN 2022). The ideology and practice of *ruscism*, aimed at cultural and physical destruction of Ukraine and its people, meet a strong physical and intellectual resistance in Ukraine.

A relatively new term *schizofascism*, in parallel to the terms *Ruscism* and *Russian Nazism,* was proposed by Russo-American philosopher Mikhail Epstein at the beginning of Russia's aggression against Ukraine in 2014. This term was included into Epstein's *Projective Dictionary of the Humanities* (Epstein 2017); it was also used and developed by Snyder (2022b). *Schizofascism* is defined as "fascism under the guise of fight against fascism .... [it] is a split worldview, a kind of caricature of fascism, but a serious,

---

6   Besides etymology, "рашист" (ruscist) rhymes with "фашист" (fascist).

dangerous, aggressive caricature" (Epstein 2017: 261; my translation from Russian).

A temporary sculptural installation "Застрелись" ("Shoot yourself," with the characteristic letter Z, Russian military symbol) (Fig. 1), which appeared on Taras Shevchenko Boulevard in the capital city of Kyiv in summer 2022 (sculptor Dmytro Iv), attracted much attention of Ukrainian media and was discussed on social platforms. The inscription under the name of this installation, which addresses the President of the RF, records the popular neologism *Putler* – a telling combination of the last names Putin and Hitler. The entire address reads: "History knows that war criminals have two ways: a trial or … "*Putler*, is the hint clear?"

Figure 1. Temporary sculptural installation "Застрелись" ("Shoot yourself")[7]

Prior to the start of Russia's full-scale attack on Ukraine, the supporters of the Kremlin policy towards Ukraine were broadly labelled as *vatnik(s)*: generally, less aggressive RF citizens than the *ruscists* and rather indifferent to Russia's global politics but those

---

[7] Unless otherwise noted, all photographs are made by the author.

who share their government's contempt of Western values. The Ukrainian nickname *vatnyk* (pl *vatnyky*) for the supporters of the Kremlin's policy came from the word for a piece of winter outerwear, called *vatnik* or *telogreĭka* (in Russian): a quilted cotton jacket, which was a part of the winter uniform of the Red Army soldiers.

A collective noun *vata* ("cotton wool") became the generalizing term for those Russians who despise the values of Western civilization and remain loyal to the Kremlin militaristic policy. Recently, the concept of "cotton wool" has evolved into the concept of incorrigible xenophobe, the concentrated meaning of which is embodied in the neological phrase *canned cotton wool* (Ukr. *vatna konserva*).

Also, the Ukrainian word *бавовна* (*bavovna*, cotton), denoting the material from which cotton wool is made, has become extremely popular recently as a mocking translation of Russian euphemistic term *хлопóк*, with the second syllable stressed (*khlopók*, a bang/flap/clap), which refers to frequent explosions at the ammunition depots and military bases in Russia, caused by unidentified factors.

The Russians do not want to admit their own helplessness in preventing these explosions and therefore they refer to them simply as "bangs." In the Russian language, a homograph of the word *хлопóк* (a bang) is pronounced with the first syllable stressed: *хлóпок* and has the meaning "cotton" (Ukrainian: бавовна). Ukrainians this euphemistic play on words alludes to the idea that Ukraine may secretly be behind the explosions on Russian territory. It is the word *хлóпок* that Ukrainians use to report and talk about explosions in Russia, not only among regular Ukrainians on internet platforms, but also journalists in the official media.[8]

In the background of Ukrainian television studios, behind the backs of the hosts of news programs, there is often a branch with ripe cotton as a symbol of destruction of Russian military facilities. The motto "Let's make *bavovna* great again!", which appeared on Facebook in the summer of 2022, became a humorous development

---

8   Bearing in mind that the noun *бавовна* (cotton) is semantically close to the term *вата* (cotton wool) as a derogatory name for the supporters of *Russian world*.

of the image of exploding cotton. This motto is based on the slogan of Donald Trump's presidential campaign "Let's make America great again!"

Ukrainians even proclaimed a humorous holiday, World Cotton Day: On October 7, which is the birthday of Vladimir Putin (Tys 2022). On Ukrainian news, the phrase "powerful cotton could be heard" (which means "loud explosion(s) could be heard") is repeated quite often nowadays. The image of cotton flowers entered not only art, but also everyday design, for example, women's manicures, phone covers, etc.

Depriving the original expressions of Russian *Newspeak* of their initially intended meaning and filling them with a new semantic content has proved to be an effective tool of deriding Russian propaganda.

Deconstructive translation procedures are multiple, ramified, and not infrequently intertwined. They range in their variety from the play on homonyms and homographs, such as the above example *хлопóк – хлóпок* (bang—cotton), to formal calquing with shifted contextual meaning, as in the lexeme *скрепы* (staples), to meta-derivation through translation based on pronunciation, which results in the new and absurd meanings of the formerly "meaningful" and "important" Russian concepts, for instance, «один народ» → *адіннарот* (one-for-the-mouth), «мы же братья» → *мишебратья* (mice-brothers), as well as coining new concepts by means of transcribed borrowing, in particular, *кримнашист* (the-Crimea-is-ours-believer), *іхтамнєт* (one-of-those-who-are-not-there), and so on.

Ironic word formation is a broader technique, which embraces translation, transcoding (formal calquing), a term or name borrowing, and its semantic development in the Ukrainian language. Among the newly coined neologisms are the following:

1. the verb *makronyty*, which means "to call often to no avail, talk long and pointlessly on the phone" (this neologism derives from the name of French President Emmanuel Macron);
2. the phrase *valiaty shol'tsiā* (from the name of the chancellor of Germany Olaf Scholz), which means "to be constantly

promising, but not giving anything" and is grounded on the idiom "valiãty durniã" (to do stupid things, pretending that you don't understand something);

3. the verb *chornobaïty*, which means "to do the same thing over and over without getting another result and suffer a lot because of it." Its meaning derives from the name of suburban village Chornobaïvka, near the city of Kherson in southern Ukraine. Kherson International Airport is situated in Chornobaïvka and in 2022, there was a series of Ukrainian attacks against the Russian-held airport, which began on February 27 and continued up to November 5, 2022. Chornobaïvka saw dozens of attacks on Russian positions by the Ukrainian Armed Forces, which resulted in the deaths of many Russian soldiers and the destruction of their military equipment. Because of memes on Ukrainian social media mocking Russia's repeated losses in Chornobaïvka, the village became synonymous with repeated and futile efforts.

In the deconstructive translation into Ukrainian, Russian political statements and slogans have been stripped of their initially intended meaning and imbued with a new meaning which ridicules their semantic value in various ways. The basic deconstructive translation procedures are the following: 1) neologization, 2) wordplay, 3) transcribed borrowing with a transfer of meaning, as well as 4) ironic word formation, mostly based on onomastic vocabulary, among other procedures.

5.2. Reinterpreted proverbs, new jokes, funny aphorisms and facetious quotes in digital folklore

Various genres of the verbal and syncretic arts, including new proverbs, jokes, humorous poems, etc., have been actuated immediately from the first day of the Russian invasion. The most well-pronounced are massively shared and reposted on individual, commercial, and institutional webpages. Even if they first appeared on someone's personal page, they quickly spread through social networks, lose their authorship, and enrich the treasury of Ukrainian cyber folklore.

Perhaps the most vivid example of a new proverb, which is an expansion of the traditional folk proverb, is the following:

> Українці незламні. Коли погано — плачуть, коли дуже погано — співають, коли повна дупа — сміються. Але — ніколи не опускають руки. Ukrainians are invincible. When it's bad, they cry, when it's very bad, they sing, and when it's very-very bad, they laugh. But they never give up.

This post first appeared on a private webpage of Liudmyla Pereverten' on April 12, 2022, and that very day it was broadly shared, re-appearing on several non-private pages belonging to commercial firms, such as the tourist agency "Club of positive travelers *Like Travel*" and the online store "Family Gifts," which offers embroidered and modern clothes by Ukrainian manufacturers (the store shared this post on its page "Social project *Very necessary work*"), etc.

Over the next few days, this proverb, already anonymous, entered the oral and written narratives of other authors on YouTube, Facebook and other media platforms with minor variations and abbreviations. For example, on the same day, 12 April 2022, a YouTuber nicknamed Zakhar (10K subscribers) in his post entitled "Chomu ne mozhna voiūvaty z ukraïntsīamy?" ["Why shouldn't one fight with Ukrainians?"] used a shortened version of the proverb: "Незламні. Коли погано — плачуть, коли дуже погано — співають, коли повна ср#ка — сміються!" / "Unbreakable. When it's bad, they cry, when it's very bad, they sing, when it's full of shit, they laugh!" The post gained 3,918 views on that very day (Zakhar 2022). On April 15, 2022, the post titled "Why shouldn't one fight with Ukrainians?" was reposted by a blogger under the nickname *brenik*, etc.

Beyond celebrations of Ukrainian courage, many memes play upon historical grievances between Russians and Ukrainians. Stepan Bandera (1909 — 1959, killed by a KGB agent using cyanide) was a leader of the radical wing of the Organization of Ukrainian Nationalists during World War II. His image is affiliated simultaneously with both Ukrainian resistance, independence, and nationalism and with Nazi sympathizers, depending on the viewer's perspective. In Russia, Ukrainians, particularly Ukrainian speakers are called *бандеровцы, banderovtsy,* the Bandera people (*sing* бандеровец, *fem* бандеровка). Below is an imagined dialogue between Russians and Stepan Bandera, based on an interlingual pun (from Facebook):

> Степан Бандера:
> А знаєте, як буде російською «вантаж 200»? Бандеролька.
> Stepan Bandera
> – Do you know the Russian for "cargo 200"[9]?
> – *Bander*olka (a small parcel).

"Cargo 200" is a reference to Soviet slang for war casualties, denoting the code written on trucks carrying fallen soldiers during the Afghan war.

There is a unifying method in the speaker's humorous strategy in digital folklore: to raise the level of optimism and faith in victory in spite of everything. Below are two different examples (one in Russian and the other in Ukrainian) of the most popular social media jokes that appeared in April 2022, among many other samples from the online *Collection of Ukrainian Jokes*:

Example 1 (in Russian):

> – Харьков взяли?
> – Нет.
> – Киев взяли?
> – Нет.
> – А что взяли?
> – Мясорубку взяли, миксер, кроссовки взяли и шкаф-купе взяли. (Zbirnyk 2022a)
> – Did they take over Kharkiv?
> – Nope.
> – Did they take over Kyiv?
> – Nope.
> – What did they take, then?
> – They took a meat grinder, a mixer, they took a pair of sneakers and took a sliding door wardrobe. (Collection of Ukrainian Jokes #4802)

Before making it to the *Collection of Ukrainian Jokes*, this joke appeared in several shorter versions, starting on April 2, 2022. It was posted by the user with nickname *Kolobok* (in Russian):

---

9   "Cargo 200" is a military code word used in the Soviet Union and the post-Soviet states referring to the transportation of military fatalities.

> Свежий анекдот: Киев взяли? — Нет. — Харьков взяли? — Нет. — А шо
> взяли?! — Миксер взяли, ковёр взяли...! (Kolobok 2022).
> A fresh anecdote: Did they take Kiev? — Nope. — Did they take Kharkov? —
> Nope. — What did they take? — They took a mixer, took a carpet ...!

On April 6, 2022, another version of the joke was published by Radio Liberty as part of the online reportage title: "Из России: «Киев не взяли. Взяли мясорубку, миксер и кроссовки». Соцсети — о мародерстве российских военных" ["From Russia: "Kyiv was not taken. We took a meat grinder, a mixer, and a pair of sneakers." Social networks about the looting of the Russian military"] (Radio Liberty 2022). On that very date, Russian free entertainment application АйДаПрикол published the fullest version of this joke; the same version that was included in the *Collection of Ukrainian Jokes* (Idaprikol 2022).

Example 2 (in Ukrainian):

> Втрати ворога — це як деруни зі сметаною. Їх багато, але однаково мало.
> Хочеться ще. (Zbirnyk 2022b)
> Enemy losses are like potato pancakes[10] with sour cream. There are many of
> them but still not enough. Wish there would be more. (Collection of Ukrainian Jokes #4919)

Projected confidence in victory is well reflected in the dozens of new proverbial expressions, jokes, and humorous dialogic exchanges based on puns. The following joke was one of the first to appear on social networks after February 24, 2022, and it spread across all popular networks: Facebook, Instagram, Twitter, and VKontakte, is the latter of which has been blocked in Ukraine since May 16, 2017:

> Ми така нація, що нам спочатку трохи страшно, а потім вже пох#й... а
> коли нам пох#й, то страшно всім.
> We are such a nation that at first, we get scared a little, but shortly after, we
> don't f#cking care... and when we don't f#cking care, everyone gets scared.

On March 1, 2022, the information agency "Typical Kyiv" published a rather extensive selection of the first wartime jokes under the title "*When we don't f#cking care, everyone gets scared:* What new

---

10   Potato pancakes: Ukrainian national dish.

words and expressions were added to Ukrainian folklore during the war" with the subtitle "Ukrainians know how to joke and this helps them resist the aggressor" (Typovyǐ Kyiv 2022). In the preface to this selection, digital folklore was mentioned for the first time as a special type of folklore born in social networks during the first week of the war. The above joke was quoted in full with the following reasoning: "The vital credo of Ukrainians can be put into one such phrase that characterizes their behavior in the war," and a note was made that this joke came into existence on the day of publication: "The expression appeared literally today, but describes the psychological state of the citizens of Ukraine who are literally being wiped off the face of the earth by attacking from the ground, air and sea. But as they say: "A Ukrainian fights like he plows the land." After all, in wartime, the most important thing is not to panic and not to lose optimism" (ibid.).

A lot of the wartime jokes are contingent on interlingual puns. I will exemplify this type of jokes with two examples (both in Ukrainian):

Example 3:

> Знаєте, чому росіяни нам не друзі? Тому, що друзі на дорозі не валяються.
> Do you know why Russians are not our friends? Because friends are not lying around on the road.

The above version was published on March 4, 2022, on Twitter by the user nicknamed *Софі* (Sofie 2022). The joke is based on a Russian folk proverb aboutmoney, well-known also in Ukraine, "Money does not lie under your feet (on the road)" (Poslovitsy i pogovorki n.d.). A set phrase from this proverb "… does not lie on the road (street)," which means something valuable, rare, has a wide compatibility and can be used not only with the lexeme "money," but also with any other to indicate someone or something rare, and is often extended to human beings, as in the derivative proverb: "Friends are not lying on the road." A day prior, on March 3, 2022, the first and shorter version of the new proverb was posted by *The First Private Museum of Memes on Twitter*: "Muscovites are not our friends. Because friends don't lie on the road" (Persha pryvatna memarniā 2022). It is quite likely that the user Sophie took this post as the basis for their own version of the proverb.

In a month, on April 3, 2022, a more neutral version of this proverb appeared in the title of a "portion of fresh memes that give a smile in difficult times" compiled by Oleksiy Dzyuba: *Russians are not our friends, because friends do not lie on the road. Ukrainians continue to make apt jokes during the war with Russia*" (Dzyuba 2022). A variation of the new proverb also quickly entered the Collection of Ukrainian Jokes [Zbirnyk ukraïns'kykh anekdotiv №556] (Zbirnyk 2022d). On March 26, 2022, the anecdote was published in the electronic version of the newspaper "News of Zakarpattia," in the column "Let's laugh together!" (News of Zakarpattia 2022).

Example 4:

> – Куме, а знаєте, як англійською сказати «російські війська»?
> – Hi.
> – «Рашн трупс»![11]
> – Файно.
> – My crony, dost thou know how to say "Russian troops" in English?
> – No.
> – "Russian corpses!"
> – Nice.

Visual and verbal caricatures are often combined as syncretic art on posters and billboards. Moreover, in the south-eastern regions of Ukraine, the language of this sarcastic genre can be both Russian and Ukrainian, such as the one illustrating a double-headed Russian eagle being driven away with a trident, the coat of arms of Ukraine. A caricature of an eagle chased away by a trident pitchfork appeared on a billboard in the city of Odesa on March 10, 2022. The picture was supplemented with a text in Russian, stylized at the beginning into the Biblical diction and finished with a low-colloquial pattern. This captioned cartoon, together with the inscription placed under it, circulated in numerous electronic media and on many web pages. The text is as follows:

---

11 The word "трупс" is the Anglicized plural form of Ukrainian noun "труп" that means "corpse" and would be pronounced as "troops."

Не возжелай страны
Ближнего своего,
И свободы его, и сала его,
И Крыма его —
И не застрянут у тебя
В ж#пе вилы его! (Durova 2022)
Don't covet the country
Of your neighbor,
Nor his freedom, nor his bacon,
Nor his Crimea —
If you don't want his pitchfork
To get stuck in your ass!

Allusions to the Bible and classical Ukrainian poets, especially to Taras Shevchenko, are not infrequent. The case in consideration is the following humorous variation on the theme of Shevchenko's popular verse "Zapovit" ("Yak umru, to pokhovaĭte mene na mohyli…") [My Testament], which has been spread on social media platforms, shared, and reposted multiple times. The voice of the subject in this parodistic verse, known as "Putin's Testament," is extrapolated on the RF President Vladimir Putin as the speaking persona. This verse appeared in variations on social networks as early as January 2015, and after February 24, 2022, it was topicalized with greater force. The following version of this scathing satire, with the picture of the RF president in the background, appeared online on May 1, 2022, with a link to the page of the Ministry of Defense of Ukraine (Defense of Ukraine on Twitter 2022):

Як умру, то поховайте
Мене в купі гною,
І покласти не забудьте
Униз головою.
Начепіть мені на плечі
Хоч якісь ознаки,
Щоб хоч якось відрізнялась
Голова від ср#ки.
When I die, bury me
In a pile of manure,
And do not forget to put me
Upside down.
Also pin to my shoulders
At least some insignia
To make my head somehow
Differ from my ass.

Scorching parodies of the Russian military men are appearing in large numbers to mark the notable events of the war and can be used to track down Russian hostilities in Ukraine and to compile a chronicle of Ukrainian victories. One of the witticisms of this kind refers to the stay of Russian troops on the territory of the Chornobyl nuclear power plant: they captured the plant on the first day of the full-scale war, February 24, and remained there until April 2, 2022. This anecdotal story concerns the stupidity and lack of general education on the part of Russian troops who raised the dust in the so-called "red forest" near Chornobyl nuclear power plant, dug trenches there and organized an ammunition depot at the foot of the plant, having stayed there for 36 days.

The joke was spread in social networks in different variations. On April 1, 2022, it appeared in the daily newspaper "Komsomol's'ka Pravda v Ukraïni" (KP in Ukraine), which until January 13, 2022, was printed exclusively in Russian. Below I give this anecdote in the "KP in Ukraine" version:

> До Статуту З(бройних) С(ил) Росії вирішено запровадити нове звернення. До солдатів, які перебували в радіусі 20 км від ЧАЕС, слід звертатися з часткою "фон"; у радіусі 10 км — "ваша світлість"; у радіусі 5 км — "ваше сіятельство" (Komsomol's'ka Pravda 2022).
>
> It was decided to introduce a new address to the Statute of the Armed Forces of Russia. Soldiers[12] who stayed within the radius of 20 km from the Chornobyl nuclear power plant should be addressed with the prefix "Von" [in Russian and Ukrainian "фон" means "background radiation"], those who stayed within the radius of 10 km, "Your Luminescence," and those who stayed within the radius of 5 km, "Your Radiance."

Lots of satire have been created around the globally-known exchange of the brave Ukrainian serviceman, who defended the island of Zmiïnyi in the Black Sea, with the Russian navy warship, which put forward an ultimatum:

> – Я русский военный корабль! Предлагаю сложить оружие и сдаться! Russian Warship: "I suggest you lay down your arms and surrender, otherwise you'll be hit"
>
> – Русский военный корабль, иди нах#й
>
> Ukrainian Outpost's response to the threat was telling and brief: "Russian warship, f#ck off!" (February 25, 2022).

---

12   In other versions "the orcs," which is a collective name for Russian soldiers.

Among multiple sarcastic Ukrainian "good wishes," grounded on the Ukrainian serviceman's response to the Russian warship, is the following:

> А не міг би той хлопака зі Зміїного по радіо ще й путіна послати? Може, має дар...) (Zbirnyk 2022c)
> "And that guy from Zmiїnyi, could he also send Putin to hell on the radio? Maybe he has a magic gift ...)" (Collection of Ukrainian Jokes #5076)

Losses of the enemy are often made a topic for dark humor. The following illustration (Fig. 2) from social media is a humorous interpretation of the famous painting by Ivan Shishkin "Morning in a Pine Forest," which appeared on the wrapper of Russian chocolate candies "Mishka kosolapy" ("Clumsy Bear") as early as 1913. The bear candy outlived the Russian Empire and even the Soviet Union that inherited it. A unique candy, which became recognizable thanks to Shishkin's masterpiece on its wrapper, remains widely popular and desired, though quite expensive in Putin's Russia. The humor in the inscription on its Ukrainian caricature is built on word play with the near homographs. The Ukrainian inscription reads:

New candies went on sale in Russia for the May 9th holiday:[13]
Meshki (Bags) in the Forest[14]
Unwrap and find your denazifier![15]

Figure 2.
Ukrainian caricature of the wrapper of Russian chocolate candies "Mishka kosolapy" ("Clumsy Bear")

---

13   "Victory Day" (May 9, 1945) in the "Great patriotic War" in Russia.
14   The remains of the dead bodies of Russian soldiers are packed in black bags.
15   The denazification of Ukrainians was one of the intermediate goals of Russia's so-called "special military operation" in Ukraine.

The pun is based on the play on words "meshkí", «мешкИ в лесу», *Bags in the Forest*, with the stress on the last syllable in the word «мешки» (bags), versus "míshki" from a recognizable popular candy name «мИшки в лесу», *Bears in the Forest*, with the stress on the first syllable in the word «мишки» (bears).

Putin's law that criminalized any public voice calling the war against Ukraine a "war" instead of framing it as a "special military operation," was ridiculed in one of the most popular memes responding to this censorial law shortly after the start of invasion on February 24. The meme replaces the title of Leo Tolstoy's 1867 novel *War and Peace* with "Special Military Operation and Peace" (Vasily Grogol 2022; printed in Bishara 2022). This meme spread in cyberspace, was photocopied, and posted on bulletin boards in European universities, circulated globally, etc.

Ukrainians are dismantling Russian Newspeak on social platforms using the strategies of 1) creating new narrative framings for traditional proverbs, 2) making anecdotal exchanges and stories strung on the homonymic and homographic word play, including interlingual homonymy, and contextually engendered or reversed semantic contrast, 3) generating wellerism-like ironic aphorisms, and 4) manufacturing facetious recontextualization of the *Newspeak* concepts.

5.3. Comical pictures, memes and cartoons

In this subsection, a combination of pictorial and verbal elements will be considered more closely. At that, sometimes the image alone works, or in combination with a one-word or short-phrase inscription. The comical effect lies in the strategy of paradox, which unfolds as a conceptual conflict between the image and inscription, or a cognitive conflict encoded in the image itself.

One of popular anti-Putin memes circulating on the internet (Fig. 3), "How this will end for Putin," was posted on Twitter on March 1, 2022 (Jerry Avenaim 2022):

Figure 3.   The meme "How this will end for Putin"

After a guided missile cruiser of the Russian Navy *Moskva* sank on April 18, 2022, it became "obvious" that the Ukrainian servicemen on Zmiïnyi [Snake] Island really did tell Russian warships to "go to hell." Also, a cartoon on the topic of the sunk warship *Moskva* quickly appeared on social media. The pivotal illustrated text (Fig. 4) unfolds as a dialogue between the Fish-landlord in the sunk submarine, which not unexpectedly turned out to be extremely costly, and the Fish-tenant. This version was published on April 18, 2022, on Twitter by the user nicknamed Чылік (Chylik 2022).

Fish-landlord: *$1000 plus utilities*

Fish-tenant: *kinda expensive*

Fish-landlord: *and what did you expect...*

it's Moscow

Figure 4. Cartoon on the topic of the sunk warship *Moskva*

The topic of the effectiveness of bayraktars—Turkish strike drones with a long flight duration—has also proved to be very popular in both verbal and visual humorous art in the first months of war. For instance, on April 6, 2022, a trolling-request asking if there are direct flights by Bayraktar from Kiev to Moscow appeared in Russian on the Facebook page of the company "Transport of Kiev:"

> Тут люди интересуются, летает ли Bayraktar Airlines из Киева на Москву: "Скажите, пожалуйста, а есть прямые авиарейсы Байрактаров из Киева на Москву?" (Transport of Kiev 2022)
> People are asking whether *Bayraktar Airlines* fly from Kyiv to Moscow: "Please let me know if there are direct flights by *Bayraktar* from Kyiv to Moscow?"

An example of commented visual art on the theme of bayraktars is given below (Fig. 5). The inscription reads: Seeing *Bayraktar*, the Russian tank pretended to be dead (UNIAN, March 14, 2022).

Figure 5. Comical picture with the upside-down Russian tank

A humorous visual image can be combined with a phrase-long inscription, as in Figure 6, or with a one- or two-word inscription, as in Figures 7 and 8, or devoid of verbal elements altogether, as in Figure 9 below.

Figure 6. "Careful: a f#cked-up neighbor"

While the inscription on the wall in Figure 6 reads: "Careful: a f#cked-up neighbor," the user's comment preceding the inscription is the following: "we need such a wall." The picture was posted on April 16, 2022, on Facebook by the user nicknamed *Sophie Muraly* (2022).

Figure 7. "Занавес"

The Russian word behind the curtains in Figure 7, "Занавес" is written with a substitution of the Cyrillic letter "З" ("Занавес") with the Latin letter "Z," which is a new military symbol in Russia, sported by Russians on their uniforms and tanks. The contextual meaning of the word "Занавес" is the following: "The show's all over, clear out," or, as Facebook user under nickname *LudMila Nitz* formulated: "We are leaving, we are leaving…. Curtain," indicating the end of performance for the two fans of the "classical Russian ballet" in ballerina tutus—self-proclaimed President of Belarus Lukashenka and Russian President Putin. The picture was retweeted and reposted many times, particularly on the Facebook pages of the users *Natalia Pylypiuk* (March 21, 2022), *LudMila Nitz* (March 26, 2022), *Sanasar Kuiumchian* (April 27, 2022) and others, as well as published on the Telegram channel of the same name (Занавес 2022) and reposted by Reddit from Ukrainian Memes and Art for Ukraine sites (Reddit Zahabec 2022a; 2022b).

A similar type of picture with an inscription in the background and humorous images of Presidents Lukashenka and Putin in the foreground can be seen in the following author's comic on Twitter (Fig. 8), "Pariah Olympics 2022" (Camley Cartoons 2022),which has also become quite popular in the networks.

Figure 8. "Pariah Olympics 2022"

A further illustration from public domain of the war-born art of Easter-egg painting on grenades, called "the combat Easter eggs," contains no verbal elements (Fig. 9).

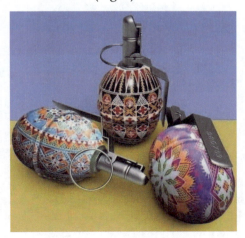

Figure 9. Lemon grenades, painted like Easter eggs.

The art appeared seven years ago in the Donbas area of anti-terrorist operation (Ukr.: ATO) among the Ukrainian military and was first publicly discussed in the reportage "The Offensive Easter eggs: The ATO fighters paint grenades with Easter patterns" on the TV News Service channel on April 11, 2015 (TSN 2015).

An entire collection of funny visual metaphors which refer to various aspects of Russian propagandistic viewpoint at the history of Ukraine can be singled out. For example, the following picture (Fig. 10) embodies the Kremlin's "concept" of the origin of Ukraine from the Union of Soviet Socialist Republics, founded by Vladimir Ulyanov-Lenin in 1922. It is grotesquely called The Monument "Vladimir Lenin founds Ukraine" (bronze, granite, Alzheimer's).

Figure 10. The Monument "Vladimir Lenin founds Ukraine" (bronze, granite, Alzheimer's)

The statue of Lenin in the above montaged picture replaces the posture of Lybid', a legendary co-founder of the city of Kyiv. The picture was posted as early as December 23, 2021, on the Facebook page of the user *Процишин Офіційний* (Protsyshyn Ofitsiĭnyĭ 2021). Since then, it has been reposted many times. Below (Fig. 11) is the picture of the real monument, erected in 1982 in a park near the Paton bridge in Kyiv in honor of the symbolic 1500th anniversary of Kyiv. It is the Monument to the founders of Kyiv: brothers Kyĭ, Shchek, Khoryv and their sister Lybid'. The official name of the monument is "Soaring Lybid'," although it is also called "The Boat."

Figure 11. "Soaring Lybid'" ("The Boat")

Ukrainians are deploying meme warfare to combat Russian disinformation and pseudohistorical declarations with their arsenal of war memes. In particular, the Twitter account Ukrainian Meme Forces (UMF), which aggregates Ukrainian counter-propaganda memes from Twitter and Reddit, was created as early as February 2022 as a semi-official tool of resistance (Ukrainian Memes Forces 2022). A deluge of funny pictures grounded on historical reminiscences is helping Ukrainians cope with their predicament with humor. "Ukrainians are greeting Russian liberators with flowers!" reads a caption above the image of Ukrainian woman threshing a frightened Russian soldier with a flower bouquet (Fig. 12), tweeted by Ukrainian Memes Forces on March 11, 2022 ("Ukrainians are greeting Russian liberators with flowers!" 2022).

Figure 12. "Ukrainians are greeting Russian liberators with flowers!"

Quite often the humor in historical reminiscences spills over into bitter satire, as in the following caricature poster "Kuzka's mother is calling!" depicting a woman-drunkard calling to "protect our rat" (i.e., Vladimir Putin) (Fig. 13).

Figure 13. "Kuzka's mother is calling!"

This poster is reminiscent of the famous poster "Motherland is calling!" depicting a symbolic Motherland in red who shows the "military oath" to the Soviet citizens (Fig. 14), from the times of the "Great Patriotic War," created by the artist Irakli Toidze at the end of June 1941.

Figure 14. "Motherland is calling!"

Kuzka's mother (Кузькина мать; *Kuzka* is a diminutive of the given name *Kuzma*), is part of the Russian proverb "to show Kuzka's mother (to someone)" [Показать кузькину мать (кому-либо)], "to teach someone a lesson," "to punish someone in a brutal way." The expression *Kuzka's mother* is a common idiomatic curse in Russian. It entered the history of the foreign relations of the Soviet Union as part of the image of Nikita Khrushchev, along with the shoe-banging incident and the phrase "We shall show you Kuzka's mother!"

(meaning "We will bury you").[16] The actual reference in Khrushchev's phrase was to a code word for the atomic bomb—a thermonuclear test device—nicknamed by its builders *Kuzka's mother*. The poster "Kuzka's mother is calling!" appeared in cyber space (on Facebook) as early as June 24, 2016, on the anniversary of Khrushchev's public use of the Russian idiom "to show Kuzka's mother" for the first time—on June 24, 1959, at the first American National Exhibition in the USSR, addressing the then US Vice President Richard Nixon.

Another popular satirical caricature, with reference to history, which was shared and reposted on the Internet, belongs to the subgenre of "family portraits" and depicts a "happy" family of Hitler, Stalin, and little Putin (Fig. 15). The motto above this "family picture" reads: "We smile and continue the fight!"

Figure 15. "We smile and continue the fight!"

---

16 The interpreter was stunned and translated literally: We shall show you the mother of Kuzma.

DECONSTRUCTION OF RUSSIA'S *NEWSPEAK*   241

Syncretic deconstruction of Russian geopolitical, cultural, and historical narratives by means of comical pictures, memes, and cartoons extends in the strategy of creating a paradox, which mostly unravels a conceptual conflict between the image and inscription (as in Fig. 7, 8, 12, 13) or a cognitive conflict encoded in the image itself (as in Fig. 3, 9, 10).

5.4. Recontextualizing national traumas during wartime: favorite poetic quotes and mystifications in the cyberspace

Many bloggers, YouTubers, and other social media users rely on the authority of Taras Shevchenko, Pavlo Tychyna, Lina Kostenko, and their ilk, as people's poets, dead and alive, and attribute to them the verses which they like and post on their pages, but which might actually belong to other poets. This phenomenon is perhaps the most widespread in the case of Lina Kostenko, our contemporary, to whom at least a dozen different verses are attributed by reference @Ліна Костенко. The authority of the folk poet in today's Ukraine is no less strong than it was a hundred or more years ago, starting from the era of National Romanticism and its national emblem Taras Shevchenko (1814-1861). Symptomatically, the presence of Lina Kostenko's name functions as a kind of talisman on social platforms. The name of a genial modern poet, a woman who has not yielded to Soviet authorities, nor was tempted by the State awards during Independence, symbolizes people's belief in the magical power of the poet's word and testifies to the high moral authority of an unwavering poet in Ukrainian society.

A new folklore genre can be singled out — poetic mystification, or poetry attributed to outstanding humanitarian authorities, such as Lina Kostenko and Taras Shevchenko, alongside their authentic texts. In this chapter, due to lack of space, I will consider only the case of Lina Kostenko on Internet platforms.

Several quotes from the historical novel in verse by Kostenko "Berestechko," which was written in 1966 — 1967 and published only in independent Ukraine, began to spread actively on social networks with the beginning of the hot phase of the war. In particular, the fragment *"Tse zh treba maty satanyns'kyy namir..."* (*"Their satan plannings..."*), which appeared on Kostenko's Facebook page on March 6, 2022, is more popular today than ever before thanks to the internet reposts. This fragment is given below:

> Це ж треба мати сатанинський намір,
> чаїть в собі невиліковний сказ,
> щоб тяжко так знущатися над нами
> та ще й у всьому звинуватить нас!
> Their satan plannings always were much rougher,
> The rabies was well hidden deep inside,
> It can't be cured, and that is why we suffer,And victim blaming just an extra bloody bite! (Translated by Olha Vakhromova, April 26, 2022b)

Other popular quotes from the novel "Berestechko" appearing on Twitter and Facebook are those: "Rozp'yato nas mizh zakhodom i skhodom…" ("Between them all we suffer the damnation")[17] and "My voïny. Ne ledari. Ne lezhni…" ("Warriors we are. No lazy. No inert"):

> Ми воїни. Не ледарі. Не лежні
> І наше діло праведне й святе
> Бо хто за що, а ми за незалежність
> Отож нам так і важко через те.
> Warriors we are. No lazy. No inert
> Our cause is saint and right,
> We stand for independence,
> This makes so tough our fight. (UCU_University, May 23, 2022)

It is a telling fact that the quoted above fragment appeared in anonymous translation into English on different social platforms: on March 19, 2022, when Lina Kostenko was celebrating her 92nd birthday, a bilingual (Russian and Ukrainian) online journal "New Time of the Country" published this stanza in the post "HB (Новое Время) to our legend Lina Kostenko." It was retweeted on the official Twitter account "Ukraine/Україна: Ukraine Government

---

17 Розп'ято нас між Заходом і Сходом.
   Що не орел — печінку нам довбе.
   Зласкався, доле, над моїм народом,
   щоб він не дався знівечить себе.
   Between them all we suffer the damnation.
   And any eagle just has our liver willed.
   Dear destiny, have mercy on my nation,
   So we won't let the horde to get us killed!
   (Translated by Olha Vakhromova, April 26, 2022a)

Organization" that very day (Ukraine/Україна 2022) and on the official page of Ukrainian Catholic University on May 23, 2022 (UCU_University 2022).

In Ukrainian, all the above stanzas from the poem "Berestechko," as well as a separate short poem "*I zhakh, i krov, i smert', i vidchaǐ...*," were published by news agency company Ukrainian Independent Information Agency (UNIAN) on Lina Kostenko's birthday (Pikulina 2022). This relatively new poem by Lina Kostenko, "*I zhakh, i krov., i smert', i vidchaǐ...*," the one directly exposing Putin's ongoing war against Ukraine, quickly became popular and recognizable by its first line. The history of its creation is worthy of separate mentioning. On March 19, 2015, Kostenko celebrated her 85th birthday. And the day before, she joined the humanitarian action "Second Front of the Anti-Terrorist Operation." Humanitarian aid and books were collected for the soldiers of the volunteer battalion "Kyiv-1" and for the children who remained in the anti-terrorist operation zone. Kostenko handed over to the front several collections of her poems with words of support. On the title page of one of her books taken to the frontline she wrote a poem by hand, "*I zhakh, i krov...*," which instantly flew around the Internet:

> І жах, і кров, і смерть, і відчай,
> І клекіт хижої орди,
> Маленький сірий чоловічок
> Накоїв чорної біди.
> Це звір огидної породи,
> Лох-Несс холодної Неви.
> Куди ж ви дивитесь, народи?!
> Сьогодні ми, а завтра — ви. (Druhyǐ front Liny Kostenko 2015)
> Horror, blood, death, and despair,
> The screeching of a vulture's horde,
> A little gray man
> Has brought a black scourge.
> This is a beast of a dreadful breed,
> The Loch Ness monster of the cold Neva.
> Which way are you looking, peoples?!
> Today's our turn, tomorrow is — yours! (Translated by Svitlana Budzhak-Jones, in open access)

Among more recent translations of Kostenko's poetry into English one can come across a poem "*Shche nazva ye, a richky vzhe nemaye...*" ("*The river's gone, the name remains*") on the Twitter page of Boris

244 LADA KOLOMIYETS

Dralyuk, tweeted on December 5, 2022, with the translator's comment: "May both the landscape of Ukraine, now scarred, and the beautiful names of its rivers and valleys, towns and villages, arise and flourish!" (Dralyuk 2022). Fans of Lina Kostenko's creative work maintain a page on Twitter, where they present her aphorisms, quotes from longer works and her short poems (@L_Kostenko).[18] Concurrently, Ukrainian media, retweets and reposts broadly attribute to Lina Kostenko such poems as "A Stolen Spring" (*Ukradena vesna*) and "When the war ends..." (*Koly zakinchytsiā viĭna...*), although the real authors of these poems are Olena Horhol'-Ihnat'iēva (2022) and Halyna Potopliāk (2022), respectively. The poem "*Ukradena vesna*" was first published on March 17, 2022, by Horhol-Ihnatieva and the poem "*Koly zakinchytsia viĭna...*" on August 23, 2022, by Potopliāk. The phenomenon of their attribution to Lina Kostenko in subsequent reposts proves the authority of Lina Kostenko as a people's poet.

These and other poems on social networks help to explicate and debunk Putin's myths about the absence of a separate Ukrainian people and its separate history. The main strategy of dissecting Putin's war crimes through poetic means is inverted and restructured opposites, for example, as in the poem "Horror, blood, death, and despair...," which metaphorically points to Putin as "the Loch Ness monster of the cold Neva" back in 2015. Poetry turns out to be extremely effective in getting to the bottom of the imperial semiotic space in Russian-Ukrainian historical relations.

6. Discussion and Conclusion

Ukrainian folk voices and genres in cyberspace have been greatly versatile ranging from ritual folklore, folk epic and small folklore genres to children's folklore and songs to post-folklore. Additionally, new genres have appeared, as well as numerous remakes of songs, poetic mystifications, and anonymous translations. The analysis of the data presented in this chapter shows that people's creativity manifested on social platforms and in electronic media emerged as an effective vehicle of deconstructing Russian neo-

---

18 See: https://twitter.com/L_Kostenko

imperial myths and propaganda and generating simultaneously a new culture of cyberwar while making their war globally visible.

Critical discourse analysis, combined with the theory of deconstruction, structural-semantic analysis and translation analysis, allows us to identify a set of strategies of deconstructing Russian *Newspeak,* peculiar to particular digital (folklore) genres and parodistic translation in the media. Linguistic deconstruction of Russian myths serves not only as an important warning about real threats, but also as a means of anticipating and combating them. In the Ukrainian deconstructive translation, the basic strategy is resorting to parody: Russian political statements and slogans are stripped of their initially intended meaning and imbued with a new meaning which ridicules their semantic value in various ways. The leading deconstructive translation procedures are neologization, wordplay, transcribed borrowing with a transfer of meaning, as well as ironic word formation. Ironic word formation, which happens to be predominantly onomastic and vocabulary-based, is a broader technique that embraces translation, transcoding (formal calquing), a term or name borrowing, and its semantic development in the Ukrainian language.

Humorous dismantling of Russian neo-imperial myths in such verbal genres of digital folklore as reinterpreted traditional proverbs, new jokes, funny aphorisms, and facetious quotes (written mainly in Ukrainian, but also occurring in Russian) proceeds by using the following strategies: creation of new narrative framings; contextual semantic development in jokes of homonyms- or homographs-based word play (including interlingual homonymy); creation of wellerism-like ironic statements/aphorisms (built on play with coherence and logic); and facetious recontextualization of the original Russian *Newspeak* concepts.

In syncretic genres of digital folklore, which represent new folklore genres, such as comical pictures, memes, and cartoons (I considered only the works of art belonging to these genres which either already became anonymous, or are in transition to anonymity), the deconstruction of Russian geopolitical, cultural, and historical narratives and reminiscences presents itself in the strategy of creating a paradox, which, more frequently, demonstrates a conceptual conflict between the image and inscription to it or, in rarer cases, a cognitive conflict encoded in the image itself (if the image is not accompanied by any inscription).

The social platforms users' experience of explicating Putin's war crimes and debunking colonial myths by poetic means has been analyzed in the case of original verses by Lina Kostenko and public mystifications of her poetry. The strategy of restructured opposites has been used by Kostenko in her original verses revealing Putin's rhetoric, and Kostenko's fans turn to the strategy of poetic mystification or attributing a poem they liked to a well-known and authoritative author in order to make the text, considered to be important, more widely distributed and more influential.

By means of deconstructive strategies spontaneously applied in humorous translation and digital folklore, Ukrainian civilians demonstrate their ability to influence the ongoing conflict in real time via virtual conversations aimed at debunking Russian militaristic myths and narratives. A deconstructive approach and humor as a tool of dismantling the Kremlin's *Newspeak* have shown their joint effectiveness on social platforms. The most popular humorous forms and genres of digital folklore, explored in this chapter, constitute a feature of contemporary people's cyberwar.

A promising prospect for further research is the analysis of parodistic translation and various genres of digital folklore within the theoretical framework of war cultures as a new stage in a cyber war, which globally engages Ukrainian communities in virtual battles, namely, as a people's cyber war. Therefore, the prospect for further research consists in the historical, linguo-semiotic, and discursive analysis of the concept of war culture from the cyberwar perspective, as a new age of cyberwar culture, in comparison with the 20th-century war cultures, starting from WWI (see Smith 2007; Horne and Kramer 2001; Audoin-Rouzeau and Becker 2003). What is new in the history of warfare is the combination of technology and participatory democracy introducing a new element—Ukrainian digital folklore, or the direct, sustained, and spontaneously unifying engagement of civilians in ways that span the globe. The methodology of further research, thus, may be extended to historical method and the method of historical analogy, classification, and typological analysis.

Bibliography:

Audoin-Rouzeau, Stéphane & Becker, Annette. (2003). *14-18: Understanding the great war*. London: Macmillan.

Bishara, Hakim. (2022). Ukrainians wage a meme war against Russia: An outpouring of memes is helping Ukrainians cope through humor that often spills over into dark satire. *Hyperallergic,* 11 March, https://hyperallergic.com/author/hakim-bishara/ (accessed 15 March 2023)

Bol'shoĭ. (2011). Bol'shoĭ akademicheskiĭ slovar' russkogo iàzyka / gl. red. A. S. Gerd [from Russ.: The great academic dictionary of the Russian language / chief editor A. S. Gerd]. Moscow; Sankt-Petersburg: Nauka, 2004–2017 (ongoing edition). Vol. 17: Plan-Podlech' / RAN. In-t lingvisticheskikh issledovaniĭ.

Brenik. (2022). Chomu ne mozħna voiūvaty z ukraïntsiàmy? [from Ukr.: Why cannot one fight with Ukrainians?]. *Livejournal,* 15 April, https://brenik.livejournal.com/76649.html (accessed 16 August 2022).

Camley Cartoons. (2022). Pariah Olympics 2022. *Twitter,* https://twitter.com/camleycartoons/status/1499378811175059456 (accessed 15 February 2023).

Charles, Ron. (2022). In Ukraine, humor has become a weapon of war. *The Washington Post,* 1 April, https://www.washingtonpost.com/books/2022/04/01/ukraine-humorina/ (accessed August 16, 2022).

Chylik. (2022). 1000 dollarov pliūs kommunal'nye [from Russ.: $1000 plus utilities]. *Twitter,* 18 April, https://twitter.com/chilikto/status/1515802940661026817 (accessed 16 August 2022).

Derrida, Jacques. (1981). *Dissemination.* Translated, with an introduction and additional notes by Barbara Johnson. Chicago: The University of Chicago Press.

Derrida, Jacques. (1979). Living on: Border lines. In *Deconstruction and criticism.* New York: Seabury Press, 75–176.

Derrida, Jacques. (1982). Margins of philosophy. Translated, with additional notes by Alan Bass. Chicago: The University of Chicago Press.

Derrida, Jacques. (1976). *Of grammatology.* Baltimore: John Hopkins University Press.

Derrida, Jacques. (1978). *Writing and difference.* Translated, with an introduction and additional notes by Alan Bass. Chicago: The University of Chicago Press.

Do Statutu. (2022) Do Statutu Z(broĭnykh) S(yl) Rosiï vyrisheno zaprovadyty nove zvernenniā… [from Ukr.: It was decided to introduce a new address to the Statute of the Armed Forces of Russia…]. *Komsomol's'ka Pravda v Ukraïni* (from Ukr.: KP in Ukraine), 1 April, htt ps://kp.ua/ua/life/a647051-vijskovo-polovij-humor-i-vid-tajhi-do-britanskikh-moriv-rosijska-armija-vsikh-tupikh (accessed 16 August 2022).

Dralyuk, Boris. (2022). *The river's gone, the name remains.* Translation of Lina Kostenko's verse "*Shche nazva ye, a richky vzhe nemaye…*," *Twitter*, 5 December, https://twitter.com/BorisDralyuk/status/159983283619 8236160 (accessed 15 February 2023).

Druhyĭ (2015). Druhyĭ front Liny Kostenko [from Ukr.: The Second Front of Lina Kostenko]. *Holos Ukraïny: Hazeta Verkhovnoï Rady Ukraïny* [from Ukr.: Voice of Ukraine: Newspaper of the Verkhovna Rada of Ukraine], 21 March, http://www.golos.com.ua/article/253032 (accessed 15 February 2023).

Durova, Dar'ia. (2022). Khoteli na Ukrainu, a poshli na***: v seti pokazali, kak "privetstvuiūt" v Odesse okkupantov. Foto [from Russ.: They wanted to go to Ukraine but went to ***: the network showed how the invaders are "welcomed" in Odessa. A photo]. *Obozrevatel*, 10 March, https://war.obozrevatel.com/hoteli-na-ukrainu-a-poshli-na -v-seti-pokazali-kak-privetstvuyut-v-odesse-okkupantov-foto.htm (accessed 15 August 2022).

Dzyuba, Oleksiy. (2022). Rosiiāny nam ne druzi. Bo druzi na dorozi ne valiāiūt'siā. Ukraïntsī prodovzhuiūt' vluchno zhartuvaty pid chas viĭny z rosiieiū [from Ukr.: Russians are not our friends, because friends do not lie on the road. Ukrainians continue to make apt jokes during the war with Russia]." 3 April, https://dev.ua/news/rosiian y-nam-ne-druzi-bo-druzi-na-dorozi-ne-valiaiutsia-ukarintsi-prodov zhuiut-vluchno-zhartuvaty-pid-chas-viiny-z-rosiieiu-1648969133 (accessed 17 August 2022).

Eggers, Dave. (2023). The profound defiance of daily life in Kyiv: In the capital, Ukrainians track the trajectory of Russian missiles on smartphone apps, but refuse to be defeated by fear. *The New Yorker*, 5 January, https://www.newyorker.com/news/dispatch/the-profo und-defiance-of-daily-life-in-kyiv (accessed 15 March 2023).

Epstein, Mikhail. (2017). *Schizofascism.* In *Proėktivnyĭ slovar' gumanitarnykh nauk* [from Russ.: Projective Dictionary of the Humanities], Epstein, Mikhail (ed). Moscow: Novoe literaturnoe obozrenie, 261–262.

Horhol'-Ihnat'iĕva, Olena. (2022). Ukradena vesna (I bude myr... I vyshni zatsvitut'...) [from Ukr.: A Stolen Spring (And there will be peace and cherry blossoms…]. *Mala Storinka*, 31 March, https://mala.storinka.o rg/олена-горголь-ігнатьєва-вірш-украдена-весна-і-буде-мир.ht ml (accessed 5 January 2023).

Horne, John & Kramer, Alan. (2001). *German atrocities, 1914: A history of denial*. Yale University Press.

Iz Rossii. (2022). Iz Rossii: "Kiev ne vziᾱli. Vziᾱli miᾱsorubku, mikser i krossovki." Sotᵴ̄seti—o marodërstve rossiïskikh voennykh [from Russ.: From Russia: "Kyiv was not taken. We took a meat grinder, a mixer, and sneakers." Social networks about the looting of the Russian military]." *Radio Liberty*, 6 April, https://ru.krymr.com/a/rossiya-ukraina-voyna-maro derstvo/31789005.html (accessed 17 August 2022).

Iūliiᾱ Bondarenko. ([2021] 2022). Philolohichne prokliᾱttiᾱ "russkoho mira"… [A philological curse of the "russian world"…] *Facebook*, 19 April, https://www.facebook.com/permalink.php?story_fbid=pfbi d02bFiovUFcRkeETC3NCdyEVFfZzKp4JCw5Ay8dAiMQKqmPkgk 5F4WqQQURMjPAjD6rl&id=100001539589047 (accessed 17 August 2022).

Jerry Avenaim. (2022). How this will end for Putin. *Twitter*, 1 March, https://twitter.com/avenaim/status/1498774563563339781 (accessed 4 February 2023).

Kak pravil'no. (N.d.). Kak pravil'no "pobediῡ," "pobezħu" ili "pobezħdu"? [from Russ.: What is the correct word for "I will win"?]. Как правильно "победю", "побежу" или "побежду"? (accessed 15 August 2022).

Khar'kov vziᾱli? (2022). Khar'kov vziᾱli?—Net… [from Russian: Did they take Kharkov?—No. …]. *Idaprikol*, 6 April, https://idaprikol.ru/pict ure/xarkov-vziali-net-kiev-vziali-net-a-cto-vziali-miasorubku-yizdF uHS9 (accessed 15 August 2022).

Kolobok. (2022). Svezhiῐ anekdot: Kiev vziᾱli?… [A fresh anecdote: Did they take Kiev? …]. *Twitter*, 2 April, https://twitter.com/kolobokushka (accessed 16 August 2022).

Koly. (2022). "Koly nam pokh#ῐ, to strashno vsim": iᾱkymy novymy slovamy ta vyrazamy popovnyvsiᾱ ukraïns'kyῐ fol'klor pid chas viῐny [from Ukr.: "When we don't f#cking care, it's scary for everyone:" What new words and expressions were added to Ukrainian folklore during the war]. *Typovyῐ Kyiv / Tipichnyῐ Kiev* [Typical Kyiv], 1 March, https://typical.kiev.ua/bez-kategori%D1%97/koly-nam-pohuj-to-s trashno-vsim-yakymy-novymy-slovamy-ta-vyrazamy-popovnyvsya -ukrayinskyj-folklor-pid-chas-vijny/ (accessed 15 August 2022).

Kormych, Borys & Malyarenko, Tetyana. (2022). Ukraine: The thin red line between freedom and perishing. *Focus Ukraine*: A blog of the Kennan Institute, 12 April, https://www.wilsoncenter.org/blog-post/ukrai ne-thin-red-line-between-freedom-and-perishing?utm_campaign=ki &utm_medium=email&utm_source=newsletter&emci=322f3a74-25 bc-ec11-997e-281878b83d8a&emdi=e669d8da-35bc-ec11-997e-281878 b83d8a&ceid=194090 (accessed 17 August 2022).

Kume. (2022). Kume, a znaiēte, iāk anhliïs'koiū skazaty "rosiïs'ki viïs'ka"?... [from Ukr.: My crony, dost thou know how to say "Russian troops" in English? ...]." *News of Zakarpattia*, 26 March, http://novzak.uz.ua/news/smijmosya-razom-164/ (accessed 16 August 2022).

Maksymiv, Sofiya. (2022). How humor helps Ukrainians withstand war atrocities. *UkraineWorld*, 21 July, https://ukraineworld.org/articles/opinions/how-humor-helps-ukrainians (accessed 16 August 2022).

Martyniuk, V. (ed). (2018). Hibrydni zahrozy Ukraini i suspil'na bezpeka. Dosvid YeEs i Skhidnoho partnerstva. Analitychnyï dokument [from Ukr.: Hybrid threats to Ukraine and public safety. Experience of the EU and the Eastern Partnership. Analytical document]. Kerivnyk proektu: V. Martyniuk. Ekspertna hrupa proektu: M. Honchar, A. Chubyk, S. Zhuk, O. Chyzhova, H. Maksak, Yu. Tyshchenko, O. Zvarych [from Ukr.: Project manager: V. Martyniuk. Project expert group: M. Honchar, A. Chubyk, S. Zhuk, O. Chyzhova, H. Maksak, Yu. Tyshchenko, O. Zvarych]. Kyiv: Center for Global Studies "Strategy XXI."

Matloff, Judith. (2022). Ukraine's latest weapon in the war: Jokes. *"We choose to see things through a comic lens. That makes it easier to live through drastic situations."* Al Jazeera, 6 September, https://www.aljazeera.co m/features/2022/9/6/ukraine-latest-weapon-in-the-war-jokes (accessed 5 January 2023).

McDonald, Christie (ed). (1995). *The ear of the Other: Otobiography, transference, translation: Texts and discussions with Jacques Derrida*. English translation by Peggy Kamuf. Lincoln and London: University of Nebraska Press.

Moskovyty. (2022). Moskovyty nam ne druzi. Bo druzi na dorozi ne valiāiūt'siā [from Ukr.: Muscovites are not our friends. Because friends don't lie on the road]. *Persha pryvatna memarnya on Twitter* [The First Private Museum of Memes on Twitter], 3 March, https://t witter.com/2pryvatmemarnya/status/1499362769963032576?lang= en (accessed 17 August 2022).

Naukovo-mystets'kyï. (2022). Naukovo-mystets'kyï forum "Muzy ne movchat'!" [from Ukr.: Scientific and artistic forum "The muses are not silent!", 20-25 June, https://padlet.com/wixengblog/671uiua3c dhch1c8 (accessed 18 August 2022).

Nazvaly. (2021). Nazvaly viĭnu viĭnoiu: Rada ukhvalyla zaiāvu pro eskalatsiiū rosiĭs'ko-ukraïns'koho konfliktu [from Ukr.: The war was called a war: the Rada adopted a Declaration on the escalation of the Russian-Ukrainian conflict]. *Hlyboka.Info*, 30 March, https://lb.ua/ne ws/2021/03/30/481114_nazvali_viynu_viynoyu_rada_uhvalila.ht ml (accessed 17 August 2022).

Novak, Dan. (2022). Humor helps Ukrainians deal with war, *VOA Learning English*, 19 June, https://learningenglish.voanews.com/a/humor-he lps-ukrainians-deal-with-war/6618420.html (accessed 18 August 2022).

Opanasyk, Myroslava. (2022). Ukrainian cartoonists merciless in Putin takedowns & portrayals of war. *Geneva Solutions*, 17 June, updated 21 June, https://genevasolutions.news/ukraine-stories/ukrainian-cart oonists-merciless-in-putin-takedowns-portrayals-of-war (accessed 18 August 2022).

Orwell, George, Hitchens, Christopher & Heath, A. M. (2003). *Animal Farm and 1984*. New York: Houghton Mifflin Harcourt.

Pam'iātnyk. (2021). Pam'iātnyk "Volodymyr Lenin zasnovuiē Ukraïnu" (bronza, hranit, Al'tšheĭmer) [from Ukr.: The Monument "Vladimir Lenin founds Ukraine" (bronze, granite, Alzheimer's)]. Facebook page, 23 December, https://www.facebook.com/ProtsyshynOfficial /photos/a.510481825815864/1735133123350722/ (accessed 17 August 2022).

Pikulina, Karina. (2022). Lini Kostenko—92: pronyzlyvi virshi ta tsytaty pro viĭnu. 19 bereznya v umovakh viĭny vydatna ukrayins'ka poetesa Lina Kostenko svyatkuye sviy den' narodzhennya [from Ukr.: Lina Kostenko is 92: poignant poems and quotes about war. On 19 March, in the conditions of war, the outstanding Ukrainian poet Lina Kostenko celebrates her birthday]. *UNIAN*, 19 March, https://www. unian.ua/society/lina-kostenko-svyatkuye-92-den-narodzhennya-v irshi-i-citati-pro-viynu-novini-ukrajini-11750761.html (accessed 5 February 2023).

Pobachyvshy. (2022). Pobachyvshy "Bayraktar," rosiĭs'kyĭ tank prykynuvsiā mertvym [from Ukr.: Seeing the *Bayraktar*, the Russian tank pretended to be dead]. *YHIAH [UNIAN]*, 14 March, https://ww w.facebook.com/UNIAN.ua/photos/a.362897783771953/51039549 22999525/?type=3 (accessed 18 August 2022).

Poslovitsȳ. (n.d.). Poslovitsȳ i pogovorki pro den'gi [from Russ.: Proverbs and sayings about money]. https://sbornik-mudrosti.ru/poslovicy-i-pogovorki-pro-dengi/ (accessed 16 August 2022).

252 Lada Kolomiyets

Potopliăk, Halyna. (2022). *Koly zakinchytsiā viĭna...* [from Ukr.: When the war ends...]. Avtors'ka poeziiā Halyny Potopliăk [Author's poetry by Halyna Potopliăk], 23 August, https://www.facebook.com/groups /1023142351408398/posts/1987857168270240/ (accessed 3 January 2023).

Pysanky. (2015). Pysanky nastupal'ni: biĭtsī ATO rozmal'ovuiūt' Velykodnimy maliūnkamy hranaty [from Ukr.: The offensive Easter eggs: The ATO fighters paint grenades with Easter patterns]. *TCH [TSN]*, 11 April, https://tsn.ua/ato/pisanki-nastupalni-biyci-ato-rozmalovuy ut-velikodnimi-malyunkami-granati-420868.html (accessed 18 August 2022).

Rashyzm. (2022). Rashyzm teper maiē svoiū ofitsiĭnu storinku u "Vikipediï." [from Ukr.: Ruscism now has its official Wikipedia page], *TCH [TSN]*, 19 April, https://tsn.ua/ato/rashizm-teper-maye-svoyu -oficiynu-storinku-u-vikipediyi-2041099.html (accessed 17 August 2022).

Rebryna, Vadym. (2022). Rada vyznala Rosiiū neonatsysts'koiū derzhavoiū-terorystom ta zaboronyla ïï propahandu [from Ukr.: The Council recognized Russia as a neo-Nazi terrorist state and banned its propaganda]. *LIHA.NOVYNY.* Informatsiĭne ahenstvo LIHABiznesinform. LIHA.NEWS. LihaBusinessInform News Agency, 14 April, https://news.liga.net/ua/politics/news/rada-pri znala-rossiyu-neonatsistskim-gosudarstvom-terroristom-i-zapretila-ego-propagandu (accessed 14 August 2022).

Reddit. (2022a). *Reddit Zahabec: Ukrainian Memes,* https://www.reddit.com /r/UkrainianMemes/comments/tpo18j/zahabec/ (accessed 4 February 2023).

Reddit. (2022b). *Reddit Zahabec: ArtForUkraine,* https://www.reddit.com/r /ArtForUkraine/ (accessed 4 February 2023).

Serov, Vadim (ed). (2003). *Encyclopedic dictionary of catchy words and expressions.* Moscow: "Lokid-Press."

Shaw, Charles. (2022). Ukraine's caustic wartime humor has surprising Soviet roots: The memes and YouTube videos represent a legacy reclaimed. *Slate* (Published by the Slate Group, a Graham Holdings Company), 3 May, https://slate.com/news-and-politics/2022/05/u kraine-wartime-humor-soviet-union-history.html (accessed 14 August 2022).

Shuvalova, Iryna. (2022). "Moskal's," "Separs," and "Vatniks:" The many faces of the enemy in the Ukrainian satirical songs of the war in the Donbas. *East/West: Journal of Ukrainian Studies*, Vol. IX, No. 1: 177-200, DOI: https://doi.org/10.21226/ewjus590

Shuvalova, Iryna. (2020). *Voices of the war in Donbas: exploring identities in the affected communities through the prism of war songs* (Doctoral dissertation, University of Cambridge).

Smith, Leonard V. (2007). The "Culture de guerre" and French historiography of the Great War of 1914–1918. *History Compass* 5 (6): 1967–1979.

Snyder, Timothy. (2022a). The war in Ukraine has unleashed a new word: In a creative play on three different languages, Ukrainians identify an enemy: "ruscism." *The New York Times*, 22 April, https://www.nytimes.com/2022/04/22/magazine/ruscism-ukraine-russia-war.html (accessed 16 August 2022).

Snyder, Timothy. (2022b). Шизофашизм России: единственный выход для РФ — проиграть войну против Украины [from Russ.: Schizofascism of Russia: the only way out for the Russian Federation is to lose the war against Ukraine]. *LIGA.net*, 9 June, https://www.liga.net/politics/opinion/shizofashizm-rossii-edinstvennyy-vyhod-dlya-rf-proigrat-voynu-protiv-ukrainy (accessed 17 August 2022).

Sofie. (2022). Znaiете, chomu rosiiа̄ny nam ne druzi? [from Ukr.: Do you know why Russians are not our friends?]. *Twitter*, 4 March, https://twitter.com/seuluum/status/1499714082886275076 (accessed 17 August 2022).

Sophie Muraly. (2022). Oberezћno y#bnutyĭ susid [from Ukr.: Careful: a f#cked-up neighbor]. *Facebook*, 16 April, https://www.facebook.com/sophie.shc/photos/a.2005602576359254/3061683237417844/ (accessed 15 August 2022).

Sukovata, Viktoriya. (2017). In the context of Bakhtin's philosophy of laughter and the post-colonial perspective: Ukrainian popular culture. *Baltic Worlds*, 1-2: 57-65.

Transport of Kiev. (2022). Tut liūdi interesuiūtsiā, letaet li Bayraktar Airlines iz Kieva na Moskvu [from Russ.: We got people interested in whether Bayraktar Airlines fly from Kiev to Moscow]. *Facebook*, 6 April, avianews.com — Aviation Today, https://www.facebook.com/avianews/photos/a.180681061971742/5282029585170172/?type=3&eid=ARCfmuQSt8CA1k1-cQTQSKsswCEfjTC2tLsEGJ-Gi1yeZGKT-JnMOIo843c7N0XSVz2X-xzwQ6zzui8T (accessed 14 August 2022).

Tys, Alina. (2022). S'ohodni — Den' bavovny: ukrayintsi pomityly pohanyy znak dlya putina. U tsey den' dyktator vidznachaye den' narodzhennya [from Ukr.: Today is Cotton Day: Ukrainians saw a bad sign for Putin. On this day, the dictator celebrates his birthday]. Radio Track: *NOVYNY* [NEWS], 7 October, https://radiotrek.rv.ua/news/sogodni---den-bavovni-ukrayinci-pomitili-poganiy-znak-dlya-putina_296261.html (accessed 1 February 2023).

Ukrainian Memes Forces @uamemesforces https://twitter.com/uamemes forces (accessed 1 February 2023).

Ukrainians. (2022). Ukrainians are greeting Russian liberators with flowers! *Tweeter*, 11 March, https://twitter.com/uamemesforces/status/1502348587421913091 (accessed 4 February 2023).

Vakhromova, Olha. (2022a). *Between them all we suffer the damnation*. Translation of Lina Kostenko's verse *"Rozp'yato nas mizh zakhodom i skhodom…,"* 26 April, https://lyricstranslate.com (accessed 24 January 2023).

Vakhromova, Olha. (2022b). *Their satan plannings always were much rougher…* Translation of Lina Kostenko's verse *"Tse zh treba maty satanyns'kyy namir…"* 26 April, https://lyricstranslate.com (accessed 24 January 2023).

Vasily Grogol. (2022). Special military operation and peace. *Instagram*, https://www.instagram.com/vasilygrogol/ (accessed 4 February 2023).

Warriors. (2022). *Warriors we are. No lazy. No inert*. A stanza by Lina Kostenko *"My voïny. Ne ledari. Ne lezhni…"* in anonymous translation. HB to our legend Lina Kostenko; Ukraine/Україна (@Ukraine) Ukraine Government Organization, March 19, https://twitter.com/Ukraine/status/1505302141174525952; reprint Ukrainian Catholic University (UCU_University), 23 May, https://twitter.com/ucu_university/status/1528629377453305857?lang=en (accessed 4 January 2023).

Wodak, Ruth & Meyer, Michael. (2012). *Methods of critical discourse analysis*. London: SAGE Publications Ltd.

Yarmolenko, Nataliya. (2022a). Internet-fol'klor rosiys'ko-ukrayins'koyi viïny: tradytsiyi ta novatorstvo [from Ukr.: Internet folklore of the Russian-Ukrainian war: traditions and innovation]. Lecture from the educational series. Bohdan Khmelnytskyi Cherkasy National University, 12 May, https://cdu.edu.ua/news/prosvitnytska-lektsiia-internet-folklor-rosiisko-ukrainskoi-viiny-tradytsii-ta-novatorstvo.html; http://ufck.univer.ck.ua/portfolios/item/1261-nataliia-yarmolenko-provela-vidkrytu-lektsiiu-pro-internetfolklor-pid-chas-viiny.html (accessed 19 August 2022).

Yarmolenko, Nataliya. (2022b). Internetlor rosiïs'ko-ukraïns'koï viïny: zhanrova ta siūzhetno-tematychna kharakterystyky [from Ukr.: Internet Folklore of the Russo-Ukrainian war: genre and plot-thematic characteristics]. Lecture-presentation. 21 June. Scientific and artistic forum "Muzy ne movchat'!" [from Ukr.: The muses are not silent!], 20-25 June, https://padlet.com/wixengblog/671uiua3cdhch1c8 (accessed 18 August 2022).

Yak umru. (2022). Yak umru, to pokhovaĭte / Mene v kupi hnoiū… [from Ukr.: When I die, bury me / In a pile of manure…]. *Defense of Ukraine on Twitter*, 1 May, https://twitter.com/defenceu/status/1520732243 785924614?lang=ar-x-fm (accessed 15 August 2022).

Yurchak, Alexei. (2005). *Everything was forever, until it was no more: The last Soviet generation*. Princeton, New Jersey: Princeton University Press.

Yurchak, Alexei. (2014). *Èto bylo navsegda, poka ne konchilos'. Poslednee sovetskoe pokolenie*. [from Russ.: Everything was forever, until it was no more: The last Soviet generation] Predisl. A. Beliāeva; per. s angl. [from Russ.: foreword by A. Beliāev; transl. from English]. Moscow: Novoe literaturnoe obozrenie.

Zakhar. (2022). Chomu ne mozħna voiūvaty z ukraïntsīāmy? [from Ukr.: Why shouldn't one fight with Ukrainians?]. *YouTube*, 12 April, https://www.youtube.com/user/navsi100zakhar (accessed 14 August 2022).

Занавес. (n.d.). Занавес [from Russ.: The show's all over, clear out]. *Telegram channel Занавес*, https://telemetr.io/en/channels/1736863111-zanaves0 (accessed 17 August 2022).

Zbirnyk. (2022a). Zbirnyk ukraïns'kykh anekdotiv №4802 [from Ukr.: Collection of Ukrainian jokes #4802], https://rozdil.lviv.ua/anekdot/an ekdot.php?id=4802 (accessed 16 August 2022).

Zbirnyk. (2022b). Zbirnyk ukraïns'kykh anekdotiv №4919 [from Ukr.: Collection of Ukrainian jokes #4919], https://rozdil.lviv.ua/anekdot/an ekdot.php?id=4919 (accessed 14 August 2022).

Zbirnyk. (2022c). Zbirnyk ukraïns'kykh anekdotiv №5076 [from Ukr.: Collection of Ukrainian jokes #5076], https://rozdil.lviv.ua/anekdot/an ekdot.php?id=5076 (accessed 15 August 2022).

Zbirnyk. (2022d). Zbirnyk ukraïns'kykh anekdotiv №556 [from Ukr.: Collection of Ukrainian jokes #556], https://rozdil.lviv.ua/anekdot/ane kdot.php?id=556 (accessed 16 August 2022).

Conclusion

Future Perspectives on Language and Power in Ukraine and Kazakhstan

Bridget Goodman

The purpose of this chapter is twofold. First, I will reflect on the lessons regarding historical and present language and power in Ukraine and Kazakhstan highlighted by the authors in this volume. After that, I will suggest directions for future research and policy on languages and power in Ukraine and Kazakhstan — directions which may also be of benefit in other countries of Eurasia and Central Asia.

Looking Back

First and foremost, it is clear from reading these chapters that it is difficult to reflect on the nature of language and power in Ukraine and Kazakhstan without considering the past role of the Soviet Union and the Russian language. As in many postcolonial contexts (e.g. English in Hong Kong or French in Morocco), the language of the Russian or Soviet colonizing power continues to occupy a meaningful place for communication in both Ukrainian and Kazakh societies. While ostensibly the power of Russian has decreased since the beginning of independence in the 1990s, in practice positioning the Ukrainian and Kazakh languages in equally or greater powerful positions in society compared to Russian is still a discursive and ideological struggle of development or strengthening of national identity. Meanwhile, the effortless continuation of Russian is a consequence and a legacy of the historical power of the Russian language.

Despite the challenges of supporting Ukrainian and Kazakh, the authors in this volume have shown innovative spaces that exist and can be created to support these languages and associated identities. Vardanian has shown that translation of literature has historically served to promote Soviet or Russian empiring ideology, but these translations can be revisited and reworked to connect better to both the original source and to modern Ukraine. Kolomiyets also sees value in translation of digital writings as a means of asserting Ukrainian identity. Like Kolomiyets, Nedashkivska shows how social media is a space for developing and reclaiming Ukrainian identity. Within the social spaces identified by both Kolomiyets and Nedashkivska, support of particular language forms becomes ideologically indexed to prestigious and modern brands or rebrands of identity. Conversely, rejection of language forms suggests a desire to adhere to current norms and values. Humor is shown in these studies to play an equally important role in asserting one's language ideology about Ukraine and the Ukrainian language, and defusing the power of the Russian language and its speakers from Russia (see also Bilaniuk 2024; Goodman 2024).

Other authors in this volume highlight the diversity of language, power, ideologies and practices at different scales of society. Soroka, Kudriavtseva and Danylenko in Ukraine and Ahn and Smagulova in Kazakhstan show that while societal tendencies are towards supporting the titular language and asserting the titular language as the language of identity, home language practices may still support the use of the Russian language or of mixing the titular language and Russian. While such practices have likely been ongoing for decades, the documentation of attitudes and practices is enhanced by an explicit awareness of diverse practices in diverse spaces.

Education is shown in this volume to be both a key space for development of language use, and a space that requires a response to further questions about how to ideologically and politically support languages and identities. In Ukraine, Melnyk argues that "language matters" but the language that matters is first and foremost Ukrainian, even in schools that offer minority languages as a language of instruction—including Russian as the language of a national minority. In Kazakhstan, Ahn and Smagulova demonstrate that while officially there is a choice between Kazakh and Russian as languages of instruction, and ideological reasons to support Kazakh-medium instruction as the language of identity development, parents may still prefer to send their children to Russian-medium schools. In both contexts, parents are confronted with a choice: a) deny their children development of the language of their national identity — the minority language in Ukraine or Kazakh in Kazakhstan; or b) deny their children further access to education and economic benefits through study in the language of power — now Ukrainian in Ukraine or Russian in Kazakhstan. Overall, these choices point to continued potential for inequalities among youth based on the choice and quality of instruction in their preferred language.

Moving Forward

I suggest two main approaches for researchers and policymakers to take in the next five years to continue to understand the interplay of language ideologies, power, and identity formation in Ukraine and Kazakhstan. First, researchers need to conduct national-level studies to see if ideologically there continues to be shifts away from the Russian language towards the titular languages. At the same time, such research needs to allow space for the range of language repertoires and language practices respondents may still engage in — practices which may or may not be aligned with stated national or individual language ideologies. Sociological surveys as Soroka, Kudriavtseva and Danylenko conducted, social media reviews as Kolomiyets and Nedashkivska conducted, and examinations of literature in translation as Vardanian conducted have been shown in this volume to be effective approaches for understanding national language tendencies.

When reporting results of such studies to policymakers, it will be important for researchers to highlight the distinctions between a) speakers who make agentive choices to use Ukrainian or Kazakh, or to mix their language with Russian, and b) speakers who feel they are not empowered to use Russian or any other national language in a particular context. Politically, it is important to refute propaganda suggesting Russian speakers' rights are being violated.

At the same time, it is important from a human rights perspective not to sweep reports of discrimination or inequality for any group under the rug.

A second direction not explored in the papers in this volume regarding education is direct observation or interviews with school staff about language ideologies and practices in the classroom. Research in Ukraine and Kazakhstan prior to the 2022 war is mixed on whether language practices in classrooms is focused on nation building through target language use (Friedman 2010), or can be multilingual, fluid and not necessarily aligned with monolingual, target-language of instruction-only goals (Goodman 2017; Wheeler 2017). While it may be difficult to safely access classrooms in Ukraine in the midst of war, it is the classroom practices and the uptake of those practices which can shape how language ideologies impact language learning, language use, and identity.

Bibliography:

Bilaniuk, Laada. (2024). Memes as antibodies: creativity and resilience in the face of Russia's war. In *Dispossession: Anthropological perspectives on Russia's war against Ukraine*, Wanner, Catherine (ed). New York: Routledge, 143–166.

Friedman, Debra A. (2010). Speaking correctly: error correction as language socialization practice in a Ukrainian classroom. *Applied Linguistics* 31(3): 346–367.

Goodman, Bridget. (2017). The ecology of language and translanguaging in a Ukrainian university. In *Translanguaging practices in higher education: beyond monolingual ideologies*, Mazak, Catherine M. and Carroll, Kevin S. (eds). Bristol: Multilingual Matters, 50–69.

Goodman, Bridget. (2024). "Russian warship, go f*ck yourself": circulating social media discourses in the 2022 Russia-Ukraine war. In *Dispossession: imperial legacies and Russia's war on Ukraine*, Wanner, Catherine (ed). New York: Routledge, 167–187.

Wheeler, L. (2017). *A linguistic ethnographic perspective on Kazakhstan's trinity of languages: language ideologies and identities in a multilingual university community.* Unpublished doctoral dissertation. University of Birmingham

Our Authors

Elise S. Ahn, PhD is the Founding Director of the International Projects Office at the University of Wisconsin–Madison. Before coming to UW–Madison, Elise worked at KIMEP University (Almaty, Kazakhstan) as an assistant professor and the director of a master's degree program in Teaching English to Speakers of Other Languages. She has numerous publications in journals like the *Journal of Language, Identity, and Education* and *World Englishes.* She is also the editor for the *Wisconsin in the World: Internationalization at the University of Wisconsin–Madison* and *Language Change in Central Asia.* She conducts research revolving around the intersection of human geography and language and education policy and planning processes; internationalization in education policy production and reform; internationalization of (higher) education; and program evaluation with a focus on Turkey and Central Asia. More information may be found at Dr. Ahn's website (elisesahn.com).

Laada Bilaniuk is a Professor in the Department of Anthropology at the University of Washington, Seattle, USA. She received her PhD in Anthropology from the University of Michigan. Her research interests include language politics and language ideology, purism and mixed languages, identity, nationalism, and popular culture. Her book, *Contested Tongues: Language Politics and Cultural Correction in Ukraine* (Cornell University Press, 2005) draws on ethnographic fieldwork and historical sources to untangle the complex sociolinguistic situation in Ukraine. Her recent publications include "Memes as antibodies: Creativity and resilience in the face of Russia's war," in *Dispossession: Anthropological Perspectives on Russia's War Against Ukraine* (Catherine Wanner, e.d., Routledge, 2024), and the journal articles "The trajectory of language laws in Ukraine: inclusions and omissions in naming and categorization since 1989" (*Acta Slavica Iaponica*, 2022), "Linguistic conversions: Nation-building on the self" (*Journal of Soviet and Post-Soviet Politics and Societies*, 2020), "Purism and pluralism: Language use trends in popular culture in Ukraine since independence," (*Harvard Ukrainian Studies*,

2017), and "Race, media, and postcoloniality: Ukraine between nationalism and cosmopolitanism" (*City & Society*, 2016). She is currently working on a book on the politics of popular culture in Ukraine.

Ihor Danylenko is Senior Lecturer at the Department of Methods of Sociological Research, the School of Sociology at V. N. Karazin Kharkiv National University (Ukraine), and a senior researcher at the V. N. Karazin Kharkiv National University Social and Humanitarian Research Centre. He has more than twenty years of experience as a sociologist at the department of methods of sociological research. As a practical researcher, he has participated in more than a hundred different projects, including such international research project as ENRI-EAST "Interplay of European, National and Regional Identities: Nations between States along the New Eastern Borders of the European Union" (2008–2012), HITT-CIS "Health in Times of Transition: Trends in Population Health and Health Policies in CIS Countries" (2009–2013), TRUEDEM "Trust in European Democracies" (2023–2025). His research interests and practical work fall into the fields of making and managing sociological / marketing / electoral projects, working as a social analyst in statistical packages and creating reports based on data storytelling.

Debra A. Friedman is Associate Professor of Second Language Studies at Indiana University Bloomington, USA. Her research focuses on the social, cultural and ideological aspects of language education in multilingual communities through the framework of language socialization. Her work on the role of language teaching in the revitalization of the Ukrainian language and the construction of national identity has been published in *Applied Linguistics, Annual Review of Applied Linguistics, Journal of Language, Identity, and Education, International Journal of Multilingualism* and several edited volumes. She is the author of *Understanding, evaluating, and conducting second language writing research* (2017) (with Charlene Polio of Michigan State University) and *Researching second language classrooms: Qualitative and mixed methods approaches* (in progress).

OUR AUTHORS 263

Bridget Goodman is Associate Professor of Multilingual Education at Nazarbayev University Graduate School of Education. She holds an MSEd in Teaching English to Speakers of Other Languages (TESOL) and a PhD in Educational Linguistics from the University of Pennsylvania. Her teaching and research interests include English Medium Education (EME) policy and practice in Ukraine and Kazakhstan, the ecology of language in Ukraine and Kazakhstan, and discourse analysis of social media. She has published on these topics in journals such as *International Journal of the Sociology of Language*, *TESOL Quarterly*, *Anthropology and Education Quarterly*, and numerous edited books. Her most recent publication on Ukraine appeared in the 2024 book *Dispossession* edited by Catherine Wanner.

Lada Kolomiyets is Doctor of Science in Translation Studies, Professor at the Taras Shevchenko National University of Kyiv, currently Visiting Professor at Dartmouth College (USA). Fulbright scholar at the University of Iowa (1996/97) and Pennsylvania State University (2017/18). An interdisciplinary researcher in literature, folklore, and translation studies, with three monographs, several textbooks for graduate students, literary anthologies, numerous chapters in collective volumes and articles in the leading peer-reviewed journals. Her books include monographs *Conceptual and Methodological Grounds of Contemporary Ukrainian Translations of British, Irish, and North American Poetry* (2004) and *Ukrainian Literary Translation and Translators in the 1920s-30s* (2013, 2nd ed. 2015), book chapters in *Translation Studies in Ukraine as an Integral Part of the European Context* (2023), *Translation under Communism* (2022), *Translation and Power* (2020), etc. She has held fellowships at Wenner-Gren Foundations, the Harris Distinguished Professorship Foundation, and others.

Natalia Kudriavtseva is Professor of Translation and Slavic Studies at Kryvyi Rih State Pedagogical University, Ukraine, and currently a fellow at the Centre for Advanced Study Sofia, Bulgaria. Her research focuses on Ukraine's language and education policies and grassroots language activism after 2014, as well as the post-2014 shift to Ukrainian among Ukraine's L1 speakers of Russian. She has authored articles and analyses in the *Journal of Multilingual and Multicultural Development*, the *Ideology and Politics Journal*, the Kennan Institute's *Focus Ukraine* blog and Germany-based *Ukraine-Analysen* and *Ukrainian Analytical Digest*. Her book chapters appeared in *Inventing Majorities. Ideological Creativity in Post-Soviet Societies* (Ibidem Verlag 2022) and *Teaching and Learning Resources for Endangered Languages* (Brill 2023). She has been a member of editorial boards of several international and Ukrainian academic journals and a fellow at the School for Advanced Study in the Social Sciences (EHESS) in Paris (2023), Hanse Institute for Advanced Study in Delmenhorst (2022-2023), Alfried Krupp Institute for Advanced Study Greifswald (2022), the University of Cambridge (2013) and Woodrow Wilson International Center for Scholars (2009).

Svitlana Melnyk is Senior Lecturer in the Department of Slavic and East European Languages and Cultures at Indiana University. She received her PhD-equivalent degree from the Department of Philology at Kyiv Taras Shevchenko University. Svitlana specializes in sociolinguistics and bilingualism. She has co-authored *Linguistic and Ethnic Diversity of Ukraine* (2010, in Ukrainian) as well as a number of articles examining language policy in Ukraine published in the *International Journal of Bilingual Education and Bilingualism, Bilingualism* and others. Her research also includes language pedagogy as well as the issue of the impact of the Russo-Ukrainian war on the Ukrainian language and communication.

Alla Nedashkivska is Professor of Slavic Applied Linguistics and the Ukrainian language program in the department of Modern Languages and Cultural Studies, and a former director of the Ukrainian Language Education Centre at the Canadian Institute of Ukrainian Studies at the University of Alberta. She publishes widely in the areas of Slavic linguistics, applied linguistics and sociolinguistics, studying political and media language, language ideologies, language identity, language attitudes and language practices, as well as language pedagogy and second language acquisition in Ukrainian. She authors Ukrainian language textbooks, one of which,

Ukrainian Through Its Living Culture (University of Alberta Press, 2010) has won the 2012 AATSEEL Book prize for "Best Contribution to Language Pedagogy," and another *Вікно у світ бізнесу: ділова українська мова / A Window into the World of Business: Ukrainian for Professional Communication* (University of Alberta Press/Pica Pica Press 2016) has received "The Inaugural University of Alberta Open Educational Resources Award" (2018). Her newest textbook project [with O. Sivachenko] *PodorozhiUA: Beginners' Ukrainian via the Blended-learning Model* is being finalized.

Juldyz Smagulova is Professor and Founding Dean of College of Human Sciences and Education at KIMEP University, Kazakhstan. She holds a Candidate of Philological Sciences degree from al-Farabi Kazakh National University and a PhD in Sociolinguistics from King's College London. Her research can be classified under three major interrelated strands: language ideology; language and education policy; and language pedagogy. These strands are held together by a common scholarly interest in multilingual contexts where different speakers have different access to linguistic and other resources. She is the co-author of *Language Change in Central Asia* (Mouton de Gruyter 2016) and the bilingual Kazakh-Russian *Dictionary of Sociolinguistics* (2020). She has more than twenty articles and book chapters published internationally and locally, including papers in journals such as *International Journal of Bilingualism, Journal of Sociolinguistics, International Journal of Bilingual Education and Bilingualism, World Englishes, International Journal of the Sociology of Language*, and *Journal of Eurasian Studies*.

Yuliia Soroka is Doctor of Science in Sociology, Professor at V. N. Karazin Kharkiv National University (Ukraine), and a senior researcher at the University of Fribourg (Switzerland). She is a sociologist of culture. Her research focuses on the processes in the symbolic space of Ukrainian society, culture and power relations. Her works on collective identities within pro-Euromaidan discourse, hate speech, dialogue as a social technology, discourse of Muslims in Ukrainian media, hostility towards IDPs, discourse of queer women in Ukrainian media were published in *Symbolic Interaction*

Journal, the *Ideology and Politics Journal*, *Sociology: Theory, Methods, Marketing Journal*, and other international and Ukrainian academic journals. She is the author of *The native, the strange, the different: a sociocultural perspective of perception of the Other* (Kharkiv 2012, in Ukrainian). She is a member of ASN (Association of the Study of Nationality), SAU (Sociological Association of Ukraine), and SWS (Sociologist for Women Society). She is a member of editorial boards of *Sociology: Theory, Methods and Marketing* and *Visnyk of V. N. Karazin Kharkiv National University. Series "Sociological studies of contemporary society: methodology, theory, methods."* She has been a fellow of the Fulbright Academic Exchange Program (2010), Scholars at Risk Program (2022-2024), and Gerda Henkel Foundation (2023-2024).

Maryna Vardanian is Professor of Translation and Slavic Studies at Kryvyi Rih State Pedagogical University (Ukraine), and Visiting Scholar at the Institute for Translation and Interpreting at Heidelberg University (Germany). Her major research interest is Ukrainian literature for children and young adults, including both Soviet and diasporic authors. Her current research project examines ideological approaches in translations of children's literature, the war and emigration via trauma studies, cultural memory studies and ecocriticism. She is the author of over seventy books, articles, papers, and book chapters published internationally and locally, including articles in international journals, such as *Children's Literature in Education, Ideology and Politics Journal, International Research in Children's Literature.* One of her latest book chapters, "Seeking Home, Discovering the Bush: The Australian Bush Envisaged in Ukrainian Children's Books" (co-authored with Lydia Kokkola), appeared as part of Palgrave Macmillan's series "Critical Approaches to Children's Literature" (2023). She is a member of several professional associations, such as International Research Society for Children's Literature, European Children's Literature Network and the Association for Slavic, East European, and Eurasian Studies.

Index

Academic Achievement 147, 155, 163

Adaptation 41, 67, 75, 89

Aesop 73

Africa 76, 77, 84, 85

Almaty 7, 22, 136, 137, 138, 142, 143, 144, 146, 148, 150, 151, 152, 154, 162, 163, 164, 165, 260

Andre Lefevere 61, 66

Aneta Pavlenko 32, 34, 57, 105, 133

Antonio Gramsci 17, 27

Asanova 162, 164

Asharshylyk 11

Assimilation 20, 35, 61, 65, 70, 72, 75, 80, 81, 89

Attribution, Iconization 168, 169, 178

Bavovna 218

Belarusian 171, 194, 198

Berestechko 240, 241, 242

Bilingual Linguistic Practices 101

Bortsi Za Voliu (Fighters For Freedom) 74

Cartoon 225, 230

Charles Clerice 75, 86

Charles Dickens 73

Chornobaïvka, A Suburban Village 220

Chornobyl Nuclear Power Plan 227

Classroom Practices 259

Colonial And Nation-Building Ideologies / Strategies In Translation 61, 68

Colonial Discourse 63, 72

Colony 21, 63, 70, 77, 83, 84, 90

Corinne A. Seals 37, 58, 106, 134

Corinne Seals 37, 58, 106, 134

Corrective Power 17, 20

Crimea 18, 19, 30, 34, 43, 106, 108, 213, 219, 226

Critical Discourse Analysis 16, 18, 24, 253

Critical Linguistics 16

Cultural Colonialism 61, 62, 69, 77

Cyberspace 201, 203, 204, 206, 208, 229, 240, 243

Daniel Defoe 73

Dark Humor 228

De Swann 164

Debra A. Friedman 7, 15, 24, 26, 30, 55, 104, 105, 132, 168, 259, 261

Debra Friedman 7, 15, 24, 26, 30, 55, 104, 105, 132, 168, 259, 261

Deconstruction 24, 200, 201, 206, 207, 212, 213, 240, 244

De-Russification 38, 173, 175, 185, 186

Digital / Cyber Folklore 24, 200, 201, 202, 204, 205, 206, 207, 220, 222, 224, 244, 245

Dirk Geeraerts 102, 132

Discourse 12, 16, 17, 25, 26, 57, 68, 74, 105, 107, 126, 128, 131, 138, 141, 191, 197, 198, 201, 211, 215, 244, 262, 264

Domestication 61, 66, 67, 83, 89, 90

Donbas 18, 19, 21, 22, 30, 34, 47, 106, 108, 113, 114, 127, 202, 235, 251, 252

Education Policy 18, 30, 35, 42, 53, 136, 162, 260, 264

English 12, 38, 44, 50, 62, 78, 82, 97, 99, 100, 101, 102, 103, 104, 110, 118, 119, 120, 121, 122, 123, 125, 126, 130, 145, 164, 205, 209, 213, 214, 215, 216, 225, 241, 242, 249, 250, 254, 256, 260, 262

Ethnic Composition 107, 142, 149

Euromaidan 18, 19, 24, 30, 34, 37, 56, 106, 264

Facebook 24, 41, 168, 180, 181, 182, 183, 187, 188, 189, 190, 192, 194, 195, 196, 204, 211, 218, 221, 222, 223, 231, 233, 235, 239, 240, 241, 248, 250, 252

Foreignization 61, 66, 67, 79, 89, 90

France 77

Free Ukrainian Language Courses 19, 49

French 20, 61, 62, 63, 75, 76, 77, 78, 81, 86, 89, 90, 91, 92, 99, 102, 118, 119, 219, 252, 256

Gabrielle Hogan-Brun 33, 55

Gentle Ukrainianization 39

George Orwell 209, 210, 250

Gideon Toury 61, 66

Great Britain 76, 81, 85, 86

Hans Christian Andersen 73

Hegemony 17, 20, 28, 99, 134

Holodomor 11, 73, 93

Homo Soveticus 70

Hong Kong 256

Identification 41, 62, 97, 104, 107, 110, 111, 114, 115, 128, 134

Identity 12, 15, 19, 20, 26, 27, 29, 33, 34, 37, 48, 56, 58, 62, 71, 72, 74, 77, 89, 102, 103, 105, 107, 128, 134, 163, 164, 165, 166, 170, 171, 175, 179, 180, 183, 184, 185, 194, 197, 198, 200, 202, 209, 256, 257, 258, 259, 260, 261, 263

Ideological Approach To Translation 63

Ideological Manipulation 63, 69, 91, 93

Ideology In Translation 89

Ildikó Orosz 30, 54

Inequality 12, 125, 138, 139, 161, 259

Instagram 24, 41, 168, 180, 181, 183, 187, 188, 189, 192, 194, 195, 204, 223, 253

István Csernicskó 30, 33, 34, 46, 54, 57, 106, 132

Ivan Dziuba 32, 54

Jacques Derrida 25, 201, 206, 207, 246, 249

Jaroslav Rudnytskyj 52, 58

John Stephens 64

Judith T. Irvine 65, 93, 101, 133, 179

Jules Verne 73, 77, 79

Kapitan Sorvi-Holova (Captain Daredevil) 79, 87

INDEX 269

Kathryn A. Woolard 21, 28, 65, 95, 99, 102, 105, 131, 134, 135, 168, 169, 195, 198

Kazakh 11, 12, 17, 22, 136, 137, 138, 139, 140, 141, 142, 143, 144, 145, 146, 147, 148, 149, 150, 151, 152, 153, 154, 155, 156, 157, 158, 159, 160, 161, 162, 164, 165, 166, 171, 256, 257, 258, 264

Kazakhstan 5, 7, 8, 11, 13, 15, 17, 18, 22, 26, 136, 137, 138, 139, 140, 141, 142, 146, 147, 150, 152, 154, 155, 161, 162, 163, 164, 165, 166, 256, 257, 258, 259, 260, 262, 264

Kharkiv Orthography 173

Kherson 45, 108, 113, 174, 181, 220

Kliasychnyi Pravopys 181, 182

Konstantin Polevoi 78, 87, 90, 91

Korean 149

Kyiv 38, 45, 49, 54, 55, 56, 57, 58, 91, 92, 94, 95, 108, 113, 114, 127, 133, 134, 174, 198, 204, 215, 217, 222, 223, 231, 235, 242, 247, 248, 249, 262, 263

Laada Bilaniuk 7, 9, 19, 26, 30, 31, 33, 41, 50, 52, 54, 105, 106, 132, 257, 259, 260

Language Attitudes 30, 37, 104, 133, 165, 263

Language Ideologies 20, 24, 25, 29, 30, 31, 36, 52, 61, 65, 69, 97, 133, 134, 168, 169, 170, 178, 183, 184, 198, 258, 259, 263

Language Ideology 9, 10, 13, 20, 50, 63, 64, 65, 70, 71, 72, 89, 98, 101, 102, 175, 184, 187, 257, 260, 264

Language Legislation 39, 47, 196

Language Policy 29, 31, 34, 36, 37, 47, 52, 55, 136, 137, 141, 142, 145, 165, 263

Language Practice 18, 21, 26, 27, 31, 34, 53, 65, 100, 108, 109, 111, 113, 114, 116, 117, 118, 123, 124, 133, 134, 171, 174, 175, 179, 191, 194, 195, 257, 258, 259, 263

Language Proficiency 38, 44, 97, 109, 110, 111, 118, 119, 120, 121, 122, 123, 126, 129, 136, 137, 161, 163

Language Repertoire 258

Language-In-Education Policy 19, 29, 30, 31, 35, 36, 43, 44, 46, 53, 163

Larysa Masenko 31, 32, 33, 56, 57, 104, 129, 133

Lawrence Venuti 61, 66

Le Capitaine Casse-Cou 20, 61, 63, 74, 75, 76, 79, 89, 91

Legitimate Language 21, 97, 98, 99, 100, 131, 134

Liliya Hrynevych 47, 48, 55, 59

Lina Kostenko 240, 241, 242, 243, 245, 247, 250, 253

Linguicide 29, 52, 57, 58

Linguistic Discrimination 98

Literacy 155, 160, 163

Literary Polysystems 69

Literature For Children And Young Adults 20, 61, 64, 91, 92, 265

Louis Boussenard 61, 63, 74, 77

Maksym Strikha 72

Margrethe B. Søvik 97, 100, 104, 134

Maria Tymoczko 66

Mark Twain 73

Marko Pavlyshyn 69

Max Weber 16, 28

Medium Of Instruction (MOI) 136, 137

Meme 189, 229, 230, 236, 246

Metropolis 21, 61, 63, 70, 77, 84, 90

Michel Foucault 17, 26

Migration 136, 137, 138, 141, 142, 148, 150, 162, 164, 166

Miguel De Cervantes 73

Mikhail Epstein 216, 247

Minority 12, 19, 29, 30, 32, 35, 36, 42, 43, 44, 45, 47, 48, 53, 56, 57, 71, 139, 140, 162, 257

Minority Language Education 30, 53

Mocking Neologism 213, 214, 215

Monica Heller 16, 27, 99, 133

Monolingual Linguistic Practices 98, 100, 101, 107, 112, 113, 123, 126, 127, 131

Morocco 256

Mykola Riabchuk 32, 38, 58

Natalia Kudriavtseva 5, 7, 15, 19, 21, 27, 30, 37, 38, 44, 49, 55, 56, 97, 105, 106, 133, 257, 258, 262

Nataliya Yarmolenko 200, 202, 253

Nationality 12, 90, 110, 114, 115, 128

Native Language 41, 43, 44, 73, 141, 192

Neo-Imperial Newspeak 206

Neologization 25, 220, 244

Norms Of Translation 61, 66

Orthography 23, 27, 32, 168, 169, 171, 173, 174, 175, 178, 180, 181, 182, 183, 185, 188, 192, 197, 198

Parodistic Translation 24, 200, 202, 205, 206, 207, 213, 244, 245

Paul Kroskrity 25, 27, 93, 102, 133, 135, 178, 197

Paul Magocsi 31, 56

Peter Hollindale 64

Pierre Bourdieu 17, 21, 26, 97, 98, 99, 100, 102, 131, 132, 134

Pisa 147, 155

Poetic Mystification 200, 201, 206, 240, 243, 245

Postcolonial Theory 61, 90, 95

Post-Soviet 10, 11, 17, 32, 40, 49, 56, 63, 165, 222

Power And Translation 61

Pravopys 73, 94, 169, 172, 173, 174, 181, 182, 197, 198

Proty Pravopysu 181, 183

Purism 10, 33, 105, 260

Rewriting In Translation 61, 66, 90

Rudyard Kipling 73

Rural 10, 22, 32, 48, 104, 108, 136, 137, 138, 139, 140, 141, 143, 146, 150, 152, 163, 165

Ruscism 216, 252

INDEX 271

Russian 5, 10, 11, 12, 17, 18, 19,
20, 21, 22, 24, 27, 29, 30, 31,
32, 33, 36, 37, 38, 39, 40, 41,
42, 43, 44, 45, 46, 47, 50, 51,
52, 53, 54, 56, 57, 58, 59, 60,
61, 62, 65, 70, 71, 72, 73, 75,
78, 79, 81, 82, 87, 88, 89, 90,
91, 93, 97, 100, 101, 102, 103,
104, 105, 106, 109, 110, 111,
112, 113, 114, 115, 116, 117,
118, 123, 125, 126, 127, 128,
129, 130, 131, 132, 133, 134,
136, 137, 138, 140, 141, 143,
144, 145, 147, 148, 149, 150,
151, 152, 153, 154, 155, 156,
157, 158, 159, 160, 161, 162,
166, 171, 172, 173, 175, 182,
183, 185, 186, 188, 189, 191,
192, 193, 194, 196, 200, 201,
203, 204, 205, 206, 207, 208,
209, 210, 211, 212, 213, 214,
215, 216, 217, 218, 219, 220,
222, 223, 224, 225, 227, 228,
229, 230, 231, 232, 233, 235,
236, 237, 238, 240, 241, 243,
244, 245, 246, 247, 248, 249,
250, 253, 256, 257, 258, 259,
263, 264

Russian Colonial Policy 72

Russification 11, 12, 19, 20, 32,
34, 42, 54, 70, 71, 72, 104,
105, 106, 171, 173

Sassen 138, 165

School Choice 18, 22, 136, 138

School Enrollment 144, 148

Segregation 136, 138, 140

Serhiy Haidai 51, 55

Shevchenko Scientific Society 74,
92, 197

Skrypnykivka 171, 173, 186

Smagulova 7, 21, 22, 136, 137,
146, 149, 161, 163, 165, 257,
264

Social Inequality 97, 98, 100, 107,
108, 111, 123, 131, 137, 146

Social Status 22, 97, 101, 110,
111, 119, 120, 124, 130

Soviet 7, 10, 11, 12, 17, 20, 32, 42,
43, 55, 57, 61, 63, 65, 69, 70,
71, 72, 75, 78, 79, 80, 81, 82,
84, 85, 86, 87, 88, 89, 90, 92,
94, 104, 137, 138, 139, 142,
143, 146, 147, 158, 171, 173,
174, 175, 185, 209, 210, 222,
238, 240, 251, 254, 256, 257,
260, 263, 265

Soviet Identity 70

Soviet Union 42, 70, 94, 147, 173,
209

Stacy Churchill 19, 26, 31, 35, 42,
43, 54

State Language 23, 29, 30, 32, 33,
34, 36, 38, 39, 41, 43, 44, 46,
47, 48, 49, 53, 59, 104, 137,
141, 163, 185

Stepan Bandera 221, 222

Stephen May 23, 24, 35, 36, 39,
57, 59, 93, 148, 168, 180, 181,
182, 197, 201, 202, 223, 226,
228, 241, 242, 243, 251, 253,
254

Stratification 136, 137, 139, 140,
142, 145, 162, 163

Survey 21, 23, 36, 41, 97, 100,
101, 108, 109, 110, 111, 114,
119, 122, 125, 126, 128, 130,
134, 136, 137, 138, 146, 147,
148, 149, 150, 152, 155, 156,
157, 162

Surzhyk 33, 105, 110

Symbolic Capital 12, 15, 23

Symbolic Power 17, 21, 22, 26, 27, 97, 98, 101, 126, 131, 132

Taras Kremin 47, 51, 52

Target Culture 62, 66, 69, 89, 207

Target Text 62, 64, 71, 80

Tatar 42, 43, 44, 45, 49, 112, 149, 171

Terry Martin 32, 56, 132

The Brothers Jacob And Wilhelm Grimm 73

The First Academic All-Ukrainian Spelling 73, 90

The Franco-Prussian War 76

The International Educational Coordinating Council 74

The Interwar Years 74

The Leonid Hlibov Association Of Children's Literature 74

The Orange Free State 76

The Russian Federation 10, 11, 51, 52, 56, 62, 156, 157, 161, 209, 210, 211, 213, 216, 252

The Second World War 74, 80

The South African War / The Anglo-Boer War / The Boer War 20, 63, 76, 77, 78, 84, 85, 86, 91

The Soviet Union 32, 56, 61, 63, 69, 70, 78, 93, 137, 138, 139, 140, 142, 143, 171, 173, 175, 210, 222, 228, 238, 256

The System Of Patronage 61, 90

The Union Of The Soviet Socialist Republics 10, 235

Tiktok 24, 41, 168, 180, 181, 182, 183, 187, 188, 189, 192, 193, 194, 195

Timothy Snyder 216, 252

Tollefson 138, 165

Translation For Children And Young Adults 61, 63

Translation Strategies 61, 65, 66, 89

Transvaal 76, 86

Uighur 144, 149

Ukraine 5, 7, 8, 11, 12, 15, 17, 18, 19, 20, 21, 23, 24, 26, 27, 29, 30, 31, 32, 34, 35, 36, 37, 38, 39, 40, 41, 42, 43, 44, 46, 47, 48, 49, 51, 52, 53, 54, 55, 56, 57, 58, 59, 60, 61, 62, 63, 65, 70, 71, 72, 73, 74, 75, 83, 84, 85, 86, 93, 97, 98, 100, 101, 103, 105, 106, 107, 108, 109, 111, 113, 116, 117, 118, 126, 127, 128, 129, 131, 132, 133, 134, 146, 157, 169, 170, 172, 173, 174, 175, 180, 181, 184, 185, 195, 197, 198, 200, 201, 202, 204, 205, 206, 208, 209, 210, 211, 212, 213, 214, 215, 216, 217, 218, 220, 223, 224, 225, 226, 227, 228, 229, 233, 235, 240, 241, 242, 243, 246, 247, 249, 250, 251, 252, 253, 254, 256, 257, 258, 259, 260, 261, 262, 263, 264, 265

Ukrainian 5, 7, 11, 12, 17, 18, 20,
21, 23, 24, 26, 27, 29, 30, 31,
32, 33, 34, 35, 36, 37, 38, 39,
40, 41, 42, 43, 44, 45, 46, 47,
48, 49, 50, 51, 52, 53, 55, 56,
57, 58, 59, 60, 61, 62, 64, 65,
69, 70, 71, 72, 73, 74, 75, 78,
79, 80, 81, 82, 83, 84, 85, 86,
88, 89, 90, 91, 92, 94, 95, 97,
100, 101, 102, 103, 104, 105,
106, 107, 108, 109, 110, 111,
112, 113, 114, 115, 116, 117,
118, 123, 125, 126, 127, 128,
129, 130, 131, 132, 133, 134,
135, 168, 169, 170, 171, 172,
173, 174, 175, 180, 181, 182,
183, 184, 185, 186, 187, 188,
189, 190, 191, 192, 193, 194,
195, 196, 197, 198, 200, 201,
202, 203, 204, 205, 206, 207,
208, 210, 211, 212, 213, 214,
215, 216, 217, 218, 219, 220,
221, 222, 223, 224, 225, 226,
227, 228, 230, 233, 235, 236,
240, 241, 242, 243, 244, 245,
248, 250, 251, 252, 253, 254,
256, 257, 258, 259, 260, 261,
262, 263, 264, 265

Ukrainian Diaspora 69, 72, 73, 74,
83, 84, 85, 94, 95, 190, 194,
195

Ukrainian Language 18, 26, 27,
30, 31, 32, 33, 34, 36, 37, 38,
39, 40, 41, 42, 43, 44, 46, 47,
48, 49, 50, 51, 52, 53, 55, 56,
57, 59, 60, 63, 71, 72, 73, 74,
83, 89, 90, 104, 112, 127, 128,
129, 131, 132, 133, 168, 169,
170, 175, 183, 184, 185, 186,
187, 188, 191, 192, 193, 194,
195, 197, 213, 219, 244, 257,
261, 263

Ukrainian Memes Forces 204, 236,
253

Ukrainian Orthography 23, 169,
171, 173, 180, 181, 184, 197

Ukrainian-Russian Bilingualism
21, 30, 33, 101, 105, 106, 126,
128, 131

Urban 17, 22, 32, 103, 108, 136,
137, 138, 139, 140, 141, 142,
150, 152, 158, 162, 163

Urbanization 136, 137, 143, 146,
150, 163

Vatnik 217

Victor Hugo 73, 81

Viktor Kubaichuk 31, 55

Vladimir Lenin 32, 235, 250

Vladimir Putin 22, 200, 210, 211,
213, 214, 216, 217, 219, 226,
228, 229, 230, 233, 234, 237,
239, 242, 243, 245, 248, 250,
252

Volodymyr Kulyk 24, 27, 30, 37,
47, 48, 56, 104, 105, 107, 127,
133

Volodymyr Rashchuk 40

Wordplay 25, 220, 244

Ye-Mova 19

Yevhen Drobiazko 75, 79, 88, 90,
91

Zbirnyk Ukraïns'kykh Anekdotiv /
Collection Of Ukrainian Jokes
204, 208, 222, 223, 225, 228,
254

Zohar Shavit 66

SOVIET AND POST-SOVIET POLITICS AND SOCIETY

Edited by Dr. Andreas Umland | ISSN 1614-3515

1 *Андреас Умланд (ред.)* | Воплощение Европейской конвенции по правам человека в России. Философские, юридические и эмпирические исследования | ISBN 3-89821-387-0

2 *Christian Wipperfürth* | Russland – ein vertrauenswürdiger Partner? Grundlagen, Hintergründe und Praxis gegenwärtiger russischer Außenpolitik | Mit einem Vorwort von Heinz Timmermann | ISBN 3-89821-401-X

3 *Manja Hussner* | Die Übernahme internationalen Rechts in die russische und deutsche Rechtsordnung. Eine vergleichende Analyse zur Völkerrechtsfreundlichkeit der Verfassungen der Russländischen Föderation und der Bundesrepublik Deutschland | Mit einem Vorwort von Rainer Arnold | ISBN 3-89821-438-9

4 *Matthew Tejada* | Bulgaria's Democratic Consolidation and the Kozloduy Nuclear Power Plant (KNPP). The Unattainability of Closure | With a foreword by Richard J. Crampton | ISBN 3-89821-439-7

5 *Марк Григорьевич Меерович* | Квадратные метры, определяющие сознание. Государственная жилищная политика в СССР. 1921 – 1941 гг | ISBN 3-89821-474-5

6 *Andrei P. Tsygankov, Pavel A. Tsygankov (Eds.)* | New Directions in Russian International Studies | ISBN 3-89821-422-2

7 *Марк Григорьевич Меерович* | Как власть народ к труду приучала. Жилище в СССР – средство управления людьми. 1917 – 1941 гг. | С предисловием Елены Осокиной | ISBN 3-89821-495-8

8 *David J. Galbreath* | Nation-Building and Minority Politics in Post-Socialist States. Interests, Influence and Identities in Estonia and Latvia | With a foreword by David J. Smith | ISBN 3-89821-467-2

9 *Алексей Юрьевич Безугольный* | Народы Кавказа в Вооруженных силах СССР в годы Великой Отечественной войны 1941-1945 гг. | С предисловием Николая Бугая | ISBN 3-89821-475-3

10 *Вячеслав Лихачев и Владимир Прибыловский (ред.)* | Русское Национальное Единство, 1990-2000. В 2-х томах | ISBN 3-89821-523-7

11 *Николай Бугай (ред.)* | Народы стран Балтии в условиях сталинизма (1940-е – 1950-е годы). Документированная история | ISBN 3-89821-525-3

12 *Ingmar Bredies (Hrsg.)* | Zur Anatomie der Orange Revolution in der Ukraine. Wechsel des Elitenregimes oder Triumph des Parlamentarismus? | ISBN 3-89821-524-5

13 *Anastasia V. Mitrofanova* | The Politicization of Russian Orthodoxy. Actors and Ideas | With a foreword by William C. Gay | ISBN 3-89821-481-8

14 *Nathan D. Larson* | Alexander Solzhenitsyn and the Russo-Jewish Question | ISBN 3-89821-483-4

15 *Guido Houben* | Kulturpolitik und Ethnizität. Staatliche Kunstförderung im Russland der neunziger Jahre | Mit einem Vorwort von Gert Weisskirchen | ISBN 3-89821-542-3

16 *Leonid Luks* | Der russische „Sonderweg"? Aufsätze zur neuesten Geschichte Russlands im europäischen Kontext | ISBN 3-89821-496-6

17 *Евгений Мороз* | История «Мёртвой воды» – от страшной сказки к большой политике. Политическое неоязычество в постсоветской России | ISBN 3-89821-551-2

18 *Александр Верховский и Галина Кожевникова (ред.)* | Этническая и религиозная интолерантность в российских СМИ. Результаты мониторинга 2001-2004 гг. | ISBN 3-89821-569-5

19 *Christian Ganzer* | Sowjetisches Erbe und ukrainische Nation. Das Museum der Geschichte des Zaporoger Kosakentums auf der Insel Chortycja | Mit einem Vorwort von Frank Golczewski | ISBN 3-89821-504-0

20 *Эльза-Баир Гучинова* | Помнить нельзя забыть. Антропология депортационной травмы калмыков | С предисловием Кэролайн Хамфри | ISBN 3-89821-506-7

21 *Юлия Лидерман* | Мотивы «проверки» и «испытания» в постсоветской культуре. Советское прошлое в российском кинематографе 1990-х годов | С предисловием Евгения Марголита | ISBN 3-89821-511-3

22 *Tanya Lokshina, Ray Thomas, Mary Mayer (Eds.)* | The Imposition of a Fake Political Settlement in the Northern Caucasus. The 2003 Chechen Presidential Election | ISBN 3-89821-436-2

23 *Timothy McCajor Hall, Rosie Read (Eds.)* | Changes in the Heart of Europe. Recent Ethnographies of Czechs, Slovaks, Roma, and Sorbs | With an afterword by Zdeněk Salzmann | ISBN 3-89821-606-3

24 *Christian Autengruber* | Die politischen Parteien in Bulgarien und Rumänien. Eine vergleichende Analyse seit Beginn der 90er Jahre | Mit einem Vorwort von Dorothée de Nève | ISBN 3-89821-476-1

25 *Annette Freyberg-Inan with Radu Cristescu* | The Ghosts in Our Classrooms, or: John Dewey Meets Ceauşescu. The Promise and the Failures of Civic Education in Romania | ISBN 3-89821-416-8

26 *John B. Dunlop* | The 2002 Dubrovka and 2004 Beslan Hostage Crises. A Critique of Russian Counter-Terrorism | With a foreword by Donald N. Jensen | ISBN 3-89821-608-X

27 *Peter Koller* | Das touristische Potenzial von Kam''janec'–Podil's'kyj. Eine fremdenverkehrsgeographische Untersuchung der Zukunftsperspektiven und Maßnahmenplanung zur Destinationsentwicklung des „ukrainischen Rothenburg" | Mit einem Vorwort von Kristiane Klemm | ISBN 3-89821-640-3

28 *Françoise Daucé, Elisabeth Sieca-Kozlowski (Eds.)* | Dedovshchina in the Post-Soviet Military. Hazing of Russian Army Conscripts in a Comparative Perspective | With a foreword by Dale Herspring | ISBN 3-89821-616-0

29 *Florian Strasser* | Zivilgesellschaftliche Einflüsse auf die Orange Revolution. Die gewaltlose Massenbewegung und die ukrainische Wahlkrise 2004 | Mit einem Vorwort von Egbert Jahn | ISBN 3-89821-648-9

30 *Rebecca S. Katz* | The Georgian Regime Crisis of 2003-2004. A Case Study in Post-Soviet Media Representation of Politics, Crime and Corruption | ISBN 3-89821-413-3

31 *Vladimir Kantor* | Willkür oder Freiheit. Beiträge zur russischen Geschichtsphilosophie | Ediert von Dagmar Herrmann sowie mit einem Vorwort versehen von Leonid Luks | ISBN 3-89821-589-X

32 *Laura A. Victoir* | The Russian Land Estate Today. A Case Study of Cultural Politics in Post-Soviet Russia | With a foreword by Priscilla Roosevelt | ISBN 3-89821-426-5

33 *Ivan Katchanovski* | Cleft Countries. Regional Political Divisions and Cultures in Post-Soviet Ukraine and Moldova| With a foreword by Francis Fukuyama | ISBN 3-89821-558-X

34 *Florian Mühlfried* | Postsowjetische Feiern. Das Georgische Bankett im Wandel | Mit einem Vorwort von Kevin Tuite | ISBN 3-89821-601-2

35 *Roger Griffin, Werner Loh, Andreas Umland (Eds.)* | Fascism Past and Present, West and East. An International Debate on Concepts and Cases in the Comparative Study of the Extreme Right | With an afterword by Walter Laqueur | ISBN 3-89821-674-8

36 *Sebastian Schlegel* | Der „Weiße Archipel". Sowjetische Atomstädte 1945-1991 | Mit einem Geleitwort von Thomas Bohn | ISBN 3-89821-679-9

37 *Vyacheslav Likhachev* | Political Anti-Semitism in Post-Soviet Russia. Actors and Ideas in 1991-2003 | Edited and translated from Russian by Eugene Veklerov | ISBN 3-89821-529-6

38 *Josette Baer (Ed.)* | Preparing Liberty in Central Europe. Political Texts from the Spring of Nations 1848 to the Spring of Prague 1968 | With a foreword by Zdeněk V. David | ISBN 3-89821-546-6

39 *Михаил Лукьянов* | Российский консерватизм и реформа, 1907-1914 | С предисловием Марка Д. Стейнберга | ISBN 3-89821-503-2

40 *Nicola Melloni* | Market Without Economy. The 1998 Russian Financial Crisis | With a foreword by Eiji Furukawa | ISBN 3-89821-407-9

41 *Dmitrij Chmelnizki* | Die Architektur Stalins | Bd. 1: Studien zu Ideologie und Stil | Bd. 2: Bilddokumentation | Mit einem Vorwort von Bruno Flierl | ISBN 3-89821-515-6

42 *Katja Yafimava* | Post-Soviet Russian-Belarussian Relationships. The Role of Gas Transit Pipelines | With a foreword by Jonathan P. Stern | ISBN 3-89821-655-1

43 *Boris Chavkin* | Verflechtungen der deutschen und russischen Zeitgeschichte. Aufsätze und Archivfunde zu den Beziehungen Deutschlands und der Sowjetunion von 1917 bis 1991 | Ediert von Markus Edlinger sowie mit einem Vorwort versehen von Leonid Luks | ISBN 3-89821-756-6

44 *Anastasija Grynenko in Zusammenarbeit mit Claudia Dathe* | Die Terminologie des Gerichtswesens der Ukraine und Deutschlands im Vergleich. Eine übersetzungswissenschaftliche Analyse juristischer Fachbegriffe im Deutschen, Ukrainischen und Russischen | Mit einem Vorwort von Ulrich Hartmann | ISBN 3-89821-691-8

45 *Anton Burkov* | The Impact of the European Convention on Human Rights on Russian Law. Legislation and Application in 1996-2006 | With a foreword by Françoise Hampson | ISBN 978-3-89821-639-5

46 *Stina Torjesen, Indra Overland (Eds.)* | International Election Observers in Post-Soviet Azerbaijan. Geopolitical Pawns or Agents of Change? | ISBN 978-3-89821-743-9

47 *Taras Kuzio* | Ukraine – Crimea – Russia. Triangle of Conflict | ISBN 978-3-89821-761-3

48 *Claudia Šabić* | „Ich erinnere mich nicht, aber L'viv!" Zur Funktion kultureller Faktoren für die Institutionalisierung und Entwicklung einer ukrainischen Region | Mit einem Vorwort von Melanie Tatur | ISBN 978-3-89821-752-1

49 *Marlies Bilz* | Tatarstan in der Transformation. Nationaler Diskurs und Politische Praxis 1988-1994 | Mit einem Vorwort von Frank Golczewski | ISBN 978-3-89821-722-4

50 *Марлен Ларюэль (ред.)* | Современные интерпретации русского национализма | ISBN 978-3-89821-795-8

51 *Sonja Schüler* | Die ethnische Dimension der Armut. Roma im postsozialistischen Rumänien | Mit einem Vorwort von Anton Sterbling | ISBN 978-3-89821-776-7

52 *Галина Кожевникова* | Радикальный национализм в России и противодействие ему. Сборник докладов Центра «Сова» за 2004-2007 гг. | С предисловием Александра Верховского | ISBN 978-3-89821-721-7

53 *Галина Кожевникова и Владимир Прибыловский* | Российская власть в биографиях I. Высшие должностные лица РФ в 2004 г. | ISBN 978-3-89821-796-5

54 *Галина Кожевникова и Владимир Прибыловский* | Российская власть в биографиях II. Члены Правительства РФ в 2004 г. | ISBN 978-3-89821-797-2

55 *Галина Кожевникова и Владимир Прибыловский* | Российская власть в биографиях III. Руководители федеральных служб и агентств РФ в 2004 г.| ISBN 978-3-89821-798-9

56 *Ileana Petroniu* | Privatisierung in Transformationsökonomien. Determinanten der Restrukturierungs-Bereitschaft am Beispiel Polens, Rumäniens und der Ukraine | Mit einem Vorwort von Rainer W. Schäfer | ISBN 978-3-89821-790-3

57 *Christian Wipperfürth* | Russland und seine GUS-Nachbarn. Hintergründe, aktuelle Entwicklungen und Konflikte in einer ressourcenreichen Region| ISBN 978-3-89821-801-6

58 *Togzhan Kassenova* | From Antagonism to Partnership. The Uneasy Path of the U.S.-Russian Cooperative Threat Reduction | With a foreword by Christoph Bluth | ISBN 978-3-89821-707-1

59 *Alexander Höllwerth* | Das sakrale eurasische Imperium des Aleksandr Dugin. Eine Diskursanalyse zum postsowjetischen russischen Rechtsextremismus | Mit einem Vorwort von Dirk Uffelmann | ISBN 978-3-89821-813-9

60 *Олег Рябов* | «Россия-Матушка». Национализм, гендер и война в России XX века | С предисловием Елены Гощило | ISBN 978-3-89821-487-2

61 *Ivan Maistrenko* | Borot'bism. A Chapter in the History of the Ukrainian Revolution | With a new Introduction by Chris Ford | Translated by George S. N. Luckyj with the assistance of Ivan L. Rudnytsky | Second, Revised and Expanded Edition ISBN 978-3-8382-1107-7

62 *Maryna Romanets* | Anamorphosic Texts and Reconfigured Visions. Improvised Traditions in Contemporary Ukrainian and Irish Literature | ISBN 978-3-89821-576-3

63 *Paul D'Anieri and Taras Kuzio (Eds.)* | Aspects of the Orange Revolution I. Democratization and Elections in Post-Communist Ukraine | ISBN 978-3-89821-698-2

64 *Bohdan Harasymiw in collaboration with Oleh S. Ilnytzkyj (Eds.)* | Aspects of the Orange Revolution II. Information and Manipulation Strategies in the 2004 Ukrainian Presidential Elections | ISBN 978-3-89821-699-9

65 *Ingmar Bredies, Andreas Umland and Valentin Yakushik (Eds.)* | Aspects of the Orange Revolution III. The Context and Dynamics of the 2004 Ukrainian Presidential Elections | ISBN 978-3-89821-803-0

66 *Ingmar Bredies, Andreas Umland and Valentin Yakushik (Eds.)* | Aspects of the Orange Revolution IV. Foreign Assistance and Civic Action in the 2004 Ukrainian Presidential Elections | ISBN 978-3-89821-808-5

67 *Ingmar Bredies, Andreas Umland and Valentin Yakushik (Eds.)* | Aspects of the Orange Revolution V. Institutional Observation Reports on the 2004 Ukrainian Presidential Elections | ISBN 978-3-89821-809-2

68 *Taras Kuzio (Ed.)* | Aspects of the Orange Revolution VI. Post-Communist Democratic Revolutions in Comparative Perspective | ISBN 978-3-89821-820-7

69 *Tim Bohse* | Autoritarismus statt Selbstverwaltung. Die Transformation der kommunalen Politik in der Stadt Kaliningrad 1990-2005 | Mit einem Geleitwort von Stefan Troebst | ISBN 978-3-89821-782-8

70 *David Rupp* | Die Rußländische Föderation und die russischsprachige Minderheit in Lettland. Eine Fallstudie zur Anwaltspolitik Moskaus gegenüber den russophonen Minderheiten im „Nahen Ausland" von 1991 bis 2002 | Mit einem Vorwort von Helmut Wagner | ISBN 978-3-89821-778-1

71 *Taras Kuzio* | Theoretical and Comparative Perspectives on Nationalism. New Directions in Cross-Cultural and Post-Communist Studies | With a foreword by Paul Robert Magocsi | ISBN 978-3-89821-815-3

72 *Christine Teichmann* | Die Hochschultransformation im heutigen Osteuropa. Kontinuität und Wandel bei der Entwicklung des postkommunistischen Universitätswesens | Mit einem Vorwort von Oskar Anweiler | ISBN 978-3-89821-842-9

73 *Julia Kusznir* | Der politische Einfluss von Wirtschaftseliten in russischen Regionen. Eine Analyse am Beispiel der Erdöl- und Erdgasindustrie, 1992-2005 | Mit einem Vorwort von Wolfgang Eichwede | ISBN 978-3-89821-821-4

74 *Alena Vysotskaya* | Russland, Belarus und die EU-Osterweiterung. Zur Minderheitenfrage und zum Problem der Freizügigkeit des Personenverkehrs | Mit einem Vorwort von Katlijn Malfliet | ISBN 978-3-89821-822-1

75 *Heiko Pleines (Hrsg.)* | Corporate Governance in post-sozialistischen Volkswirtschaften | ISBN 978-3-89821-766-8

76 *Stefan Ihrig* | Wer sind die Moldawier? Rumänismus versus Moldowanismus in Historiographie und Schulbüchern der Republik Moldova, 1991-2006 | Mit einem Vorwort von Holm Sundhaussen | ISBN 978-3-89821-466-7

77 *Galina Kozhevnikova in collaboration with Alexander Verkhovsky and Eugene Veklerov* | Ultra-Nationalism and Hate Crimes in Contemporary Russia. The 2004-2006 Annual Reports of Moscow's SOVA Center | With a foreword by Stephen D. Shenfield | ISBN 978-3-89821-868-9

78 *Florian Küchler* | The Role of the European Union in Moldova's Transnistria Conflict | With a foreword by Christopher Hill | ISBN 978-3-89821-850-4

79 *Bernd Rechel* | The Long Way Back to Europe. Minority Protection in Bulgaria | With a foreword by Richard Crampton | ISBN 978-3-89821-863-4

80 *Peter W. Rodgers* | Nation, Region and History in Post-Communist Transitions. Identity Politics in Ukraine, 1991-2006 | With a foreword by Vera Tolz | ISBN 978-3-89821-903-7

81 *Stephanie Solywoda* | The Life and Work of Semen L. Frank. A Study of Russian Religious Philosophy | With a foreword by Philip Walters | ISBN 978-3-89821-457-5

82 *Vera Sokolova* | Cultural Politics of Ethnicity. Discourses on Roma in Communist Czechoslovakia | ISBN 978-3-89821-864-1

83 *Natalya Shevchik Ketenci* | Kazakhstani Enterprises in Transition. The Role of Historical Regional Development in Kazakhstan's Post-Soviet Economic Transformation | ISBN 978-3-89821-831-3

84 *Martin Malek, Anna Schor-Tschudnowskaja (Hgg.)* | Europa im Tschetschenienkrieg. Zwischen politischer Ohnmacht und Gleichgültigkeit | Mit einem Vorwort von Lipchan Basajewa | ISBN 978-3-89821-676-0

85 *Stefan Meister* | Das postsowjetische Universitätswesen zwischen nationalem und internationalem Wandel. Die Entwicklung der regionalen Hochschule in Russland als Gradmesser der Systemtransformation | Mit einem Vorwort von Joan DeBardeleben | ISBN 978-3-89821-891-7

86 *Konstantin Sheiko in collaboration with Stephen Brown* | Nationalist Imaginings of the Russian Past. Anatolii Fomenko and the Rise of Alternative History in Post-Communist Russia | With a foreword by Donald Ostrowski | ISBN 978-3-89821-915-0

87 *Sabine Jenni* | Wie stark ist das „Einige Russland"? Zur Parteibindung der Eliten und zum Wahlerfolg der Machtpartei im Dezember 2007 | Mit einem Vorwort von Klaus Armingeon | ISBN 978-3-89821-961-7

88 *Thomas Borén* | Meeting-Places of Transformation. Urban Identity, Spatial Representations and Local Politics in Post-Soviet St Petersburg | ISBN 978-3-89821-739-2

89 *Aygul Ashirova* | Stalinismus und Stalin-Kult in Zentralasien. Turkmenistan 1924-1953 | Mit einem Vorwort von Leonid Luks | ISBN 978-3-89821-987-7

90 *Leonid Luks* | Freiheit oder imperiale Größe? Essays zu einem russischen Dilemma | ISBN 978-3-8382-0011-8

91 *Christopher Gilley* | The 'Change of Signposts' in the Ukrainian Emigration. A Contribution to the History of Sovietophilism in the 1920s | With a foreword by Frank Golczewski | ISBN 978-3-89821-965-5

92 *Philipp Casula, Jeronim Perovic (Eds.)* | Identities and Politics During the Putin Presidency. The Discursive Foundations of Russia's Stability | With a foreword by Heiko Haumann | ISBN 978-3-8382-0015-6

93 *Marcel Viëtor* | Europa und die Frage nach seinen Grenzen im Osten. Zur Konstruktion ‚europäischer Identität' in Geschichte und Gegenwart | Mit einem Vorwort von Albrecht Lehmann | ISBN 978-3-8382-0045-3

94 *Ben Hellman, Andrei Rogachevskii* | Filming the Unfilmable. Casper Wrede's 'One Day in the Life of Ivan Denisovich' | Second, Revised and Expanded Edition | ISBN 978-3-8382-0044-6

95 *Eva Fuchslocher* | Vaterland, Sprache, Glaube. Orthodoxie und Nationenbildung am Beispiel Georgiens | Mit einem Vorwort von Christina von Braun | ISBN 978-3-89821-884-9

96 *Vladimir Kantor* | Das Westlertum und der Weg Russlands. Zur Entwicklung der russischen Literatur und Philosophie | Ediert von Dagmar Herrmann | Mit einem Beitrag von Nikolaus Lobkowicz | ISBN 978-3-8382-0102-3

97 *Kamran Musayev* | Die postsowjetische Transformation im Baltikum und Südkaukasus. Eine vergleichende Untersuchung der politischen Entwicklung Lettlands und Aserbaidschans 1985-2009 | Mit einem Vorwort von Leonid Luks | Ediert von Sandro Henschel | ISBN 978-3-8382-0103-0

98 *Tatiana Zhurzhenko* | Borderlands into Bordered Lands. Geopolitics of Identity in Post-Soviet Ukraine | With a foreword by Dieter Segert | ISBN 978-3-8382-0042-2

99   *Кирилл Галушко, Лидия Смола (ред.)* | Пределы падения – варианты украинского буду-
щего. Аналитико-прогностические исследования | ISBN 978-3-8382-0148-1

100 *Michael Minkenberg (Ed.)* | Historical Legacies and the Radical Right in Post-Cold War Central
and Eastern Europe | With an afterword by Sabrina P. Ramet | ISBN 978-3-8382-0124-5

101 *David-Emil Wickström* | Rocking St. Petersburg. Transcultural Flows and Identity Politics in the St. Petersburg
Popular Music Scene | With a foreword by Yngvar B. Steinholt | Second, Revised and Expanded Edition |
ISBN 978-3-8382-0100-9

102 *Eva Zabka* | Eine neue „Zeit der Wirren"? Der spät- und postsowjetische Systemwandel 1985-2000 im Spiegel
russischer gesellschaftspolitischer Diskurse | Mit einem Vorwort von Margareta Mommsen | ISBN 978-3-8382-0161-0

103 *Ulrike Ziemer* | Ethnic Belonging, Gender and Cultural Practices. Youth Identitites in Contemporary Russia |
With a foreword by Anoop Nayak | ISBN 978-3-8382-0152-8

104 *Ksenia Chepikova* | ‚Einiges Russland' - eine zweite KPdSU? Aspekte der Identitätskonstruktion einer post-
sowjetischen „Partei der Macht" | Mit einem Vorwort von Torsten Oppelland | ISBN 978-3-8382-0311-9

105 *Леонид Люкс* | Западничество или евразийство? Демократия или идеократия? Сборник статей
об исторических дилеммах России | С предисловием Владимира Кантора | ISBN 978-3-8382-0211-2

106 *Anna Dost* | Das russische Verfassungsrecht auf dem Weg zum Föderalismus und zurück. Zum
Konflikt von Rechtsnormen und -wirklichkeit in der Russländischen Föderation von 1991 bis 2009 | Mit einem Vorwort von Ale-
xander Blankenagel | ISBN 978-3-8382-0292-1

107 *Philipp Herzog* | Sozialistische Völkerfreundschaft, nationaler Widerstand oder harmloser Zeit-
vertreib? Zur politischen Funktion der Volkskunst im sowjetischen Estland | Mit einem Vorwort von Andreas Kappeler | ISBN
978-3-8382-0216-7

108 *Marlène Laruelle (Ed.)* | Russian Nationalism, Foreign Policy, and Identity Debates in Putin's
Russia. New Ideological Patterns after the Orange Revolution | ISBN 978-3-8382-0325-6

109 *Michail Logvinov* | Russlands Kampf gegen den internationalen Terrorismus. Eine kritische Bestands-
aufnahme des Bekämpfungsansatzes | Mit einem Geleitwort von Hans-Henning Schröder und einem Vorwort von Eckhard Jesse
| ISBN 978-3-8382-0329-4

110 *John B. Dunlop* | The Moscow Bombings of September 1999. Examinations of Russian Terrorist Attacks at
the Onset of Vladimir Putin's Rule | Second, Revised and Expanded Edition | ISBN 978-3-8382-0388-1

111 *Андрей А. Ковалёв* | Свидетельство из-за кулис российской политики I. Можно ли делать добро
из зла? (Воспоминания и размышления о последних советских и первых послесоветских годах) | With a foreword by Peter
Reddaway | ISBN 978-3-8382-0302-7

112 *Андрей А. Ковалёв* | Свидетельство из-за кулис российской политики II. Угроза для себя и окру-
жающих (Наблюдения и предостережения относительно происходящего после 2000 г.) | ISBN 978-3-8382-0303-4

113 *Bernd Kappenberg* | Zeichen setzen für Europa. Der Gebrauch europäischer lateinischer Sonderzeichen in der
deutschen Öffentlichkeit | Mit einem Vorwort von Peter Schlobinski | ISBN 978-3-89821-749-1

114 *Ivo Mijnssen* | The Quest for an Ideal Youth in Putin's Russia I. Back to Our Future! History, Modernity, and
Patriotism according to Nashi, 2005-2013 | With a foreword by Jeronim Perović | Second, Revised and Expanded Edition |
ISBN 978-3-8382-0368-3

115 *Jussi Lassila* | The Quest for an Ideal Youth in Putin's Russia II. The Search for Distinctive Conformism in
the Political Communication of Nashi, 2005-2009 | With a foreword by Kirill Postoutenko | Second, Revised and Expanded Edi-
tion | ISBN 978-3-8382-0415-4

116 *Valerio Trabandt* | Neue Nachbarn, gute Nachbarschaft? Die EU als internationaler Akteur am Beispiel ihrer
Demokratieförderung in Belarus und der Ukraine 2004-2009 | Mit einem Vorwort von Jutta Joachim | ISBN 978-3-8382-0437-6

117 *Fabian Pfeiffer* | Estlands Außen- und Sicherheitspolitik I. Der estnische Atlantizismus nach der wiedererlang-
ten Unabhängigkeit 1991-2004 | Mit einem Vorwort von Helmut Hubel | ISBN 978-3-8382-0127-6

118 *Jana Podßuweit* | Estlands Außen- und Sicherheitspolitik II. Handlungsoptionen eines Kleinstaates im Rah-
men seiner EU-Mitgliedschaft (2004-2008) | Mit einem Vorwort von Helmut Hubel | ISBN 978-3-8382-0440-6

119 *Karin Pointner* | Estlands Außen- und Sicherheitspolitik III. Eine gedächtnispolitische Analyse estnischer Ent-
wicklungskooperation 2006-2010 | Mit einem Vorwort von Karin Liebhart | ISBN 978-3-8382-0435-2

120 *Ruslana Vovk* | Die Offenheit der ukrainischen Verfassung für das Völkerrecht und die europäi-
sche Integration | Mit einem Vorwort von Alexander Blankenagel | ISBN 978-3-8382-0481-9

121 *Mykhaylo Banakh* | Die Relevanz der Zivilgesellschaft bei den postkommunistischen Transformationsprozessen in mittel- und osteuropäischen Ländern. Das Beispiel der spät- und postsowjetischen Ukraine 1986-2009 | Mit einem Vorwort von Gerhard Simon | ISBN 978-3-8382-0499-4

122 *Michael Moser* | Language Policy and the Discourse on Languages in Ukraine under President Viktor Yanukovych (25 February 2010–28 October 2012) | ISBN 978-3-8382-0497-0 (Paperback edition) | ISBN 978-3-8382-0507-6 (Hardcover edition)

123 *Nicole Krome* | Russischer Netzwerkkapitalismus Restrukturierungsprozesse in der Russischen Föderation am Beispiel des Luftfahrtunternehmens „Aviastar" | Mit einem Vorwort von Petra Stykow | ISBN 978-3-8382-0534-2

124 *David R. Marples* | 'Our Glorious Past'. Lukashenka's Belarus and the Great Patriotic War | ISBN 978-3-8382-0574-8 (Paperback edition) | ISBN 978-3-8382-0675-2 (Hardcover edition)

125 *Ulf Walther* | Russlands „neuer Adel". Die Macht des Geheimdienstes von Gorbatschow bis Putin | Mit einem Vorwort von Hans-Georg Wieck | ISBN 978-3-8382-0584-7

126 *Simon Geissbühler (Hrsg.)* | Kiew – Revolution 3.0. Der Euromaidan 2013/14 und die Zukunftsperspektiven der Ukraine | ISBN 978-3-8382-0581-6 (Paperback edition) | ISBN 978-3-8382-0681-3 (Hardcover edition)

127 *Andrey Makarychev* | Russia and the EU in a Multipolar World. Discourses, Identities, Norms | With a foreword by Klaus Segbers | ISBN 978-3-8382-0629-5

128 *Roland Scharff* | Kasachstan als postsowjetischer Wohlfahrtsstaat. Die Transformation des sozialen Schutzsystems | Mit einem Vorwort von Joachim Ahrens | ISBN 978-3-8382-0622-6

129 *Katja Grupp* | Bild Lücke Deutschland. Kaliningrader Studierende sprechen über Deutschland | Mit einem Vorwort von Martin Schulz | ISBN 978-3-8382-0552-6

130 *Konstantin Sheiko, Stephen Brown* | History as Therapy. Alternative History and Nationalist Imaginings in Russia, 1991-2014 | ISBN 978-3-8382-0665-3

131 *Elisa Kriza* | Alexander Solzhenitsyn: Cold War Icon, Gulag Author, Russian Nationalist? A Study of the Western Reception of his Literary Writings, Historical Interpretations, and Political Ideas | With a foreword by Andrei Rogatchevski | ISBN 978-3-8382-0589-2 (Paperback edition) | ISBN 978-3-8382-0690-5 (Hardcover edition)

132 *Serghei Golunov* | The Elephant in the Room. Corruption and Cheating in Russian Universities | ISBN 978-3-8382-0570-0

133 *Manja Hussner, Rainer Arnold (Hgg.)* | Verfassungsgerichtsbarkeit in Zentralasien I. Sammlung von Verfassungstexten | ISBN 978-3-8382-0595-3

134 *Nikolay Mitrokhin* | Die „Russische Partei". Die Bewegung der russischen Nationalisten in der UdSSR 1953-1985 | Aus dem Russischen übertragen von einem Übersetzerteam unter der Leitung von Larisa Schippel | ISBN 978-3-8382-0024-8

135 *Manja Hussner, Rainer Arnold (Hgg.)* | Verfassungsgerichtsbarkeit in Zentralasien II. Sammlung von Verfassungstexten | ISBN 978-3-8382-0597-7

136 *Manfred Zeller* | Das sowjetische Fieber. Fußballfans im poststalinistischen Vielvölkerreich | Mit einem Vorwort von Nikolaus Katzer | ISBN 978-3-8382-0757-5

137 *Kristin Schreiter* | Stellung und Entwicklungspotential zivilgesellschaftlicher Gruppen in Russland. Menschenrechtsorganisationen im Vergleich | ISBN 978-3-8382-0673-8

138 *David R. Marples, Frederick V. Mills (Eds.)* | Ukraine's Euromaidan. Analyses of a Civil Revolution | ISBN 978-3-8382-0660-8

139 *Bernd Kappenberg* | Setting Signs for Europe. Why Diacritics Matter for European Integration | With a foreword by Peter Schlobinski | ISBN 978-3-8382-0663-9

140 *René Lenz* | Internationalisierung, Kooperation und Transfer. Externe bildungspolitische Akteure in der Russischen Föderation | Mit einem Vorwort von Frank Ettrich | ISBN 978-3-8382-0751-3

141 *Juri Plusnin, Yana Zausaeva, Natalia Zhidkevich, Artemy Pozanenko* | Wandering Workers. Mores, Behavior, Way of Life, and Political Status of Domestic Russian Labor Migrants | Translated by Julia Kazantseva | ISBN 978-3-8382-0653-0

142 *David J. Smith (Eds.)* | Latvia – A Work in Progress? 100 Years of State- and Nation-Building | ISBN 978-3-8382-0648-6

143 *Инна Чувычкина (ред.)* | Экспортные нефте- и газопроводы на постсоветском пространстве. Анализ трубопроводной политики в свете теории международных отношений | ISBN 978-3-8382-0822-0

144 *Johann Zajaczkowski* | Russland – eine pragmatische Großmacht? Eine rollentheoretische Untersuchung russischer Außenpolitik am Beispiel der Zusammenarbeit mit den USA nach 9/11 und des Georgienkrieges von 2008 | Mit einem Vorwort von Siegfried Schieder | ISBN 978-3-8382-0837-4

145 *Boris Popivanov* | Changing Images of the Left in Bulgaria. The Challenge of Post-Communism in the Early 21st Century | ISBN 978-3-8382-0667-7

146 *Lenka Krátká* | A History of the Czechoslovak Ocean Shipping Company 1948-1989. How a Small, Landlocked Country Ran Maritime Business During the Cold War | ISBN 978-3-8382-0666-0

147 *Alexander Sergunin* | Explaining Russian Foreign Policy Behavior. Theory and Practice | ISBN 978-3-8382-0752-0

148 *Darya Malyutina* | Migrant Friendships in a Super-Diverse City. Russian-Speakers and their Social Relationships in London in the 21st Century | With a foreword by Claire Dwyer | ISBN 978-3-8382-0652-3

149 *Alexander Sergunin, Valery Konyshev* | Russia in the Arctic. Hard or Soft Power? | ISBN 978-3-8382-0753-7

150 *John J. Maresca* | Helsinki Revisited. A Key U.S. Negotiator's Memoirs on the Development of the CSCE into the OSCE | With a foreword by Hafiz Pashayev | ISBN 978-3-8382-0852-7

151 *Jardar Østbø* | The New Third Rome. Readings of a Russian Nationalist Myth | With a foreword by Pål Kolstø | ISBN 978-3-8382-0870-1

152 *Simon Kordonsky* | Socio-Economic Foundations of the Russian Post-Soviet Regime. The Resource-Based Economy and Estate-Based Social Structure of Contemporary Russia | With a foreword by Svetlana Barsukova | ISBN 978-3-8382-0775-9

153 *Duncan Leitch* | Assisting Reform in Post-Communist Ukraine 2000–2012. The Illusions of Donors and the Disillusion of Beneficiaries | With a foreword by Kataryna Wolczuk | ISBN 978-3-8382-0844-2

154 *Abel Polese* | Limits of a Post-Soviet State. How Informality Replaces, Renegotiates, and Reshapes Governance in Contemporary Ukraine | With a foreword by Colin Williams | ISBN 978-3-8382-0845-9

155 *Mikhail Suslov (Ed.)* | Digital Orthodoxy in the Post-Soviet World. The Russian Orthodox Church and Web 2.0 | With a foreword by Father Cyril Hovorun | ISBN 978-3-8382-0871-8

156 *Leonid Luks* | Zwei „Sonderwege"? Russisch-deutsche Parallelen und Kontraste (1917-2014). Vergleichende Essays | ISBN 978-3-8382-0823-7

157 *Vladimir V. Karacharovskiy, Ovsey I. Shkaratan, Gordey A. Yastrebov* | Towards a New Russian Work Culture. Can Western Companies and Expatriates Change Russian Society? | With a foreword by Elena N. Danilova | Translated by Julia Kazantseva | ISBN 978-3-8382-0902-9

158 *Edmund Griffiths* | Aleksandr Prokhanov and Post-Soviet Esotericism | ISBN 978-3-8382-0963-0

159 *Timm Beichelt, Susann Worschech (Eds.)* | Transnational Ukraine? Networks and Ties that Influence(d) Contemporary Ukraine | ISBN 978-3-8382-0944-9

160 *Mieste Hotopp-Riecke* | Die Tataren der Krim zwischen Assimilation und Selbstbehauptung. Der Aufbau des krimtatarischen Bildungswesens nach Deportation und Heimkehr (1990-2005) | Mit einem Vorwort von Swetlana Czerwonnaja | ISBN 978-3-89821-940-2

161 *Olga Bertelsen (Ed.)* | Revolution and War in Contemporary Ukraine. The Challenge of Change | ISBN 978-3-8382-1016-2

162 *Natalya Ryabinska* | Ukraine's Post-Communist Mass Media. Between Capture and Commercialization | With a foreword by Marta Dyczok | ISBN 978-3-8382-1011-7

163 *Alexandra Cotofana, James M. Nyce (Eds.)* | Religion and Magic in Socialist and Post-Socialist Contexts. Historic and Ethnographic Case Studies of Orthodoxy, Heterodoxy, and Alternative Spirituality | With a foreword by Patrick L. Michelson | ISBN 978-3-8382-0989-0

164 *Nozima Akhrarkhodjaeva* | The Instrumentalisation of Mass Media in Electoral Authoritarian Regimes. Evidence from Russia's Presidential Election Campaigns of 2000 and 2008 | ISBN 978-3-8382-1013-1

165 *Yulia Krasheninnikova* | Informal Healthcare in Contemporary Russia. Sociographic Essays on the Post-Soviet Infrastructure for Alternative Healing Practices | ISBN 978-3-8382-0970-8

166 *Peter Kaiser* | Das Schachbrett der Macht. Die Handlungsspielräume eines sowjetischen Funktionärs unter Stalin am Beispiel des Generalsekretärs des Komsomol Aleksandr Kosarev (1929-1938) | Mit einem Vorwort von Dietmar Neutatz | ISBN 978-3-8382-1052-0

167 *Oksana Kim* | The Effects and Implications of Kazakhstan's Adoption of International Financial Reporting Standards. A Resource Dependence Perspective | With a foreword by Svetlana Vlady | ISBN 978-3-8382-0987-6

168 *Anna Sanina* | Patriotic Education in Contemporary Russia. Sociological Studies in the Making of the Post-Soviet Citizen | With a foreword by Anna Oldfield | ISBN 978-3-8382-0993-7

169 *Rudolf Wolters* | Spezialist in Sibirien Faksimile der 1933 erschienenen ersten Ausgabe | Mit einem Vorwort von Dmitrij Chmelnizki | ISBN 978-3-8382-0515-1

170 *Michal Vit, Magdalena M. Baran (Eds.)* | Transregional versus National Perspectives on Contemporary Central European History. Studies on the Building of Nation-States and Their Cooperation in the 20th and 21st Century | With a foreword by Petr Vágner | ISBN 978-3-8382-1015-5

171 *Philip Gamaghelyan* | Conflict Resolution Beyond the International Relations Paradigm. Evolving Designs as a Transformative Practice in Nagorno-Karabakh and Syria | With a foreword by Susan Allen | ISBN 978-3-8382-1057-5

172 *Maria Shagina* | Joining a Prestigious Club. Cooperation with Europarties and Its Impact on Party Development in Georgia, Moldova, and Ukraine 2004–2015 | With a foreword by Kataryna Wolczuk | ISBN 978-3-8382-1084-1

173 *Alexandra Cotofana, James M. Nyce (Eds.)* | Religion and Magic in Socialist and Post-Socialist Contexts II. Baltic, Eastern European, and Post-USSR Case Studies | With a foreword by Anita Stasulane | ISBN 978-3-8382-0990-6

174 *Barbara Kunz* | Kind Words, Cruise Missiles, and Everything in Between. The Use of Power Resources in U.S. Policies towards Poland, Ukraine, and Belarus 1989–2008 | With a foreword by William Hill | ISBN 978-3-8382-1065-0

175 *Eduard Klein* | Bildungskorruption in Russland und der Ukraine. Eine komparative Analyse der Performanz staatlicher Antikorruptionsmaßnahmen im Hochschulsektor am Beispiel universitärer Aufnahmeprüfungen | Mit einem Vorwort von Heiko Pleines | ISBN 978-3-8382-0995-1

176 *Markus Soldner* | Politischer Kapitalismus im postsowjetischen Russland. Die politische, wirtschaftliche und mediale Transformation in den 1990er Jahren | Mit einem Vorwort von Wolfgang Ismayr | ISBN 978-3-8382-1222-7

177 *Anton Oleinik* | Building Ukraine from Within. A Sociological, Institutional, and Economic Analysis of a Nation-State in the Making | ISBN 978-3-8382-1150-3

178 *Peter Rollberg, Marlene Laruelle (Eds.)* | Mass Media in the Post-Soviet World. Market Forces, State Actors, and Political Manipulation in the Informational Environment after Communism | ISBN 978-3-8382-1116-9

179 *Mikhail Minakov* | Development and Dystopia. Studies in Post-Soviet Ukraine and Eastern Europe | With a foreword by Alexander Etkind | ISBN 978-3-8382-1112-1

180 *Aijan Sharshenova* | The European Union's Democracy Promotion in Central Asia. A Study of Political Interests, Influence, and Development in Kazakhstan and Kyrgyzstan in 2007–2013 | With a foreword by Gordon Crawford | ISBN 978-3-8382-1151-0

181 *Andrey Makarychev, Alexandra Yatsyk (Eds.)* | Boris Nemtsov and Russian Politics. Power and Resistance | With a foreword by Zhanna Nemtsova | ISBN 978-3-8382-1122-0

182 *Sophie Falsini* | The Euromaidan's Effect on Civil Society. Why and How Ukrainian Social Capital Increased after the Revolution of Dignity | With a foreword by Susann Worschech | ISBN 978-3-8382-1131-2

183 Valentyna Romanova, Andreas Umland *(Eds.)* | Ukraine's Decentralization. Challenges and Implications of the Local Governance Reform after the Euromaidan Revolution | ISBN 978-3-8382-1162-6

184 *Leonid Luks* | A Fateful Triangle. Essays on Contemporary Russian, German and Polish History | ISBN 978-3-8382-1143-5

185 *John B. Dunlop* | The February 2015 Assassination of Boris Nemtsov and the Flawed Trial of his Alleged Killers. An Exploration of Russia's "Crime of the 21st Century" | ISBN 978-3-8382-1188-6

186 *Vasile Rotaru* | Russia, the EU, and the Eastern Partnership. Building Bridges or Digging Trenches? | ISBN 978-3-8382-1134-3

187 *Marina Lebedeva* | Russian Studies of International Relations. From the Soviet Past to the Post-Cold-War Present | With a foreword by Andrei P. Tsygankov | ISBN 978-3-8382-0851-0

188 *Tomasz Stępniewski, George Soroka (Eds.)* | Ukraine after Maidan. Revisiting Domestic and Regional Security | ISBN 978-3-8382-1075-9

189 *Petar Cholakov* | Ethnic Entrepreneurs Unmasked. Political Institutions and Ethnic Conflicts in Contemporary Bulgaria | ISBN 978-3-8382-1189-3

190 *A. Salem, G. Hazeldine, D. Morgan (Eds.)* | Higher Education in Post-Communist States. Comparative and Sociological Perspectives | ISBN 978-3-8382-1183-1

191 *Igor Torbakov* | After Empire. Nationalist Imagination and Symbolic Politics in Russia and Eurasia in the Twentieth and Twenty-First Century | With a foreword by Serhii Plokhy | ISBN 978-3-8382-1217-3

192 *Aleksandr Burakovskiy* | Jewish-Ukrainian Relations in Late and Post-Soviet Ukraine. Articles, Lectures and Essays from 1986 to 2016 | ISBN 978-3-8382-1210-4

193 *Natalia Shapovalova, Olga Burlyuk (Eds.)* | Civil Society in Post-Euromaidan Ukraine. From Revolution to Consolidation | With a foreword by Richard Youngs | ISBN 978-3-8382-1216-6

194 *Franz Preissler* | Positionsverteidigung, Imperialismus oder Irredentismus? Russland und die „Russischsprachigen", 1991–2015 | ISBN 978-3-8382-1262-3

195 *Marian Madeła* | Der Reformprozess in der Ukraine 2014-2017. Eine Fallstudie zur Reform der öffentlichen Verwaltung | Mit einem Vorwort von Martin Malek | ISBN 978-3-8382-1266-1

196 *Anke Giesen* | „Wie kann denn der Sieger ein Verbrecher sein?" Eine diskursanalytische Untersuchung der russlandweiten Debatte über Konzept und Verstaatlichungsprozess der Lagergedenkstätte „Perm'-36" im Ural | ISBN 978-3-8382-1284-5

197 *Victoria Leukavets* | The Integration Policies of Belarus and Ukraine vis-à-vis the EU and Russia. A Comparative Analysis Through the Prism of a Two-Level Game Approach | ISBN 978-3-8382-1247-0

198 *Oksana Kim* | The Development and Challenges of Russian Corporate Governance I. The Roles and Functions of Boards of Directors | With a foreword by Sheila M. Puffer | ISBN 978-3-8382-1287-6

199 *Thomas D. Grant* | International Law and the Post-Soviet Space I. Essays on Chechnya and the Baltic States | With a foreword by Stephen M. Schwebel | ISBN 978-3-8382-1279-1

200 *Thomas D. Grant* | International Law and the Post-Soviet Space II. Essays on Ukraine, Intervention, and Non-Proliferation | ISBN 978-3-8382-1280-7

201 *Slavomír Michálek, Michal Štefansky* | The Age of Fear. The Cold War and Its Influence on Czechoslovakia 1945–1968 | ISBN 978-3-8382-1285-2

202 *Iulia-Sabina Joja* | Romania's Strategic Culture 1990–2014. Continuity and Change in a Post-Communist Country's Evolution of National Interests and Security Policies | With a foreword by Heiko Biehl | ISBN 978-3-8382-1286-9

203 *Andrei Rogatchevski, Yngvar B. Steinholt, Arve Hansen, David-Emil Wickström* | War of Songs. Popular Music and Recent Russia-Ukraine Relations | With a foreword by Artemy Troitsky | ISBN 978-3-8382-1173-2

204 *Maria Lipman (Ed.)* | Russian Voices on Post-Crimea Russia. An Almanac of Counterpoint Essays from 2015–2018 | ISBN 978-3-8382-1251-7

205 *Ksenia Maksimovtsova* | Language Conflicts in Contemporary Estonia, Latvia, and Ukraine. A Comparative Exploration of Discourses in Post-Soviet Russian-Language Digital Media | With a foreword by Ammon Cheskin | ISBN 978-3-8382-1282-1

206 *Michal Vit* | The EU's Impact on Identity Formation in East-Central Europe between 2004 and 2013. Perceptions of the Nation and Europe in Political Parties of the Czech Republic, Poland, and Slovakia | With a foreword by Andrea Pető | ISBN 978-3-8382-1275-3

207 *Per A. Rudling* | Tarnished Heroes. The Organization of Ukrainian Nationalists in the Memory Politics of Post-Soviet Ukraine | ISBN 978-3-8382-0999-9

208 *Kaja Gadowska, Peter Solomon (Eds.)* | Legal Change in Post-Communist States. Progress, Reversions, Explanations | ISBN 978-3-8382-1312-5

209 *Pawel Kowal, Georges Mink, Iwona Reichardt (Eds.)* | Three Revolutions: Mobilization and Change in Contemporary Ukraine I. Theoretical Aspects and Analyses on Religion, Memory, and Identity | ISBN 978-3-8382-1321-7

210 *Pawel Kowal, Georges Mink, Adam Reichardt, Iwona Reichardt (Eds.)* | Three Revolutions: Mobilization and Change in Contemporary Ukraine II. An Oral History of the Revolution on Granite, Orange Revolution, and Revolution of Dignity | ISBN 978-3-8382-1323-1

211 *Li Bennich-Björkman, Sergiy Kurbatov (Eds.)* | When the Future Came. The Collapse of the USSR and the Emergence of National Memory in Post-Soviet History Textbooks | ISBN 978-3-8382-1335-4

212 *Olga R. Gulina* | Migration as a (Geo-)Political Challenge in the Post-Soviet Space. Border Regimes, Policy Choices, Visa Agendas | With a foreword by Nils Muižnieks | ISBN 978-3-8382-1338-5

213 *Sanna Turoma, Kaarina Aitamurto, Slobodanka Vladiv-Glover (Eds.)* | Religion, Expression, and Patriotism in Russia. Essays on Post-Soviet Society and the State. ISBN 978-3-8382-1346-0

214 *Vasif Huseynov* | Geopolitical Rivalries in the "Common Neighborhood". Russia's Conflict with the West, Soft Power, and Neoclassical Realism | With a foreword by Nicholas Ross Smith | ISBN 978-3-8382-1277-7

215 *Mikhail Suslov* | Geopolitical Imagination. Ideology and Utopia in Post-Soviet Russia | With a foreword by Mark Bassin | ISBN 978-3-8382-1361-3

216 *Alexander Etkind, Mikhail Minakov (Eds.)* | Ideology after Union. Political Doctrines, Discourses, and Debates in Post-Soviet Societies | ISBN 978-3-8382-1388-0

217 *Jakob Mischke, Oleksandr Zabirko (Hgg.)* | Protestbewegungen im langen Schatten des Kreml. Aufbruch und Resignation in Russland und der Ukraine | ISBN 978-3-8382-0926-5

218 *Oksana Huss* | How Corruption and Anti-Corruption Policies Sustain Hybrid Regimes. Strategies of Political Domination under Ukraine's Presidents in 1994-2014 | With a foreword by Tobias Debiel and Andrea Gawrich | ISBN 978-3-8382-1430-6

219 *Dmitry Travin, Vladimir Gel'man, Otar Marganiya* | The Russian Path. Ideas, Interests, Institutions, Illusions | With a foreword by Vladimir Ryzhkov | ISBN 978-3-8382-1421-4

220 *Gergana Dimova* | Political Uncertainty. A Comparative Exploration | With a foreword by Todor Yalamov and Rumena Filipova | ISBN 978-3-8382-1385-9

221 *Torben Waschke* | Russland in Transition. Geopolitik zwischen Raum, Identität und Machtinteressen | Mit einem Vorwort von Andreas Dittmann | ISBN 978-3-8382-1480-1

222 *Steven Jobbitt, Zsolt Bottlik, Marton Berki (Eds.)* | Power and Identity in the Post-Soviet Realm. Geographies of Ethnicity and Nationality after 1991 | ISBN 978-3-8382-1399-6

223 *Daria Buteiko* | Erinnerungsort. Ort des Gedenkens, der Erholung oder der Einkehr? Kommunismus-Erinnerung am Beispiel der Gedenkstätte Berliner Mauer sowie des Soloveckij-Klosters und -Museumsparks | ISBN 978-3-8382-1367-5

224 *Olga Bertelsen (Ed.)* | Russian Active Measures. Yesterday, Today, Tomorrow | With a foreword by Jan Goldman | ISBN 978-3-8382-1529-7

225 *David Mandel* | "Optimizing" Higher Education in Russia. University Teachers and their Union "Universi-tetskaya solidarnost'" | ISBN 978-3-8382-1519-8

226 *Mikhail Minakov, Gwendolyn Sasse, Daria Isachenko (Eds.)* | Post-Soviet Secessionism. Nation-Building and State-Failure after Communism | ISBN 978-3-8382-1538-9

227 *Jakob Hauter (Ed.)* | Civil War? Interstate War? Hybrid War? Dimensions and Interpretations of the Donbas Conflict in 2014–2020 | With a foreword by Andrew Wilson | ISBN 978-3-8382-1383-5

228 *Tima T. Moldogaziev, Gene A. Brewer, J. Edward Kellough (Eds.)* | Public Policy and Politics in Georgia. Lessons from Post-Soviet Transition | With a foreword by Dan Durning | ISBN 978-3-8382-1535-8

229 *Oxana Schmies (Ed.)* | NATO's Enlargement and Russia. A Strategic Challenge in the Past and Future | With a foreword by Vladimir Kara-Murza | ISBN 978-3-8382-1478-8

230 *Christopher Ford* | Ukapisme – Une Gauche perdue. Le marxisme anti-colonial dans la révolution ukrai-nienne 1917-1925 | Avec une préface de Vincent Présumey | ISBN 978-3-8382-0899-2

231 *Anna Kutkina* | Between Lenin and Bandera. Decommunization and Multivocality in Post-Euromaidan Ukraine | With a foreword by Juri Mykkänen | ISBN 978-3-8382-1506-8

232 *Lincoln E. Flake* | Defending the Faith. The Russian Orthodox Church and the Demise of Religious Pluralism | With a foreword by Peter Martland | ISBN 978-3-8382-1378-1

233 *Nikoloz Samkharadze* | Russia's Recognition of the Independence of Abkhazia and South Ossetia. Analysis of a Deviant Case in Moscow's Foreign Policy | With a foreword by Neil MacFarlane | ISBN 978-3-8382-1414-6

234 *Arve Hansen* | Urban Protest. A Spatial Perspective on Kyiv, Minsk, and Moscow | With a foreword by Julie Wilhelmsen | ISBN 978-3-8382-1495-5

235 *Eleonora Narvselius, Julie Fedor (Eds.)* | Diversity in the East-Central European Borderlands. Memories, Cityscapes, People | ISBN 978-3-8382-1523-5

236 *Regina Elsner* | The Russian Orthodox Church and Modernity. A Historical and Theological Investigation into Eastern Christianity between Unity and Plurality | With a foreword by Mikhail Suslov | ISBN 978-3-8382-1568-6

237 *Bo Petersson* | The Putin Predicament. Problems of Legitimacy and Succession in Russia | With a foreword by J. Paul Goode | ISBN 978-3-8382-1050-6

238 *Jonathan Otto Pohl* | The Years of Great Silence. The Deportation, Special Settlement, and Mobilization into the Labor Army of Ethnic Germans in the USSR, 1941–1955 | ISBN 978-3-8382-1630-0

239 *Mikhail Minakov (Ed.)* | Inventing Majorities. Ideological Creativity in Post-Soviet Societies | ISBN 978-3-8382-1641-6

240 *Robert M. Cutler* | Soviet and Post-Soviet Foreign Policies I. East-South Relations and the Political Economy of the Communist Bloc, 1971–1991 | With a foreword by Roger E. Kanet | ISBN 978-3-8382-1654-6

241 *Izabella Agardi* | On the Verge of History. Life Stories of Rural Women from Serbia, Romania, and Hungary, 1920–2020 | With a foreword by Andrea Pető | ISBN 978-3-8382-1602-7

242 *Sebastian Schäffer (Ed.)* | Ukraine in Central and Eastern Europe. Kyiv's Foreign Affairs and the International Relations of the Post-Communist Region | With a foreword by Pavlo Klimkin and Andreas Umland| ISBN 978-3-8382-1615-7

243 *Volodymyr Dubrovskyi, Kalman Mizsei, Mychailo Wynnyckyj (Eds.)* | Eight Years after the Revolution of Dignity. What Has Changed in Ukraine during 2013–2021? | With a foreword by Yaroslav Hrytsak | ISBN 978-3-8382-1560-0

244 *Rumena Filipova* | Constructing the Limits of Europe Identity and Foreign Policy in Poland, Bulgaria, and Russia since 1989 | With forewords by Harald Wydra and Gergana Yankova-Dimova | ISBN 978-3-8382-1649-2

245 *Oleksandra Keudel* | How Patronal Networks Shape Opportunities for Local Citizen Participation in a Hybrid Regime A Comparative Analysis of Five Cities in Ukraine | With a foreword by Sabine Kropp | ISBN 978-3-8382-1671-3

246 *Jan Claas Behrends, Thomas Lindenberger, Pavel Kolar (Eds.)* | Violence after Stalin Institutions, Practices, and Everyday Life in the Soviet Bloc 1953–1989 | ISBN 978-3-8382-1637-9

247 *Leonid Luks* | Macht und Ohnmacht der Utopien Essays zur Geschichte Russlands im 20. und 21. Jahrhundert | ISBN 978-3-8382-1677-5

248 *Iuliia Barshadska* | Brüssel zwischen Kyjiw und Moskau Das auswärtige Handeln der Europäischen Union im ukrainisch-russischen Konflikt 2014-2019 | Mit einem Vorwort von Olaf Leiße | ISBN 978-3-8382-1667-6

249 *Valentyna Romanova* | Decentralisation and Multilevel Elections in Ukraine Reform Dynamics and Party Politics in 2010–2021 | With a foreword by Kimitaka Matsuzato | ISBN 978-3-8382-1700-0

250 *Alexander Motyl* | National Questions. Theoretical Reflections on Nations and Nationalism in Eastern Europe | ISBN 978-3-8382-1675-1

251 *Marc Dietrich* | A Cosmopolitan Model for Peacebuilding. The Ukrainian Cases of Crimea and the Donbas | With a foreword by Rémi Baudouï | ISBN 978-3-8382-1687-4

252 *Eduard Baidaus* | An Unsettled Nation. Moldova in the Geopolitics of Russia, Romania, and Ukraine | With forewords by John-Paul Himka and David R. Marples | ISBN 978-3-8382-1582-2

253 *Igor Okunev, Petr Oskolkov (Eds.)* | Transforming the Administrative Matryoshka. The Reform of Autonomous Okrugs in the Russian Federation, 2003–2008 | With a foreword by Vladimir Zorin | ISBN 978-3-8382-1721-5

254 *Winfried Schneider-Deters* | Ukraine's Fateful Years 2013–2019. Vol. I: The Popular Uprising in Winter 2013/2014 | ISBN 978-3-8382-1725-3

255 *Winfried Schneider-Deters* | Ukraine's Fateful Years 2013–2019. Vol. II: The Annexation of Crimea and the War in Donbas | ISBN 978-3-8382-1726-0

256 *Robert M. Cutler* | Soviet and Post-Soviet Russian Foreign Policies II. East-West Relations in Europe and the Political Economy of the Communist Bloc, 1971–1991 | With a foreword by Roger E. Kanet | ISBN 978-3-8382-1727-7

257 *Robert M. Cutler* | Soviet and Post-Soviet Russian Foreign Policies III. East-West Relations in Europe and Eurasia in the Post-Cold War Transition, 1991–2001 | With a foreword by Roger E. Kanet | ISBN 978-3-8382-1728-4

258 *Paweł Kowal, Iwona Reichardt, Kateryna Pryshchepa (Eds.)* | Three Revolutions: Mobilization and Change in Contemporary Ukraine III. Archival Records and Historical Sources on the 1990 Revolution on Granite | ISBN 978-3-8382-1376-7

259 *Mikhail Minakov (Ed.)* | Philosophy Unchained. Developments in Post-Soviet Philosophical Thought. | With a foreword by Christopher Donohue | ISBN 978-3-8382-1768-0

260 *David Dalton* | The Ukrainian Oligarchy After the Euromaidan. How Ukraine's Political Economy Regime Survived the Crisis | With a foreword by Andrew Wilson | ISBN 978-3-8382-1740-6

261 *Andreas Heinemann-Grüder (Ed.)* | Who Are the Fighters? Irregular Armed Groups in the Russian-Ukrainian War since 2014 | ISBN 978-3-8382-1777-2

262 *Taras Kuzio (Ed.)* | Russian Disinformation and Western Scholarship. Bias and Prejudice in Journalistic, Expert, and Academic Analyses of East European, Russian and Eurasian Affairs | ISBN 978-3-8382-1685-0

263 *Darius Furmonavicius* | LithuaniaTransforms the West. Lithuania's Liberation from Soviet Occupation and the Enlargement of NATO (1988–2022) | With a foreword by Vytautas Landsbergis | ISBN 978-3-8382-1779-6

264 *Dirk Dalberg* | Politisches Denken im tschechoslowakischen Dissens. Egon Bondy, Miroslav Kusý, Milan Šimečka und Petr Uhl (1968-1989) | ISBN 978-3-8382-1318-7

265 *Леонид Люкс* | К столетию «философского парохода». Мыслители «первой» русской эмиграции о русской революции и о тоталитарных соблазнах XX века | ISBN 978-3-8382-1775-8

266 *Daviti Mtchedlishvili* | The EU and the South Caucasus. European Neighborhood Policies between Eclecticism and Pragmatism, 1991-2021 | With a foreword by Nicholas Ross Smith | ISBN 978-3-8382-1735-2

267 *Bohdan Harasymiw* | Post-Euromaidan Ukraine. Domestic Power Struggles and War of National Survival in 2014–2022 | ISBN 978-3-8382-1798-7

268 *Nadiia Koval, Denys Tereshchenko (Eds.)* | Russian Cultural Diplomacy under Putin. Rossotrudnichestvo, the "Russkiy Mir" Foundation, and the Gorchakov Fund in 2007–2022 | ISBN 978-3-8382-1801-4

269 *Izabela Kazejak* | Jews in Post-War Wrocław and L'viv. Official Policies and Local Responses in Comparative Perspective, 1945-1970s | ISBN 978-3-8382-1802-1

270 *Jakob Hauter* | Russia's Overlooked Invasion. The Causes of the 2014 Outbreak of War in Ukraine's Donbas | With a foreword by Hiroaki Kuromiya | ISBN 978-3-8382-1803-8

271 *Anton Shekhovtsov* | Russian Political Warfare. Essays on Kremlin Propaganda in Europe and the Neighbourhood, 2020-2023 | With a foreword by Nathalie Loiseau | ISBN 978-3-8382-1821-2

272 *Андреа Пето* | Насилие и Молчание. Красная армия в Венгрии во Второй Мировой войне | ISBN 978-3-8382-1636-2

273 *Winfried Schneider-Deters* | Russia's War in Ukraine. Debates on Peace, Fascism, and War Crimes, 2022–2023 | With a foreword by Klaus Gestwa | ISBN 978-3-8382-1876-2

274 *Rasmus Nilsson* | Uncanny Allies. Russia and Belarus on the Edge, 2012-2024 | ISBN 978-3-8382-1288-3

275 *Anton Grushetskyi, Volodymyr Paniotto* | War and the Transformation of Ukrainian Society (2022–23). Empirical Evidence | ISBN 978-3-8382-1944-8

276 *Christian Kaunert, Alex MacKenzie, Adrien Nonjon (Eds.)* | In the Eye of the Storm. Origins, Ideology, and Controversies of the Azov Brigade, 2014–23 | ISBN 978-3-8382-1750-5

277 *Gian Marco Moisé* | The House Always Wins. The Corrupt Strategies that Shaped Kazakh Oil Politics and Business in the Nazarbayev Era | With a foreword by Alena Ledeneva | ISBN 978-3-8382-1917-2

278 *Mikhail Minakov* | The Post-Soviet Human | Philosophical Reflections on Social History after the End of Communism | ISBN 978-3-8382-1943-1

279 *Natalia Kudriavtseva, Debra A. Friedman (Eds.)* | Language and Power in Ukraine and Kazakhstan. Essays on Education, Ideology, Literature, Practice, and the Media | With a foreword by Laada Bilaniuk | ISBN 978-3-8382-1949-3

280 *Paweł Kowal, Georges Mink, Iwona Reichardt (Eds.)* | The End of the Soviet World? Essays on Post-Communist Political and Social Change | With a foreword by Richardt Butterwick-Pawlikowski | ISBN 978-3-8382-1961-5

281 *Kateryna Zarembo, Michèle Knodt, Maksym Yakovlyev (Eds.)* | Teaching IR in Wartime. Experiences of University Lecturers during Russia's Full-Scale Invasion of Ukraine | ISBN 978-3-8382-1954-7

282 *Oleksiy V. Kresin* | The United Nations General Assembly Resolutions. Their Nature and Significance in the Context of the Russian War Against Ukraine | Edited by William E. Butler | ISBN 978-3-8382-1967-7

283 *Jakob Hauter* | Russlands unbemerkte Invasion. Die Ursachen des Kriegsausbruchs im ukrainischen Donbas im Jahr 2014 | Mit einem Vorwort von Hiroaki Kuromiya | ISBN 978-3-8382-2003-1

ibidem.eu